Mr. Bojangles, Dance

Mr. Bojangles, Dance

Jerry Jeff Walker, Sammy Davis, Jr., and the Song That Made Nixon Cry

RYAN B. CASE

McFarland & Company, Inc., Publishers
Jefferson, North Carolina

LIBRARY OF CONGRESS CATALOGUING-IN-PUBLICATION DATA

Names: Case, Ryan B., 1980– author.
Title: Mr. Bojangles, dance : Jerry Jeff Walker, Sammy Davis, Jr.,
and the song that made Nixon cry / Ryan B. Case.
Description: Jefferson, North Carolina : McFarland & Company, Inc.,
Publishers, 2024. | Includes bibliographical references and index.
Identifiers: LCCN 2023057614 | ISBN 9781476692883 (paperback : acid free paper) ∞
ISBN 9781476650555 (ebook)
Subjects: LCSH: Walker, Jerry Jeff. Mr. Bojangles (Song) | Walker, Jerry Jeff. |
Davis, Sammy, Jr., 1925–1990. | Singers—United States—Biography. | Nixon, Richard M.
(Richard Milhous), 1913–1994. | BISAC: MUSIC / Genres & Styles / Country & Bluegrass
Classification: LCC ML420.W172 C3 2024 | DDC 782.42164092/2 [B]—
dc23/eng/20240109
LC record available at https://lccn.loc.gov/2023057614

BRITISH LIBRARY CATALOGUING DATA ARE AVAILABLE

ISBN (print) 978-1-4766-9288-3
ISBN (ebook) 978-1-4766-5055-5

© 2024 Ryan B. Case. All rights reserved

*No part of this book may be reproduced or transmitted in any form
or by any means, electronic or mechanical, including photocopying
or recording, or by any information storage and retrieval system,
without permission in writing from the publisher.*

Front cover: Sammy Davis, Jr., hugging Richard Nixon at the 1972 Republican National
Convention in Miami (Richard Nixon Presidential Library and Museum)

Printed in the United States of America

*McFarland & Company, Inc., Publishers
Box 611, Jefferson, North Carolina 28640
www.mcfarlandpub.com*

For my best ladies, Sarah and Ramona

I think that to create great music is one of the highest aspirations man can set for himself.
—Richard M. Nixon

Table of Contents

Acknowledgments   ix
Preface: Looking for Bojangles   1

Part 1

1. "Love at first sight"   5
2. Who Is Uncle Will Mastin?   7
3. *Holiday in Dixieland*   11
4. "An honest lawyer"   16
5. "That's my actor!"   22
6. *Rufus Jones for President*   27
7. "Dancing down the barriers"   33
8. "A quiet game"   36
9. "Are you a registered voter in California?"   44
10. "A time of pocket change"   52

Part 2

11. "Drifting, poor, and searching"   61
12. "How can I follow this guy?"   67
13. "When your star is up"   73
14. "A blind song-and-dance man"   78
15. "The most dangerous man in America"   84
16. Don't You Have Enough Problems?   90
17. "A call from Chicago"   96
18. "God is on our side"   104

19. "We gotta have laughs"	109
20. "Too many words … strange words"	114

Part 3

21. "The folk process"	117
22. "Would you buy a used car from this man?"	120
23. "Get Sammy"	126
24. "A real clown's act"	135
25. "I'll buy the night"	142
26. "As long as you win"	148
27. "Weirdest day so far"	158
28. My Own Worst Nightmare	166
29. "Folkies born in a new age"	174

Part 4

30. "Like some song you can't unlearn"	177
31. "They're not colorblind"	185
32. "How did that happen?"	191
33. What Were They Doing?	198
34. "As far uptown as I'm ever going to get"	202
35. "All kinds of prisons"	209
36. The Party of the Century	216
37. "Foolish in her eyes"	224
Chapter Notes	229
Bibliography	239
Index	243

Acknowledgments

This project was a labor of love that never would have come to fruition without the help of many people, and I'd like to thank them now. Kathleen Campbell at the Country Music Hall of Fame and Museum in Nashville guided me through the museum's Jerry Jeff Walker collections. Carla Braswell, Dorissa Martinez, and Ryan Pettigrew of the Richard Nixon Presidential Library and Museum in Yorba Linda, California, all provided me with invaluable help in uncovering this story. Brittany Silva at the New Orleans Public Library helped me track down records from the old First Precinct jail. Newspapers.com is truly a treasure of the modern world when it comes to research; I'm grateful to all the journalists who wrote about these men over the years. I also am largely indebted to the authors of two wonderful books, John Farrell and Wil Haygood. Farrell's award-winning 2017 portrait of Nixon and Haygood's thoroughly researched 2003 account of Sammy's life and career served as guideposts for me as I went looking for deeper meaning in the story of "Bojangles." And both are excellent starting points for anyone interested in further reading.

Dr. Robert Hunt, professor emeritus of history at Middle Tennessee State University, has been a source of constant encouragement. He convinced me that one did not have to have a doctorate degree to tell good stories. He read an early version of this draft and gave me invaluable advice. The final product is immensely better because of his input.

Dr. John Shoffeitt, a close friend of mine, also read an early draft of this text, and his kind words and suggestions were a needed jumping-off point. Likewise, Steven Afton Wolfe, my brother from another mother, read the manuscript with a creative eye and discerning input.

My whole family has always been very supportive of my creative endeavors and deserves my eternal gratitude. My father read an early draft and offered helpful guidance, while my mother, sister, and brother all politely listened to me drone on about "Mr. Bojangles" for years.

You would not be reading these sentences if it were not for my wife of thirteen years, Sarah. She is the smartest person I know and was not about to let me get away with anything less than my best. She dove into my chapters in a way that only she could, knowing me so well. Her edits forced me to think more carefully about aspects of the story I had overlooked and had me questioning things I thought I knew. She is the love of my life, and I never would have completed this book without her.

I also would like to thank Gary Mitchem and the whole team at McFarland for taking a chance on this project and putting it out in the world.

And last but not least, I have to thank my dearly departed best friend, my sweet dog Ramona. She was the absolute best girl ever and sat at my feet as I typed almost every word in this book. Taking her on walks after a long day of writing helped clear my head and refocus my energy. Like Bojangles, I will miss her forever.

Preface:
Looking for Bojangles

When I was a kid in 1980s Alabama, there was a corny joke people used to tell. A family-friendly way to break the ice that got a few chuckles.

"What do you get if you play a country song backward?" my coach or youth leader at church would ask. "Your wife comes home, your truck gets fixed, and your dog comes back to life!"

The part about the dog came from the song "Mr. Bojangles," written by Jerry Jeff Walker. In 1965, when he was just 23 years old, Walker was arrested for public intoxication and taken to the New Orleans drunk tank, where he met an old man who went by that moniker. Stuck in jail for the weekend, they passed their time telling stories, and Walker was enthralled as the man who called himself Bojangles painted a picture of his life. A life spent "drifting, poor, and searching," as Walker wrote.

Bojangles had worked the minstrel shows and county fairs that roamed the hinterland of America in the first part of the twentieth century. He told tales of good times and ex-wives. He talked of hitchhiking and the open road. But tales of his carefree existence were interlaced with moments of pain, chief among them losing his dog that he called his best friend and made part of his act. Finally admitting that his best days were behind him, he conceded that most of his run-ins with the law were avoidable; "I drinks a bit," he said. As the atmosphere in the cell darkened, one of the other men asked Bojangles to lighten the mood with a dance. He adjusted his clothes and danced a jig while the weekend drunks clapped in time.

Walker immortalized the man with a 6/8 waltz and an internal rhyme scheme. He composed the song on the road but began performing it around Greenwich Village in the mid-sixties. The song became a minor hit in New York and landed Walker a record deal.

The Nitty Gritty Dirt Band rode the song up the country music charts in 1970, and the tune has been covered by countless artists in the intervening years. Harry Belafonte, Bob Dylan, Neil Diamond, and Whitney Houston are among the more famous artists to put their spin on it. Nina Simone had Walker's favorite take. But undoubtedly the most famous version was recorded by Sammy Davis, Jr.

For years it was a staple of his live show and a fan favorite. He acted out the song on stage. Donning a derby hat and twirling a cane, he would unbutton his shirt as the song swelled to a crescendo. The old hoofer down and out, coming undone before your eyes. The performance so affected Richard Nixon, the latter once told a reporter, that it had reduced him to tears.

Jerry Jeff Walker is the embodiment of one of the great American myths, the idea that you can escape the life you are born into and reinvent yourself as something totally new. Born Ron Crosby, he left home at twenty years old and changed his name. After a few years on the road, he found what he called "the big bonanza" in a New Orleans jail cell. He was a millionaire a few short years later.

Sammy Davis, Jr., also represents this foundational American archetype, though with a unique expression. He was raised in boarding houses and the back stages of vaudeville theaters, his father and business partner having "bartered away his childhood," in the words of one biographer, for years of dancing on the edge of stardom. Once Sammy hit it big, self-reinvention came naturally. He had a Peter Pan–like imagination and was never one to let reality stand in the way of ambition. He came of age in the land of make-believe and, from Judaism to Nehru jackets, Sammy was his own man. Spurned by Jack Kennedy, he would embrace Dick Nixon.

Americans like to believe people can pull themselves up by their bootstraps, as the saying goes—the idea being that if you work hard, you will get ahead. Richard Nixon did just that. The son of a California grocer, he was determined to transform his lot in life. His all-encompassing ambition led him to excel in school and the navy. He parlayed his young achievements into a seat in Congress and then became the youngest vice president in U.S. history, on his way to being elected president twice.

American history is full of stories about self-reinvention, a defining trait of the American ethos. Walker, Davis, and Nixon all pursued self-reinvention with enviable results but also at a staggering cost. All three men lived their own versions of a country song; the tune played forward toward disaster at certain points in their lives, reversed course toward elation at others. Three markedly different men connected by sheer ambition. And a song.

What exactly is inside this process of self-reinvention, and why does it matter? The story of these three unique people and a classic song offers some answers. From the Country Music Hall of Fame in Nashville to the Richard Nixon Presidential Library in Yorba Linda, California, from Harlem to New Orleans, I chased the ghost of Bojangles. The journey took me from the Country Music Hall of Fame in Nashville to the Richard Nixon Presidential Library and Museum in California. From Harlem to New Orleans, I chased the ghost of Bojangles. This is the story I found.

PART 1

1

"Love at first sight"

Jerry Jeff Walker was walking down Decatur Street in the French Quarter section of New Orleans. It was the early morning hours of July 5, 1965. Early morning for most people, it was the late night for Jerry Jeff. He had been playing guitar in the bars and on the street corners of New Orleans for hours and was in a carefree mood.[1]

A handful of people were having coffee and beignets on the open-air patio outside the Café Du Monde. Jerry Jeff passed a woman on the sidewalk outside the coffeehouse, and he fell in love. He felt fate had intervened in his life in a marvelous and unprecedented way, and he was not going to let the moment pass him by.

As she walked past, he turned around and called after her. "You are so beautiful! I could love you the rest of my life!"

The dark-haired woman stopped and slowly turned around to see her admirer. "Now that's a big crock of shit," she replied.

"Don't mince words, tell me how you really feel."

"You're drunk, and that's just a come-on line."

Jerry Jeff was drunk. But he also felt fate was calling him to this woman.

"Don't you believe in love at first sight?" he said. "The possibility that you can see someone and know instantly that this is it?"

"It hasn't happened lately," she said and stared at him blankly.

"You're not trying," he replied. "Wait a minute, let's get someone to testify to true love."

Jerry Jeff walked onto the patio of Café Du Monde and went to the first couple he saw.

"What about you, young man? Stand up and defend my right to tell this beautiful lady there is true love at first sight!"

The couple laughed at the scene and Jerry Jeff was emboldened. A naturally theatrical fellow, Jerry Jeff was about to put on a show. He grabbed an empty chair from the young couple's table and climbed on top. He began preaching to the open-air congregants of Café Du Monde.

"Who in this whole place will stand beside me and testify that love at first sight is alive and well in this world?"

A waiter ran over to demand that the drunken man get off the table and leave, but Jerry Jeff was not deterred. He continued, screaming about the virtue of love at first sight.

The woman stood right outside the patio fence, watching the whole spectacle go down. Maybe she thought for a moment that he was kind of cute. Maybe she thought it was fate and she should give this gregarious fool a chance. Maybe she genuinely thought he was an idiot but just kept watching the display, curious where it would go. Whatever she thought, she stood there and watched Jerry Jeff proselytize about true love to the startled patrons of Café Du Monde drinking coffee at dawn.

Finally, as Jerry Jeff was getting ramped up, a voice came from beside her.

"We'd love you to get off that table." It was Officer David Glaudi and his partner, Ferdinand Marziale.

"How 'bout you, sir?" Jerry extended his proposition to the cops. "You have been summoned to defend my right to tell this young woman that I love her."

"Down. Right now," Officer Marziale said, letting it be known there would be no count to three.

The struggle that followed was a bit of a blur to all involved. "You're under arrest" were the only words Jerry Jeff remembered hearing.

Handcuffed in the back of the car as Officer Glaudi started the engine, Jerry Jeff looked back. Standing on the sidewalk outside of Café Du Monde was the most beautiful woman he had ever seen. She smiled and waved goodbye. Jerry Jeff thought he was being driven away from the woman he was fated to spend his life with. Jerry Jeff Walker was not being driven away from his fate, though. He was being driven toward it.[2]

2

Who Is Uncle Will Mastin?

In the 1840s the minstrel show took America by storm. White men painted their faces black with burnt cork and staged musicals. The shows were performed in theaters and opera houses, and were part of the traveling carnivals and tent shows that toured the country. They had their greatest popularity in northern cities, but the new art form was performed everywhere from the California gold fields to the White House. The minstrel show was the first distinctly American form of show business.

Most early minstrel shows glorified the common white man as someone who could do anything and portrayed slaves as happy and content in their master's care. The minstrel show propagated many of the stereotypes about non-white Americans that would persist long after the format's popularity waned.

In the beginning, the show followed no script. It was a series of self-contained song-and-dance numbers and comedic skits, each vying to be considered the standout performance of the night. The minstrels wore baggy mismatched clothes and shoes that were too big. The shows encouraged foot stomping and audience sing-alongs, a far cry from the typical dramatic theater productions of the time.

One of the most famous minstrels of the day was a man named Thomas Rice. He heard a Black stableman in the South singing a tune while he worked, and Thomas recognized a hit. He bought the stableman's clothes and stole his song. He soon was leading a stage show, singing, "Weel about and turnabout and do jis so. Eb'ry time I weel about, I jump Jim Crow."

The song featured a shuffle-and-hop dance step that soon became the most popular of its time. The tune became one of the first hit songs in America and Thomas Rice made a career out of Jim Crow. The meaning of "Jim Crow" would change considerably in the twentieth century, but its roots as a tool of oppression can be found in the early minstrel show.

The minstrel show evolved throughout the 1850s and comedy became just as important as music to the show's success. Minstrelsy's comedic focus was typically anti-intellectual and anti-elitist. The master of ceremonies would speak in precise English and then be mocked by the blackface performers. The jokes were pun-filled and allowed the audience to feel superior to the pompous MC. Jokes about firemen in red suspenders and chickens crossing the road to get to the other side left early minstrel audiences howling with laughter in theater aisles.

The Civil War changed the setting of minstrelsy. At the conclusion of the bloody conflict, the public wanted to forget the plantation narrative. But the shows did not change their portrayal of Blacks in general. There were still no positive portrayals of Blacks in the shows; they were still portrayed as happy imbeciles. The larger trend in minstrelsy during the 1870s and '80s was a move to a larger, more choreographed show. The topical humor and songs moved away from slaves and plantation life and on to immigration. The last decades of the nineteenth century saw unprecedented waves of immigration into the United States, and the minstrel show helped shaped public opinion about Americans' new countrymen. Germans drank lager beer and ate sausage, the Irish drank whiskey and started fights, and Asians all talked funny and wore pigtails.

Before the war, even free Black men in the North had few rights that were consistently observed, and the Fugitive Slave Act of 1850 made the concept of being a free Black man an endangered idea. After the war, show business became one avenue for Black men to make something of themselves. There was limited opportunity in general, but great possibility in show business.[1]

By the mid–1870s Black minstrel troupes were touring every corner of the country as well as Europe. Sam Lucas made his stage debut in 1869 at the age of nineteen and quickly developed into America's first African American star. He broke barriers for African Americans throughout his career. He starred in the first non-minstrel Black musical, titled *Out of Bondage*, about Black men and their journey from slavery to freedom. He taught himself guitar and was "the most celebrated minstrel in the United States." He was the first Black man to play the title role in a serious dramatic production of *Uncle Tom's Cabin*, eventually becoming the first Black man ever to star in a motion picture, in the same role. When he died in 1916, he was celebrated as "The Grand Old Man of the Negro Stage."[2]

By the turn of the twentieth century, the minstrel show was still a widely popular form of entertainment in the United States. The shows' music evolved from folky numbers picked on banjo to jazzy piano-based songs. The fusion of American melodies and African rhythms created a new style known as ragtime. Ragtime songs further perpetuated the minstrel stereotypes about African Americans, but they also spawned the "Negro musical." These new shows combined ragtime and minstrelsy along with showcasing African American dances. While the subject matter perpetuated the stereotypes, the shows did broaden the range of characters African Americans played and provided new opportunities in a world of limits.

Bert Williams and George Walker epitomized the duality of limitations and opportunity for African Americans in show business at the turn of the century. Williams set about to become an entertainer in 1893. He studied piano and went to work touring with a Hawaiian song-and-dance group before touring northern California lumber camps in a minstrel troupe. Williams attempted to become "a serious singer" but soon realized that "acting the nigger" was the only way he would find success in show business. Later that year he met George Walker in San Francisco and the two men found their contrasting styles made for a great two-man show. Over the next sixteen years the pair would rise to the zenith of show business, starring on Broadway.

They began touring in a show they produced titled *The Two Real Coons*. In the show they played on all the minstrel stereotypes, with Walker taking on the role of the "darkie" and the lighter-skinned Williams, wearing blackface, in the role of the "dandy." The show was a hit and was soon playing at the biggest theaters in New York and Boston. The show featured the men doing the cakewalk, a high-strutting dance step that had become a national sensation.

In 1902 they set about touring the country with their new act, *A Lucky Coon*. The show was a national success and the following year opened on Broadway. Williams and Walker had not broken out of minstrel stereotypes, but they had broadened the appeal of the Negro musical and shown that Blacks could run a first-rate musical company. The two remained one of America's biggest show-business draws for nearly a decade until Walker fell ill in 1909 and died two years later. Williams continued performing and became the first Black performer to be featured in the Ziegfeld Follies, the most popular show of the time.

Williams was a tragic figure. He rose to the greatest heights of American entertainment yet had to use the back door at hotels. He was a sensitive man and the institutional racism of early-twentieth-century America hurt him deeply, yet he had no recourse. W.C. Fields remarked upon his death in 1922, "Bert Williams was the funniest man I ever saw, and the saddest man I ever knew." He became an alcoholic and died at forty-seven.[3]

Show business made little impact on African Americans as a whole in the late nineteenth and early twentieth centuries. But it was one of the only jobs that provided the slimmest measure of hope to young Black men looking at a lifetime of sharecropping or factory work. A common practice among the various white traveling shows of the late nineteenth century was to have Black children sing in what were known as "pick" choruses to open their shows. And that is how Will Mastin got his start.

Francis T. Mastin fought in the War of 1812. Several years later, he caught what the papers called Alabama Fever and left Virginia for the new territory. He prospered among the hills of northern Alabama and left over sixty enslaved people to his son Gustavus. Sally Mastin was born a slave in the household of Gustavus Mastin in either 1856 or '57. The 1860 Census puts her at three years old.[4] The circumstances of Sally's freedom are lost to history, but by the 1880 Census, she had a two-year-old boy of her own and was listed as living in downtown Huntsville, Alabama.[5]

Sally Mastin would have seen little in the form of opportunity for her young son in the last decades of nineteenth-century Alabama. So, as a child, Will joined up as a "pick" in a white minstrel show and left home. The details of his early years of traveling are unknown; he said that when times were lean, he worked as a horse groomer.

Little is known of Will Mastin's life before he turned forty. He rarely spoke of his early life as he grew older except to say that he was always in show business. He surely would have heard about the success of people like Sam Lucas and Bert Williams in his line of work. He might have believed he could do the same.

It is known that by his mid-twenties he was working in various road shows as an actor and dancer. He was backstage at a theater in San Francisco during the great earthquake of 1906. By 1915 he was producing his own show in Harlem called *Over the Top*, a vaudeville-type act that featured a contortionist and eight dancing girls. In 1917 he joined the 369th Infantry Regiment out of Harlem but never ended up in Europe. And sometime around 1923 he saw a young man named Sam Davis dance the Charleston, and he offered him a job.[6]

3

Holiday in Dixieland

Sam Davis stood six feet three inches tall. He was an even-tempered man with perfect teeth and a show-business smile. Born in Wilmington, North Carolina, he was the descendant of slaves. He had a passion for fedora hats, and as a young man in Wilmington he went into a white-owned store and tried on some of the selections. The white clerk admonished him and told him to take the hat off.

"To hell with your hat!" Sam Davis fired back at the clerk. He tossed the hat on the ground and walked out of the store.

When he returned home, he told his mother about his impulsive act of protest. Rosa Davis told him to pack his things. She drove him to the train station and bought him a one-way ticket to New York City. Rosa knew what happened to young Black men in Wilmington who caused a scene.[1]

Wilmington was once a triumph of local democracy. In the years following the Civil War, the Black population gained the franchise and exercised it decisively. By the late 1890s half the city aldermen were African American. In 1898, furor erupted over a newspaper editorial about sexual relations between the races and a race riot ensued. It killed upwards of two dozen Blacks and quashed the political power African Americans had found in local government. By 1920 there were no Black city officials and life as a young Black man in Wilmington was a life under constant threat of violence.

In New York, Sam Davis worked any job he could to get by. He was an elevator man at the Roseland dance hall, he drove a cab, he worked as a shoeshine man and as a stoker on the Erie Railroad. But his passion was dancing. He started entering dance contests and winning. His specialty was the Charleston, a dance craze that swept the country in the 1920s. Will Mastin saw Davis dance and offered him a job in the show he was producing, *Holiday in Dixieland*.

Holiday in Dixieland was in the same genre as the shows produced by Bert Williams and George Walker. It featured song-and-dance numbers and comedic skits that played on the classic stereotypes common in all Black revues. The show toured the South and Midwest as part of the newly formed Theatre Owners Booking Association.

T.O.B.A. was run by a group of white men who monopolized and profited off African American entertainment acts. They controlled the bookings for what became known as the "Chitlin' Circuit." Performers often complained of the conditions on the circuit and gave the acronym a new meaning, Tough on Black Asses. Mastin saw that getting in good with T.O.B.A. meant keeping the show running and his troupe employed. Throughout the early twenties, Mastin and Davis toured the circuit with a group of thirteen other singers and dancers. One of them was a woman named Elvira Sanchez.[2]

"My mother was born in San Juan. So I'm Puerto Rican, Jewish, colored and married to a white woman. When I move into a neighborhood, people start running four ways at the same time," Sammy Davis, Jr., once joked to *Playboy* magazine.[3]

Advertisement for *Holiday in Dixieland* from the *Madison* (N.J.) *Eagle* in Madison, January 22, 1926 (Newspapers.com).

3. Holiday in Dixieland 13

It wasn't true, though. Sammy's mother was born in New York City in 1884. Her father had emigrated from Cuba only a few years before. In mid-twentieth-century America, being of Cuban ancestry was not something Sammy wanted to admit.

Elvira Sanchez was born in 1905 to parents Louisa and Marco in New York City. Louisa's father had returned to Cuba in 1898 to fight for his adopted country in the Spanish–American War. He never returned. Louisa was only fourteen. She married Marco Sanchez and had two children that survived before Marco, a raging alcoholic, was struck down by cirrhosis of the liver shortly after Elvira's birth. Having lost her father and husband in the span of a decade, Louisa Sanchez became bitter and angry but also resilient.

She found work as the personal maid to Broadway star Laurette Taylor. The job provided income and security for the single mother of two as well as ancillary perks. Louisa would often come home with stories of the Broadway lights that would enthrall her children. Sometimes the famous actress would send gifts for the kids. On occasion Louisa would travel with Taylor and dine at fancy restaurants. She had a light enough complexion that most often she would pass as white. She loathed being considered non-white and became enraged when someone would question her about it.[4]

In 1915 Louisa moved her two children to Harlem because rent was cheaper than in other parts of Manhattan. Harlem was about to undergo one of the great demographic shifts in American history as waves of African Americans began moving into the neighborhood. Langston Hughes, Duke Ellington, and Fats Waller all came to Harlem in the early 1920s. The work that incubated there would fundamentally alter American popular culture.

Elvira and her sister grew up just five blocks from the Lafayette Theatre, in the epicenter of the Harlem Renaissance. Her mother wanted nothing to do with the new Harlem scene. Her world was attached to downtown, the Broadway lights, the fancy restaurants, and Laurette Taylor. But her daughters saw Harlem coming alive and were awestruck. Both Elvira and her sister, Julia, landed jobs as chorus girls at the Lafayette Theatre when they were still in their early teens.

Elvira learned a variety of dance steps, but her specialty was the soft shoe, a form of tap dancing that does not require special shoes and creates the rhythm by sliding. She made $18.50 a week and often did eight shows a day.

"At the end of one show you'd be downstairs and hear—fifteen minutes!—and you'd have to get ready for the next one," she once told an interviewer.

The frenetic pace and carnival-like energy expanded her sense of what was possible. She worked alongside legends of the Harlem Renaissance like Ellington and Jimmie Lunceford. At night she would have drinks and walk the streets with her fellow chorus girls, men calling after them everywhere they went.

In 1924 she met Will Mastin. Will needed a new chorus girl for his show and Elvira won the job. Her mother was angry when Elvira told her of her plans to join the traveling show.

"I don't want you to go into show business because you will bring back a baby!" Louisa warned her daughter.

Elvira could not see past the bright lights, though. She wanted to be a star and she thought Will Mastin was her ticket. At nineteen years old, she joined the cast of *Holiday in Dixieland* and left New York on a train.

As the show rolled along from town to town, Will kept everything organized and everyone fed. They toured the Chitlin' Circuit of the South and "all the fine hotels" in New England. There was ample time for a young girl living her dream to fall in love, and Sam Davis and Elvira Sanchez became inseparable as 1924 turned to 1925. She became pregnant that spring and remained with the chorus until she was almost due. On December 8, 1925, Elvira Sanchez gave birth to a boy in Harlem General Hospital. She named him after his father, with no middle name: Sammy Davis, Jr.

Elvira remained in Harlem through the early months of 1926 but soon was back out on the road with Will and the ensemble. For the new year Will put together a new show titled *Struttin' Hannah from Savannah*. The production grew to a cast of twenty-four members and told the story of a couple playing the numbers racket in New Orleans. Sam and Elvira's young son was left in the company of friends in Brooklyn.[5]

Rosa Davis followed her son to New York City not long after the incident in the hat store. She had become estranged from her husband and wanted a new start. She worked as a cook for a white couple in Brooklyn and sold moonshine on the side to make ends meet. New York was a much different place than Wilmington, North Carolina, and Rosa Davis carried a pistol in her purse everywhere she went. The situation with her new grandson perturbed her. She did not feel comfortable with the arrangement her son and his new wife had left her grandchild in. One day she decided she must retrieve the child.

She went to Brooklyn and knocked on doors for hours until she found the right apartment. When she looked in, she saw her grandson dirty and lying on the ground, a dog jumping around next to him. She barged in and grabbed the child. She rushed over to the sink to wash him and, with her pistol out, said no one should get near them. She cleaned and clothed the boy and took him with her back to Harlem. She wrote her son in a letter, "I

3. Holiday in Dixieland

never saw a dirtier child in my life. They leave Sammy alone all day, so I've taken him with me. I'm going to make a home for that child."[6]

She walked the streets of Harlem with young Sammy in a baby carriage, bottles of moonshine concealed underneath, a pistol in her purse. At night she would play jazz records on her Victrola and Sammy would hold on to the bedpost, a toddler trying to catch the beat.[7]

Meanwhile on the road, Sam and Elvira's love affair continued as they toured the country in Will Mastin's vaudeville troupe. In 1927 she became pregnant again and in early 1928 gave birth to the couple's second child, a daughter they named Ramona. The baby was left in the care of Louisa Sanchez and the two headed back out on the road. Soon Sam and Elvira began to drift apart and later that year Elvira left Sam and Will to work in a rival production.

Sam Davis loved his son and was afraid that Elvira would attempt to take him from the care of Rosa. His mother and Elvira never got along and now that he and Elvira were separated, he feared losing his child. So, he returned to Harlem and declared his intention to take Sammy on the road with him. Rosa protested, saying the child was too young, but Sam insisted.

Rosa accompanied them to the train station and Sammy waved to her as they pulled away. When the train headed into the tunnel and his grandmother was out of sight, the three-year-old boy turned and asked his father where they were going. Sam Sr. smiled and said, "We are going into show business, son."[8]

4

"An honest lawyer"

In the spring of 1925, twelve-year-old Richard Nixon was lying on his stomach in the living room of his Aunt Jane Beeson's home in Lindsay, California. He was reading the newspaper. The nearby Elk Hills oil reserves were caught up in the Teapot Dome scandal that had gripped the country. The Warren Harding administration had been exposed as thoroughly corrupt upon the former president's death and the papers were full of stories about crooked lawyers, civil servants, and bribes. Unprompted, young Richard queried his aunt.

"You know what I'm going to be when I grow up?" he asked.
"No, what, Richard?" Aunt Beeson responded.
"When I grow up, I'm going to be an honest lawyer so things like that can't happen."[1]

Richard had been sent to live with his aunt to train for a very different field of endeavor. He had been taking piano and violin lessons since the age of seven. His mother and others in their small community of Yorba Linda believed him incredibly talented. "He had a natural ear," his mother would tell interviewers years later. He was sent to study with his aunt, who was a professional music teacher. By the end of his stay, he was a proficient piano player. He learned Bach and Beethoven pieces as well as his mother's favorite, "Rustle of Spring." His aunt agreed with his mother that Richard could become a professional musician if he wanted.

Richard Nixon was a fastidious and eager student, but music could never hold his full attention. He would fall in and out of practice routines and eventually gave up the violin. As a teenager he came to think he looked silly holding it under his chin. He would maintain a dilettantish approach to the piano, banging out show tunes at parties later in life as a sort of parlor trick. But the life of a professional musician seems not to have been one Richard Nixon ever entertained seriously as a young man. He was gripped by politics.

By the age of seven Richard was a regular reader of the newspaper and did not own a single comic book. His cousin Merle West remembered once walking to school with Richard and a group of classmates. Richard was "explaining the merits of some candidate and the issues he represented. I didn't understand a word he said," West recalled.

"Where does a boy of seven pick up such ideas?" she asked her older sister.

The elder West cousin knew the answer. "Frank, of course."[2]

Frank Nixon was born in southern Ohio in 1878. His grandfather had died for the Union at Gettysburg. His great great-grandfather crossed the Delaware with Washington and fought at Trenton. Frank Nixon's childhood was quick and hard. His mother died when he was seven. His father remarried but Frank did not take to his new stepmom. At age fourteen he left home and roamed westward. He spent the late 1890s and early years of the twentieth century drifting around the country working odd jobs. At various points he was employed as a carpenter, sheep rancher, telephone line operator, painter, potato farmer, and oil roustabout. He was an argumentative person who was quick to anger and had trouble holding a job more than a year. In 1907 he decided to try his luck in California and, after being fired from a job in Los Angeles, found work on a farm in Whittier. On Valentine's Day in 1908 he met Hannah Milhous and four months later they were married.

Hannah was Frank's opposite in almost every way. Seven years his junior, she was quiet, reserved, and devoutly religious. Her ancestors were Germans who had gone to England to fight for Oliver Cromwell in the fifteenth century. They were given an estate in Ireland as payment for their services and wound up becoming Quaker converts of William Penn. By 1729, the first of the Milhous clan had made its way to America. Their religious convictions made them abolitionist. In the mid–nineteenth century the family lived in Ohio and their house served as a stop on the Underground Railroad. In 1897, drawn by the temperate climate and cheap land, Hannah's father moved his family of eleven to Whittier, California, a new town fifteen miles north of Los Angeles founded by Quaker poet John Greenleaf Whittier.[3]

In Whittier, the Milhous family prospered in the nursery business. Hannah's kin did not understand her decision to marry a drifting farmhand.

"They would look down on Uncle Frank. I could feel that keenly because he wasn't well educated and had a gruff manner," a Milhous niece would recall. Hannah's younger sister carved a note in a tree the day after their wedding, reading "Hannah is a bad girl."[4]

But by all accounts, the opposites-attract theory of love seemed to work for Frank and Hannah. In 1909 Hannah gave birth to Harold, the first of five boys.

Soon after their marriage Frank purchased a parcel of land southeast of Whittier in Yorba Linda. He bought some lemon trees from his father-in-law's nursery, and he planted a lemon grove.

Their second child, Richard, came on an unusually cold Southern California night in 1913. In his first three years, the family lived with no electricity and Richard survived bouts of measles and cholera. As a toddler, he was thrown from a horse-drawn wagon. The result was a scar on his head that would leave him combing his hair back instead of parting it for the rest of his life. His brother Don was born in 1914 and Arthur arrived four years later. (The fifth boy, Edward, was not born until 1930.)

Nixon spent his first nine years in wild California, roaming the canyons and hillsides with his brothers. He attended a one-room schoolhouse where he excelled, skipping the second grade. In the years before shopping malls and urban sprawl, Yorba Linda had its idyllic charms. But the sweet smell of orange blossoms in the spring were tempered by the fierce Santa Ana winds that swept the land in the fall, and Frank's dream of becoming a citrus rancher was fading fast. Frank was stubborn and would not take any advice. Among the many mistakes he made as a novice orchard owner, he refused to use fertilizer. In 1922, he cut his losses and sold the farm.

As the lemon grove failed, Frank noticed more and more automobiles passing through town. The family moved back to Whittier, where they opened a roadside gas station and store.

Richard Nixon's childhood home in Yorba Linda, California, in 2021 (photograph by the author).

4. "An honest lawyer" 19

Whittier sits about ten miles northwest of Yorba Linda. Today they are both part of the Los Angeles metropolitan area, but in 1922 they were worlds apart. Whittier had wide paved roads and a college. There were shops and a theater.

"There was quite a bit of money in town. Dick didn't have any of it. But between the oil men and the people in the ranching business it was a very successful little isolated community," one of Nixon's friends would remember.[5]

Frank Nixon was able to capitalize on the growth of the community, and the grocery became a modest success. All the boys worked in the business, and Frank was a hard taskmaster. Richard woke up at 4 a.m. most days to drive into Los Angeles and buy produce for the store before heading to high school.

"Frank had a temper and didn't always control it like he should," a neighbor of the Nixons would recall. He would berate the children and spank them with belts when they aroused his ire. As they grew older, he would "thump" them, as he called it, hitting the young boys on the back of the head.[6]

Hannah, on the other hand, kept her emotions in check. A devout Quaker, she believed in a personal relationship with God. She spoke the old-world language, using "thee" and "thou" when addressing her sons. At night she said her prayers in a closet.

"I tried not to yell at my children, it does something to them," she would say.[7] Instead, she punished her boys with the silent treatment. "She had an iron hand inside a velvet glove," Richard's high school girlfriend would remember.[8] Nixon would recall how he feared his mother's "look" more than his father's belt.

"I just can't stand it," the youngest child, Arthur, would say of his mother's punishment. "Tell her to give me a spanking."[9]

Frank's anger would often express itself in the form of politics. He would rant and rave around their home, adopting a particular form of 1920s Republican populism. His views were what one biographer called "more intense than consistent." He voted for Woodrow Wilson in 1916 and Warren Harding four years later. He switched to Bob La Follette's Progressive Party in 1924 and then back to the Republicans, voting for Herbert Hoover twice before endorsing FDR's second term in 1936.[10]

His other sons had little interest in Frank's political rants, but Richard was fascinated. He absorbed his father's musings about wasteful government and crooked businessmen. About corporate stores run by Jews, allegedly bent on destroying hard-working folks like the Nixons.

In 1925 the Nixons' fourth child, Arthur, became ill. "Just a case of indigestion, we thought," his brother Richard said, writing later in life.

"He began to become sleepy; he did not want to eat; he wanted to rest and sleep." A week later, on August 11, Arthur died. Frank saw it as a sign from God and began closing the store on Sundays.[11]

The family was devastated and still recovering when in 1927 the eldest son, Harold, was diagnosed with tuberculosis. They decided to take him to a sanitarium in Prescott, Arizona. The dry mountain air was said to be good for patients suffering from tuberculosis. A whole industry of sanitariums flourished in Prescott by promising the cure was simple mountain air. In 1928, Hannah accompanied Harold to Prescott, hoping for a miracle.

She rented a house on Apache Drive just north of town in an area known as Pinecrest. The house had electricity, indoor plumbing, and a screened-in front porch for convalescents to sit on and take in the supposedly life-saving climate. Hannah moved into the house with her son and took in three other tubercular boarders to afford the rent. They stayed for over two years, leaving Frank and the other two boys to tend the store. In the summers, Frank and the kids would drive the fourteen hours from Whittier to stay with Hannah and Harold.

Prescott, Arizona, sits about a mile above sea level in the Bradshaw Mountains range. Founded in 1864 and named after the popular nineteenth-century historian William H. Prescott, the town was officially incorporated on July 4, 1880. The town has had many famous residents over the course of its existence. Arizona senator and Republican presidential candidate Barry Goldwater lived there, as did New York City mayor Fiorello La Guardia and radio personality Don Imus. Local legend claims that Virgil Earp was living in Prescott in 1879 when he told his younger brother Wyatt and his friend Doc Holliday about a boomtown not far away, a place called Tombstone.

In 1888, Prescott became the first place in the United States to charge admission to rodeos and formalize the competition with trophies and prizes. What began as a local "Cowboy Contest" grew into a multi-day, carnival-like festival featuring amusement rides and games in addition to the rodeo competition. In 1913 the name was changed to Frontier Days and the celebration became the town's signature attraction.

The Frontier Days celebration in Prescott grew every year, and by the 1920s games of chance were played in an area of the festival known as Slippery Gulch. The most successful game in Slippery Gulch was the Wheel of Fortune, in which contestants spun a wheel hoping to win prizes like hams or cured bacon. In the back, behind the tent, was the real action: poker and dice games lubricated with bootleg alcohol.

Running the operation outside the Wheel of Fortune tent in 1928 was a fifteen-year-old kid who had come to Prescott for the summer to help

4. "An honest lawyer"

his mother care for his tubercular brother. The kid's game became one of the most popular in town that summer as he stood outside the tent barking for customers. The young man was learning the particulars of drawing a crowd and of selling dreams to people. He even managed to convince his devout Quaker grandmother of eighty-one to take a spin on the Wheel of Fortune, and she won a ham. He was so good at the job in 1928 that he was asked to work it again in 1929.

Richard Nixon made a dollar an hour as a carnival barker at the Slippery Gulch Rodeo during his summers in Prescott, good money for a teenager in the 1920s. The experience did more than just provide income to help the family, though—it was a real-world education that was far different from his years of Quaker upbringing, and it would stick with him.[12]

5

"That's my actor!"

On March 6, 1933, one day before Hannah Nixon's forty-eighth birthday, Harold died in the upstairs bedroom of the Nixon home. Hannah would tell interviewers later in life that after Richard's brothers died, he "felt a kind of guilt that Harold and Arthur were dead and that he was alive." She said from that point forward he tried to become "three sons in one."[1]

Richard Nixon had always been a go-getter. He excelled in high school and was offered a tuition scholarship to Harvard, but living expenses and the need to help at the family business kept him from going east for higher education. In the fall of 1930 he entered Whittier College, a small school of four hundred students about 20 miles from the family home. Whittier was a school that promoted itself as having a "Christian culture without sectarian bias." Chapel was mandatory for students and smoking on campus was frowned upon. It was the perfect environment for Richard Nixon to thrive in, and he did. He majored in history and government and was involved in just about every extracurricular activity the school provided. All while rising daily at 4 a.m. to make his produce runs.

He was immediately popular on campus; he was elected president of the freshman class with 90 percent of the vote. But he was passed over to join the most prestigious group on campus, the Franklins. Fraternities were not allowed on the devout campus at Whittier, but literary societies were. And the only literary society in the fall of 1930 at Whittier College was the Franklins. Limited in number to thirty members, the society was chock-full of the wealthiest students and Nixon was not selected, so he started his own.

The Orthogonians were the brainchild of transfer student Dean Triggs, who felt that Whittier needed a rival men's society. With the blessing of English professor Albert Upton, Triggs approached Nixon about helping him form the club and the gregarious freshman enthusiastically answered the call. Nixon was elected the first president of the Orthogonians. While the Franklins took their yearbook photos in tuxedos and

5. "That's my actor!"

held four-course dinners, the Orthogonians wore open-collar white shirts and called themselves "the bean boys."

At Whittier College, Nixon developed a lifelong love of football. He played all four seasons, never rising above third string and never getting put in save for the final inconsequential moments of a game already lost or won. Coach Wallace "Chief" Newman, a man Nixon would cite again and again throughout his political career as a major influence on his life, described the young benchwarmer as "a pretty awkward kid." Still, Nixon remained so popular among the student body that at the end of one particularly lopsided game the crowd began to chant, "Put Nixon in! Put Nixon in!" A roar echoed throughout the stadium as number 23 ran onto the field. Richard Nixon then promptly incurred an offside penalty.

Nixon excelled on the debate team, though, honing a skill that would take him to the halls of power. "He was a merciless opponent," his teacher would recall. "He would so fluster the other speaker with his steady attack that his opposition would become emotional and stop thinking clearly." He won a *Reader's Digest* debate championship in 1933 by arguing for an expansion of presidential power.

Young Nixon also had a passion for drama. His college girlfriend once remarked that if he and not gone into politics he could have made a career as a leading man. He acted in the many plays produced by the college throughout the year. Professor Upton directed many of them and recalled teaching Nixon how to cry on demand: "I showed him how to get up a good cry, told him that if you got your throat acting up, you'd get tears in your eyes."[2]

In 1952, when Dwight Eisenhower decided to keep Nixon on the ticket as the vice-presidential candidate following the famous "Checkers" speech, Nixon emotionally put his head on Sen. William Knowland's shoulder and wept as the cameras rolled. Back in Whittier, his old English professor and drama coach Albert Upton screamed at the television, "That's my boy! That's my actor!"

In his senior year, Nixon was elected class president on a platform of bringing dances to the pious campus. That summer the incoming student body president met with the board of trustees. He told them students were going to dance regardless and so they might as well do it on campus, where they could be better supervised. To the shock of many in the community, Nixon convinced the board to relent on the no-dancing policy. He had just fulfilled his first campaign promise and the whole town heard about the audacious young student politician. People were shocked that a twenty-one-year-old student had brought such a radical change to the conservative campus. As football coach Chief Newman would say of Nixon, "Guts. I'll say that for Nixon. He had guts."[3]

Nixon graduated in the spring of 1934, during the depths of the Depression. The California economy had boomed in the 1920s, but those days were long gone. By 1934 the Dust Bowl was enveloping the Great Plains, turning once prosperous farmers into roving bands of migrants looking for work. National advertising that had once promoted California as the promised land now came with a footnote: "Advise anyone not to come seeking employment."

Nixon would often portray himself as a man with humble roots, and it is true that the Nixon family was not the wealthiest in Southern California. But the Nixon grocery continued to turn a profit even in the darkest days of the Depression. Nixon's cousin Jessamyn West put it this way: "The idea that the key to Nixon was his early poverty is ridiculous. The Nixons had a grocery store, two cars, and sent their son to college. By some they were considered rich."

The family was generous, letting customers run tabs for food even when it was apparent the debt would stay on the family's books for some time. Once during those early years of the Depression, they caught a regular customer shoplifting food for her family. She was a fellow Quaker and mother of two. Frank Nixon wanted to call the police. But Richard could not stand the thought of "what it will do to those boys to hear their mother is a thief." He convinced his mother to discreetly address the issue with the woman. She did, and the woman confessed. "It took months and months, but eventually she paid us every cent. Richard was right," Hannah Nixon would later recall.[4]

Nixon knew the prospects that awaited him upon graduation, and they were few, even for a college man. So, he set his sights on law school. James Buchanan Duke, a businessman who had made a fortune in the tobacco industry, left $24 million to Trinity College when he died. The small Methodist school in Durham, North Carolina, took the money as well as its patron's name and set its sights on becoming one of the best universities in the South. In 1934 it offered twenty-five scholarships to its law school. Nixon's application came with glowing reviews from the Whittier College faculty. The president of Whittier, Walter Dexter, wrote to the dean of Duke's law school, "I cannot recommend him too highly because I believe that Nixon will become one of America's important, if not great leaders."[5]

Dick Nixon had never been east of the Rocky Mountains when in the fall of 1934 he arrived in the "medieval cathedral town" of Durham. He had been granted one of the twenty-five scholarships. The competition in law school was tough. The scholarships were awarded on a yearly basis and fewer were given every year. You had to perform better and better if you wanted to stay in. Nixon was not fazed. He graduated third in his class. His time at law school was formative in many ways. He encountered for the first time poor Southern whites and even poorer Southern Blacks living in poverty in the North Carolina countryside. His scholarship paid for his tuition, but not his room and board. He took up residence in a tool shed until a maintenance man found him and convinced him he would freeze to death if he didn't move. By Christmas of 1934 he was living in a boarding house that provided accommodations that were only slightly better. He shared a room with four other men. They had one stove to heat their room through the North Carolina winter.[6]

All his roommates were Southerners and Nixon began to hear a viewpoint very different from the one he had grown up around. In Whittier, as president of the Orthogonians, Nixon had championed the membership of William Brock, the only Black man on the small school's campus. In the American South of the 1930s he found an unquestioned system of racial segregation. He was shocked at the racial realities of North Carolina, and he argued against Jim Crow in debates at Duke. He was considered one of the most liberal members of his law class. One fellow law student from Tennessee called him "the man least likely to succeed in politics" because of his attitude on race relations.[7]

One incident from Nixon's time in law school was an interesting bit of foreshadowing of the young man's ultimate place in history. In the summer of 1936, at the close of Nixon's second year in law school, he was working in the library with fellow student Frederick Albrink. The hours flew by and before they knew it, it was nighttime. They ran into Nixon's roommate Bill Perdue. The three men began discussing their apprehension about final grades for the semester, which were to be posted any day. Their scholarships and, in the depths of the Depression, their ability to continue in law school hung in the balance. Perdue suggested they go get some food, and the trio left the library. Walking past the dean's office on the way to dinner, their pace slowed.

"Well, the grades must be there by now," one of them remarked.

They tried the door, but it was locked. The transom at the top had been left open due to the heat of the early June day. Nixon and Albrink lifted Perdue, the smallest of the three men, up and through the open transom. He unlocked the door and the three men ruffled through the drawers and file cabinets until they found the grades.

They "didn't take any, didn't change any," Albrink said. When asked about the incident years later, Perdue would simply say he did not recall the affair, but, with a wink and a smile, added the caveat, "I have legal training."

Nixon would never publicly admit anything about the story. The break-in allowed Nixon to see that his grades had fallen, but he was still sixth in the class and would be eligible for tuition in his final year. It was an illuminating moment regarding the character of Richard Nixon. he was a man so consumed with ambition but also self-doubt and paranoia that he was prone to reckless behavior that could destroy him, a pattern of action that would continue for his entire life.[8]

It was Christmas break in 1936 and Nixon, Perdue, and their friend Harland Leathers drove to New York City to prospect for jobs in the still depressed economy. They stayed at the YMCA and took in a Broadway play. They applied for jobs at all the big corporate law firms. They returned to Durham to finish their last semester of law school and over the first few weeks of 1937 Perdue and Leathers were offered jobs, but Nixon was not. He graduated that spring third in his class and a member of the national law honor society, but with no job prospects. The whole family, including his eighty-eight-year-old grandmother, drove cross-country to see the pride of the family graduate. After the ceremony he took what little belongings he had brought with him, loaded the family car, and headed home to California.

Richard Nixon had a successful academic career by any standard. He was president of his class in high school, college, and law school. He was involved in every on-campus activity one could think of. Yet he had no close friends. In large groups of people he was charming and endearing, but on a more personal basis he could not let his guard down. Even Bill Perdue, a man he shared a room with for two years, did not feel he really knew him, and after graduation they never wrote to each other or made other efforts to stay in touch. His life at age twenty-four had been a straight line of success. He had a drive and ambition that were unparalleled, but, from his debate-team partners to his fellow football benchwarmers, from his counterparts in theater productions to the members of the literary society he created and the men he lived in close quarters with for almost three years during law school, all shared one memory of Richard Nixon when they were asked to recall him once he had achieved national fame: they did not really know him.[9]

6

Rufus Jones for President

The pattern was predictable. Train stations gave way to hotel rooms and boarding houses. A weeklong engagement in some town. The actors and dancers idling away the day until showtime. The chorus girls fawning over the young child. In the evening, little Sammy would watch the show from the wings. Post-show, Sam looked after the boy. They played games and listened to the radio. Sammy loved tales of cops and robbers; *Dragnet* was his favorite radio program. Sometimes Sam wanted a drink after a performance and Will would watch the child. During their nights together on the road, the young child and fifty-year-old man formed an emotional bond. Will would make funny faces at Sammy and the young child would mimic him.[1]

Sammy was at an impressionable age and soon began mimicking the show he saw every night. The troupe had a day off in Asheville, North Carolina, and pianist Obie Smith was rehearsing on an upright piano in the boarding house. Little Sammy sat and listened. When he heard parts of the show, he began acting them out. Smith continued to play, and Sammy proceeded to perform the entire eighty-minute show in the parlor of the boarding house. One by one, cast members began coming in and watching him, including his father and Will. When Sammy finished, Will Mastin was laughing and proclaimed they would find a spot in the show for the precocious child.[2]

Struttin' Hannah from Savannah contained a scene in which the lead actress sang "Sonny Boy," a song Al Jolson had made a hit. Jolson was the most popular vaudeville performer of the late twenties. He wore blackface and a straw hat. It only took him a few minutes and a bag of makeup to go from middle-aged white man to Jim Crow caricature, and early-twentieth-century audiences ate it up. One day Will saw little Sammy looking inquisitively at the burnt cork and clown-white makeup strewn about backstage. He kneeled down to Sammy's height and painted the child's face, giving him exaggerated white lips. He looked like a mini–Al Jolson, and Will had an idea.

Sammy was sent on stage during the lead actress's rendition of "Sonny Boy" and climbed onto her lap. From the side of the stage Will made funny faces at Sammy, rolling his eyes, shaking his head, and holding his nose as the singer hit her high note, and Sammy mimicked it all. The audience howled with laughter. As he left the stage, his father and uncle congratulated him on his standout performance. "You're a born mugger son, a born mugger," they told him.[3]

Sammy's bit part in *Struttin' Hannah* became a regular feature of the show. Soon others would follow. Sammy would make his entrance by peeking out from behind a curtain made to look like a fence, Hannah inquiring, "Are you a little kid or a midget?"[4] In another bit, one of the actors would feign anger at Mastin and "quit" the show. Mastin, looking perturbed, would scan the audience and find another performer, strategically placed, holding a sleeping Sammy on her lap.

"Wake that boy up," Mastin would proclaim, and that was Sammy's cue. He would bound through the audience and up on stage. He'd do his dance, "a little paddle roll," as one of the troupe remembered it years later. The applause was deafening and addictive, and it left a deep impression on the boy.[5]

In early 1929 the troupe had a booking at the Standard Theatre in Philadelphia. The theater was sponsoring a children's dance contest on a fortuitous day off for the ensemble. Sammy entered and won the $10 prize. Sammy recalled in his first autobiography that his father took him "straight over to A.S. Beck's shoe store and bought me a pair of black pumps with taps." Sammy was only three years old.[6]

In October of 1929 the stock market crashed, plunging the country into a deep depression. The Great Depression affected Black entertainers as much if not more than any other group. Work dried up for Will Mastin and his cast of twenty-four. They had rolled along throughout the 1920s as working entertainers, feeling like they were on the edge of stardom. The Depression hastened an end to the good times for people all over the world, and Sam Davis soon had to call home to Rosa, asking for a loan. She would not give it. She told him he should come back to Harlem with her young grandson if he could not make ends meet on the road, so he did.

Back in Harlem, times were tough. African Americans who had found so much promise in the preceding decade were hit hardest by the early years of the Depression. The famous writer W.E.B. Du Bois went bankrupt and lost his house.[7] The once glittering lights of the Black theaters dimmed. Almost half of Harlem's two hundred thousand people were out of work. Forty-six Harlem residents died of starvation in 1931 alone.[8]

When Sam Davis arrived home, his son burst into the apartment eager to show his "mama" his new shoes and his dance steps. Rosa was ecstatic to see her grandson and complimented his dance moves, calling him "a real dancer now." Rosa looked after him as Sam attempted to find work. Every day he left the apartment and every night he returned with nothing. He did not want to do anything but be an entertainer. With jobs scarce and competition tough, he found no work. One day a telegram arrived from Will Mastin offering employment in a new show.[9]

Mastin was a realist and he saw the changing winds. He had begun to steadily move his shows away from minstrel stereotypes and toward a more variety-based act. *Vaudeville* is a variation on a French word that translates as "street songs." The format was billed as "something for everybody"[10] and by the early twentieth century it had become the most popular form of entertainment in America. Will Mastin's acts often straddled the line between minstrel show and vaudeville and by the early thirties his performers were billed simply as Will Mastin's Gang. The troupe's size varied from five to fifteen, depending on the size of the venue and the pay, but from the time of his telegram there was always a spot for Sam Davis and his young son.

Elvira showed up at one of their engagements. Five-year-old Sammy did not know who she was, having not seen his mother in three years. She took him on a walk through town and attempted to bond with the boy. She offered to buy him ice cream, but he declined. She went into a toy store and bought a ball so she could play catch with him. Sammy had never played

Advertisement for Will Mastin & Gang from the *Bangor* (Maine) *Daily News*, October 7, 1933 (Newspapers.com).

catch. He had very limited interaction with children his own age; his life was the traveling show. She tossed the ball and it hit Sammy in the cheek. Sammy had no interest in the game.

They returned to the theater and Sammy was excited to see that the show had not started yet; he wanted his mother to see him perform. He went out that night in blackface and tap shoes, and the audience cheered the five-year-old boy. After the performance the proud boy looked around for his mother, but she was gone. Sammy started to cry. He would not see his mother again for almost twenty years, at which point he was well on his way to becoming a star.[11]

The attention Sammy received was not all positive. Lawyer Elbridge T. Gerry founded the Society for the Prevention of the Cruelty to Children in 1875. Gerry's grandfather and namesake was one of the signers of the Declaration of Independence, and the practice of "gerrymandering" congressional districts is named for him. The younger Gerry believed children should be in school, and his society actively tracked down parents who did not educate their children and had them arrested. To avoid this society of "do-gooders," as Sam and Will called it, they would have Sammy hide in backstage closets and underneath beds in boarding houses. They would often put the Jolson blackface on him, dress him in a suit and tie, put a cigar in his mouth, and say he was a forty-year-old midget. Sammy was told to call Will "uncle" to keep up the appearance of the trio as a family, a habit he would keep for the rest of his life.

Twice in the early thirties, Sam Davis was busted by the "Gerry Society" and hauled into court. The second time, he skipped town before the court appearance, but Rosa went, and the judge awarded her custody. She let Sam and Will know that Sammy would not be going anywhere without her permission. Will had the troupe booked in Boston the following week and Sammy begged his grandmother to let him go. She loved her grandson and recognized his talent. She relented on the condition that Sam and Will made sure the young child received a daily dose of Scott's Emulsion, a brand of cod liver oil, to keep him from catching cold. Sam and Will cared for Sammy as best they could and knew how while on the road. They found tutors to teach him the fundamentals of reading and writing but not much else. Sammy never would have any formal education and as an adult would avoid personalizing autographs to avoid misspelling names.[12]

Sammy's most thorough biographer wrote that Will and Sam Sr. "gave little Sammy everything. And with that, they bartered away his childhood."[13]

Through the early years of the Depression, Sam and his son would head home to Harlem when work was scarce. They would stay at Rosa's apartment on Eighth Avenue and 141st Street until Will sent word of a new booking, and then they would head for the train station.

In 1933 Will landed Sammy a job in the talkies, as the old-timers called them. In the early days of motion pictures, featured films were often accompanied by fifteen- or twenty-minute shorts. *Rufus Jones for President* was one of these, and Sammy was given the title role. The film plays on the basic minstrel-show stereotypes, with plenty of jokes about pork chops and watermelon. The plot centers around a dream that the movie's star, Ethel Waters, has after Sammy falls asleep on her lap. She dreams he becomes president of the United States, a concept that would have seemed quite fanciful to a motion-picture audience in 1933.

In the dream, the Capitol is full of African American senators shooting dice. As the Chief Justice swears in little President Sammy, the oath of office is administered in rhyme over ragtime music: "Make a law without no loops / that there will be no lock on the chicken coops. / Swear to me that you will choose / for the national anthem 'The Memphis Blues.' / Swear that the watermelon vines / are public property at all times." Sammy dances in a top hat and, in between the Chief Justice's rhymes, puts his hand on the Bible and says, "I do, I do" in rhythm to the music.[14]

The film was successful, with one Hollywood paper calling Sammy "talented." Soon another film offer came, this time from Lita Grey Chaplin. Her divorce from Charlie Chaplin, arguably America's first movie star, had made headlines the world over. By the early thirties she had burned through all her divorce settlement money and was producing and starring in small films. She cast Sammy in another short, titled *Seasoned Greetings*. She was so impressed with Sammy that she tried to adopt him. She told Sam and Will she would take him to Hollywood and make him a star. Will was wary of the talking pictures, though, and he knew that the lovable child was becoming the star of his vaudeville show. Will decided the child's future was on the road with him, not in the movies. Sammy would not star in another movie for twenty-five years.[15]

By the time he was ten years old, Sammy had seen every part of America and most of Canada by train. When he was nine, Will took him to see the legendary vaudevillian Bill "Bojangles" Robinson, the most famous African American performer of the era. Robinson was a tap dancer of the first order. He made $3,500 a week performing at the Palace in New York. He and Will were the same age and had come up the same way; both had joined "pick" choruses as children. According to Sammy's first book, Will saved Bojangles's life one night when a gun was pulled during a poker game.

Sammy watched Bojangles perform and was in awe. Robinson's act was a massive contrast to what Sammy did with his father and uncle. Will,

Sam, and Sammy were a "flash dance" act. They would hit the stage and amaze audiences with dancing that was graceful, acrobatic, and athletic. Sammy described what they did as "arms and legs flying six ways to the moon." But Robinson glided casually across the stage; hands in his pockets, he would go "up and down a flight of stairs like he was taking a stroll to the music."[16] Will took Sammy backstage to meet Bojangles after the show. The boy traded tap steps with the legend and marveled at the number of shoes in Robinson's closet. He would always speak of how Robinson had taught him to "talk to the audience with your feet."[17]

As the decade advanced, the talking pictures and radio were replacing the variety show. Old theaters were converting to movie houses and Will was having a harder time staying booked. He cut the size of the act to gain better bookings. One by one, dancers were cut in an attempt to make ends meet. Sam Sr. never worried about his job, though; his son was fast becoming the star of the show. Soon the act was billed as the Will Mastin Trio. The late thirties were the leanest years of Sammy's life, with one stretch of unemployment lasting five months. Sammy recalled that his father sold almost everything of value that they owned, but he refused to sell the radio. It was "the last link between us and show business," he said.

At night they would listen to popular radio programs that interviewed the stars of the day and Sammy was enthralled. Having grown up backstage and in urban alleys on the edge of stardom, Sammy looked up to celebrities and was fascinated by their glamorous lifestyle. He listened intently as they talked about new homes with golf courses and swimming pools. Sammy could not swim, but he knew he wanted a house with a swimming pool. "When they talked show business they weren't dreaming as we always were," he wrote. Sometimes he and his father would walk from Harlem just to gawk at the celebrities disembarking from their limos and entering the club.

Bookings were few and far between, but in 1941 the Trio landed a gig as the opening act for Tommy Dorsey at the Michigan Theater in Detroit. The main vocalist, a young white man in his twenties, stuck out his hand and greeted them as they walked in. "Hi'ya," he said. "My name is Frank, and I sing with Dorsey."[18]

"That might sound like nothing much, but the average top vocalist in those days wouldn't give the time of day to a Negro supporting act," Sammy would recall years later.[19] He watched the man, ten years his senior, perform over the next three days and was awestruck. The singer took a liking to the young dancer as well. The two hung out backstage and ate dinner together. Sammy Davis, Jr.'s, opening act for Tommy Dorsey left an indelible impression on Frank Sinatra, and it would change the Trio's lives forever.

7

"Dancing down the barriers"

In his 1965 autobiography, Sammy relates a dramatic story of his sixteenth birthday party and the radio bulletin announcing the Japanese bombing of Pearl Harbor. He says he and his father raced to the recruitment office to volunteer their services, only to be told they were too young and too old, respectively, to join up. In reality, no such scene took place. Will Mastin found increased bookings as the American home front changed to a wartime posture in the early 1940s. But in December of 1943 Sammy turned eighteen. Early in 1944, he received his draft notice backstage at a club in Reno, Nevada.

Sam and Will had created a sheltered life for Sammy. He had experienced very few encounters with racism. His life was theaters, hotels, and trains. He socialized with dancers, actors, and singers. He had very little understanding of the outside world. Sam and Will knew this and feared for his entry into the army. They knew men who had gone off to Europe and the Pacific and not come back. Will remembered World War I and the countless performers who came back missing limbs. In the summer of 1944, they bought Sammy a wristwatch to take with him to basic training.[1]

"We always had the reputation as the best dressed act in show business. Can't let 'em think different about us in the army," Will told Sammy.

On August 19, 1944, Sammy Davis, Jr., reported to basic training at Fort Warren in Cheyenne, Wyoming.

Sammy was aware that being Black made him subject to a different set of rules. He had overheard the slights at hotels and restaurants during his life on the road. But nothing prepared him for what he found when Uncle Sam came calling. Shortly before Sammy arrived in Wyoming, the army desegregated its transportation and recreation facilities. It is clear from what he wrote and said for the rest of his life that the army is where the sheltered showbiz kid had his eyes opened to the reality of race relations in America. It is where he was first called "nigger."

A soldier named Jennings was Sammy's most frequent sparring partner. Sammy related stories of his fellow PFC tricking him into drinking urine and crushing the watch Sam and Will had bought for him, saying, "Aww, don't carry on, boy, you can always steal another one." Sammy was shocked at the level of anger that came from his fellow white soldiers. He did not understand.

"Overnight the world looked different," he said. "It wasn't one color anymore."[2]

Something else happened to Sammy in the U.S. Army that would fundamentally change his life. He was ashamed of his lack of formal education and wrote "high school graduate" on his induction papers. This was far from accurate. He was barely literate. The absolute shock of army life left Sammy crying in his bunk the first night. His company master sergeant, Gene Williams, heard him and tried to persuade him everything would be all right. He told him, "A man can do anything he wants to if he tries. Give the army a try. You have any serious problems, come see me." Sammy started going to see Sergeant Williams, who noticed his obvious lack of education and encouraged the young PFC to read more. Williams had a large collection of books and began lending them to Sammy. He read Oscar Wilde and Mark Twain. He read William Shakespeare and Carl Sandburg's multi-volume biography of Abraham Lincoln. Sammy bought a pocket dictionary and would look up words he did not know. When he finished a book, he and Sergeant Williams would discuss it.

Williams knew of Sammy's entertainment background and encouraged him to perform in the Friday night variety shows held in the white service club. It did not take long for Sammy Davis, Jr., to become the star performer at Fort Warren. Without his father and Will, he was free to improvise and try out his talents. "He'd emcee the whole show. He'd run the whole thing. It was his show," recalled one of his bandmates from the army, Abe Lafferty.[3] He sang and he tap-danced and left the crowd roaring in laughter with his impersonations of Edward G. Robinson, Jimmy Cagney, and Frank Sinatra. The whites that made up the audience cheered Sammy, and he was confused about why those outside the show hated him so much. He began to live his whole life for the two hours on stage every week. He said, "I could stand on that stage, facing the audience, knowing I was dancing down the barriers between us."[4]

Yet barriers remained. As his profile at the fort grew, the target on his back got bigger. Four white soldiers lured him away from his bunk by leaving a message that the captain in charge of the weekly shows needed to see him. When he showed up, they jumped him, dragged him to a latrine, and beat him. They ripped his shirt and wrote "coon" in white paint across his chest. They wrote "nigger" on his forehead. They busted his nose and left him on the floor bleeding.

Sammy's time in the army was one the biggest factors in making

7. "Dancing down the barriers"

"Little Sammy" the flash dancer into Sammy Davis, Jr., the star. Performing with the army band boosted his confidence as a performer and allowed him to branch out and become more multifaceted in his performances. His coming to grips with the reality of racism in America hardened him in a way that was necessary for him to be more broadly successful when he returned to show business. It also provided the context for his social activism in later years.

Sammy never left Fort Warren while he was in the army. He was sent back through basic training three times, by his telling. On May 30, 1945, a little over nine months after Uncle Sam came calling, he was released. His official army discharge papers state he was "incapacitated for military service because frequent and severe headaches render him unable to perform military service."[5] The war had been over in Europe for three weeks and two nuclear explosions would end it in the Pacific two months later. He boarded a train and headed for Los Angeles, where Will and Sam Sr. were performing as a duo.

8

"A quiet game"

In April 1944 a crowd of over a thousand Allied servicemen watched as a plane landed on the small runway at Green Island in the South Pacific. The arrival of the plane was supposed to be a morale booster to the servicemen. It was carrying an American hero, Charles Lindbergh. Lindbergh was a pioneer in American aviation and one of the most famous men alive in 1944. None of the troops paid Lindbergh much mind, though. He disembarked the plane with a brown-haired female nurse who drew catcalls and whistles.

"I'm telling you, she could have been a chimpanzee ... but she was female, and they hadn't seen one in a long time," Richard Nixon would recall in 1983.

The commanding officer invited Nixon to a private dinner to be held in Lindbergh's honor that evening. Nixon declined the invitation; he was hosting a poker game.[1]

Richard Nixon's journey from third in his class at Duke's law school to the best poker player in the navy was a formative and yet relatively mundane experience. In the summer of 1937, he rode back across the country with his family after graduating Duke and arrived in Whittier with no job. He was bitter about his rejection from the big East Coast law firms. He applied to the FBI, and his file shows he aced the interviews. But at the end of his application, someone wrote "not qualified" and his recommended appointment as special agent never happened.[2]

Whittier had grown considerably in the years Nixon had spent on the East Coast and the town was becoming a suburb of Los Angeles. It was still a small town at heart, and who you knew still mattered. Nixon's grandfather on the Milhous side had been friends with Thomas Bewley's grandfather back in Indiana. Thomas Bewley was a partner at one of the biggest law firms in Whittier. Hannah Nixon used her family connections to secure Richard a job at Wingert and Bewley.

He was tasked with handling overflow cases at the law firm on a percentage basis. It wasn't his ideal job, but, with the Great Depression still raging, Nixon had an office and a title. It was something, and he did his best to view it as an opportunity. Thomas Bewley was quoted often in later life saying he could never recall Nixon having lost a case. He may never have lost a case for Bewley, but his first assignment did not end well.

He was given a complex civil case in which a woman, Marie Schee, was suing her uncle over repayment of a $2,000 loan. The uncle owned a home worth $6,500. Nixon arranged an execution sale, but did not research the history of the title. Once the sale had been approved, it was discovered the home had multiple liens on it. Countersuits were filed and, in the end, Schee lost everything. She then filed a malpractice suit against Nixon and the law firm. They settled out of court for $4,800. Nixon may not have technically lost the case, but his career was off to a less than promising start.

From then on, Nixon was mostly tasked with divorce cases. Nixon would shed most of his Quaker upbringing in the coming years, but he was never quite comfortable talking about sex. In 1959, recalling his first divorce case, he said, "This good-looking girl, beautiful really, began talking to me about her intimate marriage problems.... I turned fifteen colors of the rainbow." He was more suited for the personal injury accident cases, but there was little money in them. He took on some tax cases in which he excelled, and Tom Bewley came to view him as a hard worker and forgot about his initial blunder.

As part of his work at the law firm, Nixon drew up incorporation papers for a new company, Citra-Frost. The company's officers believed it had the technology to freeze orange juice and ship it back east. They convinced Nixon to invest his savings and serve as president of the company. He, in turn, convinced others to invest. Nixon secured a contract with a shipping company, but the first shipment spoiled before making it to market. The technology was not sound. Nixon worked hard to make a success of the orange juice business, often helping to pick and squeeze the fruit himself. A year and half later, the company went belly-up. Nixon lost all his meager savings up to that point.

Nixon's ambition remained all-encompassing. He was intent on improving his station in life, and on becoming three sons in one to his mother. He began to throw himself into all sorts of civic associations. He became a member of the 20–30 Club, a young professionals group that had chapters all over the country. He attended the national convention in San Francisco and supported a friend of his to be nominated as national president of the club. He ordered a case of brandy and champagne and made French 75's for the delegates while attempting to sway their votes to his man.

He got himself elected president of the Orange County Association of

Cities, the Duke Alumni of California, and the Whittier College Alumni Association. He was good at politics, and others were taking notice. He wrote a speech titled "Nine Old Men." It was an indictment of FDR and his plan to pack the Supreme Court. He drove around Southern California giving his speech to various Rotary and Kiwanis clubs. Jeff Wingert, the other half of the law partnership he worked for, told his daughter that Richard Nixon "was a better politician than he was a lawyer," and added, "That boy will be President of the United States someday if he wants to."

Nixon was a talented actor and he liked performing. He had not done much acting since his days at Whittier College, but when a community theater was looking for someone to play the district attorney in an upcoming play, his friend Wallace Black suggested Nixon try out for the part. "If you get up there on stage and make a good lawyer, it might bring you some business," Black claims to have told Nixon. Nixon auditioned for the part and got it. The director said he had "above-average acting skills." He enjoyed being on stage again, and early in 1938 he auditioned for another play. It was a murder mystery titled *The Dark Tower*, and it would change his life forever.[3]

Thelma Catherine Ryan lived a hardscrabble existence before she met Richard Nixon. She was born March 16, 1912, in Ely, Nevada. Her father was a man chasing fortune in the West. He had been a surveyor and worked on a whaling ship. He spent much of his adult life prospecting for gold. He called his new child "Pat" because she was born late in the night just hours before St. Patrick's Day. Her mother, Kate Bender, had already lost one husband when, in 1909, she met Will Ryan. They lived in absolute poverty in the Nevada desert with Ryan finding steady work as a timekeeper in a silver mine. Kate did not want to lose another husband. She pleaded with Ryan to move the family to California and try their hand at farming. A year after Pat was born, Will agreed and the family relocated to Artesia, about twenty miles south of Los Angeles.

In California, the Ryan family set up shop on a piece of land and began growing everything they could. Tomatoes and corn and beets and cabbage—the temperate climate of Southern California gave a truck farmer many options. Things were not always sunny in the Ryan household, though. Will drank heavily when things went poorly, and the family remained on the edge of poverty for all of Pat's young life. In 1926, when Pat was just fourteen, her mother died. Almost immediately after Kate's death, her father came down with black lung, a common affliction among veteran miners. Pat became his main caretaker. She and her brothers worked side jobs and made a pact to keep things running so the state would not assign them a guardian. The three siblings managed to stay together, graduate from high school, and all receive scholarships to college. In 1930, Will Ryan died. Thelma Catherine Ryan was eighteen and, in honor of her father, legally changed her name to Patricia.

Pat went on to earn a degree from the University of Southern California while working as a janitor at a local bank and a model in a downtown Los Angeles department store. At age twenty-four she graduated college and landed a job as a teacher in Whittier. For the first time in her life, she held a single job that paid her bills and gave her money for recreation.[4]

In January of 1938, Pat was having dinner with her friend and fellow teacher Elizabeth Cloes at the Hoover Hotel in downtown Whittier. Cloes lobbied Pat to try out for a play being put on at Whittier Community Theatre. Pat had dabbled in acting a bit at USC and even had a bit part in a Hollywood film, though her lines ended up on the cutting-room floor. Cloes thought Pat would be perfect for the part of Daphne in *The Dark Tower*. After much cajoling, Pat walked with her friend over to the church where auditions were being held. She read for the part and got it. She got something else too, the attention of a young lawyer in town.

All his life, Richard Nixon would repeat the story of how he "fell in love at first sight."[5] While it certainly may be true that he fell for Patricia Ryan upon first meeting her, the feeling was far from mutual. He offered to drive Elizabeth Cloes and Pat home after the auditions and, as the two ladies climbed into his 1935 Chevy, Pat made Elizabeth sit in the middle. Nixon was undeterred and, as he dropped them off, he asked Pat for a date. She said she was much too busy.

The scene repeated itself throughout the rehearsals for the play. By opening night, she had relented and agreed to accompany Dick to the Kiwanis Club. It was their first official date. Patricia Ryan liked Dick Nixon in many respects. "He was handsome in a strong way ... he had a wonderful quality in his voice," she would say later in life. But she was not ready to settle down. After a childhood spent in abject poverty and her formative years spent working two and even three jobs to improve her lot in life, she was ready to enjoy some of her hard-won freedom. She wanted to travel and was not ready to be tied down with the responsibilities of having a husband and family. So, she repeatedly turned down Richard Nixon's advances.[6]

Nixon was still undeterred. He wrote letters fawning over her beauty and telling her he intended to marry her. He sent roses on her birthday. She, in turn, tried to set him up with her friend. Richard Nixon had learned that persistence pays, and he kept after Pat Ryan for more than a year. As 1938 turned to 1939, she began to realize that Dick Nixon was not going away. They began going on more dates and talking about what they wanted out of life. They were an ambitious pair and talked of how they longed for the world beyond Whittier, California. In March of 1940, Nixon drove Pat up Highway 101 and turned off onto a dirt road. They made their way to a cliff overlooking the San Clemente coastline. Richard Nixon proposed marriage and Pat Ryan accepted.

Part of Pat's developing admiration for Nixon was due to his ambition. She had eventually been charmed by his persistence and seemed to understand, though she would not admit it for years, that he was indeed a better politician than lawyer. They married in June of 1940 and as a honeymoon took a road trip to Mexico. When they returned, Nixon began looking for ways out of their small California town. He applied for law jobs everywhere from Los Angeles to Havana. His chance came in October 1941.

Franklin Roosevelt signed an executive order creating the Office of Price Administration (OPA) in August of 1941. The agency was tasked with bringing some stability to the consumer prices of staple goods and helping to stave off inflation. The newly created government agency was hiring attorneys as fast as they could find them when a Duke alumnus suggested his old pal from the class of '37. Richard and Pat Nixon jumped at the chance to move to Washington. A month later, the Japanese attacked Pearl Harbor and the United States entered World War II. The event allowed the Nixons to frame their departure from Whittier as patriotic duty, though in reality they had been planning the escape for over a year.

The couple arrived in D.C. on Richard Nixon's twenty-ninth birthday, after a harrowing drive through an ice storm in the Blue Ridge Mountains. He walked on his first day at the OPA into what a historian would later call "utter chaos" as the new bureaucracy struggled with the monumental task of rationing and controlling prices barely a month after the Japanese attack.[7] Dick Nixon soon became disillusioned. He found that he was two salary tiers below his old classmate at Duke even though he had more experience and a better academic record, a fact he could never get over. It wasn't the first or last time he felt slighted by a system that rewarded connections. "Nixon was uncomfortable among the liberals, the Eastern law-school graduates, the Jews he rubbed shoulders with on the job.... He never quite fit in," his immediate supervisor, Thomas Harris, would remember.

Nixon became ideologically opposed to the work of the OPA. He had been an opponent of New Deal liberalism his whole life, but working inside the bureaucracy cemented his views. He would often talk of his work at the OPA as formative in his political thinking. He began to see liberal bureaucrats as less interested in protecting the public from price gouging as they were in controlling the profits of large corporations. He would talk of it often during his eight runs for public office. Historian Stephen Ambrose called his time at the OPA his "Road to Damascus experience."[8]

8. "A quiet game"

Nixon left the OPA after just six months on the job. His decision was not all that unique. Many young men his age were leaving their jobs in mid-1942 to support Uncle Sam's mission. Richard Nixon did not have to go. His job at the OPA entitled him to a deferment, as did his birth into the Quaker religion. He never really considered it, though. He knew American politicians were expected to serve in the military, and this was his generation's moment of service. His mother and father hated the idea of him going against his pacifist Quaker upbringing, but the decision was made.

That August he boarded a train and headed to Rhode Island for naval officer training. After a grueling few months, he was shipped to Ottumwa Naval Air Station in Iowa. "A runway that ended in a cornfield," Nixon would later recall. This was not the kind of active duty that made future politicians.

When Nixon saw an announcement seeking men his age for sea duty, he immediately put in his papers and applied. The orders came through and he reported to the naval station in San Francisco, next stop the South Pacific. Pat followed him to San Francisco, where she found a job with the Office of Civilian Defense and a small apartment on Divisadero Street. Dick Nixon would send a letter to her nearly every day he was stationed in the South Pacific.

Before embarking for San Francisco, they dropped their car in Whittier and the entire Nixon family went to the depot to see Richard off. The group included Nixon's younger brother, thirteen-year-old Eddie, Thomas Bewley, and several family friends. They had a solemn breakfast, "a painful meal full of sad silences," Nixon would later say. Nixon bid his old boss and family adieu and told his young sibling to take good care of his mother. As the train pulled away, Nixon looked back to see his mother straight-faced and expressionless while his father began to cry.[9]

Nixon shipped out for the South Pacific on the USS *President Monroe* on May 31, 1943. He was a commissioned officer but had barely ever set foot on a ship before he sailed out of San Francisco Bay that spring. He would talk of his military service often on his way to becoming president of the United States, but it was a skill he learned on the ship en route to the war zone that launched his political career. The long journey to the islands where he would spend the next year and a half was monotonous. To pass the time, the sailors played poker. Dick Nixon had seen the game played in his days as a carnival barker in Prescott and played himself occasionally in college and law school. It was on the USS *Monroe*, however, that he honed his skills. By the time Nixon arrived in the South Pacific, he was obsessed with the game.

His first post was at New Caledonia, overseeing the flight plans for cargo planes bringing in supplies and flying home the dead and wounded.

The base was far behind the front lines and there was no chance for military heroics. The days were routine and dull. A few months later, his unit was moved to Bougainville, an island only recently captured by American forces. Here he endured Japanese bombing raids. Nothing more than his tent was ever destroyed, though these bombing raids would be spoken of in harrowing fashion in his official campaign literature. He did participate in the invasion of Green Island, but with the rear guard. By the time Nixon and his men arrived, the Japanese were in full retreat. He noted in his memoir that the only danger on Green Island came from "the ever-present giant centipedes."[10]

Green Island was a supply base for the U.S. military, with an enormous amount of material passing through. Nixon set up Nick's Snack Shack to serve his fellow men stationed on the island and those passing through on their way to or from combat. Edward McCaffrey, another naval officer stationed on the island, described it this way:

> Nick was able to wheedle the supplies for his Snack Shack from other outfits that were better stocked.... Nick would swap anything. Just a small trade would set in motion a series of bigger trades.... Some of the items on the menu were not on the government issue list; an occasional bottle of whiskey ... which he doled out among men without regard to the rank.

Not surprisingly, Nick's Snack Shack became a very popular destination on Green Island.[11]

As with the Wheel of Fortune game in Prescott, the real action was in the back of the Snack Shack. While in Prescott, Nixon had mostly watched. His Quaker upbringing and his young age kept him from participating. On Green Island, Nixon was the host. In 1960 an unidentified "Wall Street man" who claimed to have served with Nixon on Green Island told a reporter, "Nick ran a twenty-four-hour poker game there. He was a hell of a poker player. But

Richard Nixon in the navy, 1945 (courtesy Richard Nixon Presidential Library and Museum).

that wasn't the way he made his money. He made it by letting us play in the back room. He took a cut out of each pot."[12] Another man who was stationed on the island said, "A hundred Navy officers will tell you Nick never lost a cent at poker." Yet another, Lester Wroble, claimed that while Nixon never lost, he was never the big winner, either; he just "seemed to always end up 30 or 60 dollars ahead."[13] Wroble recalled how Nixon had a "passion for analysis; he always played it cautious."[14] Fellow soldier James Udall recalled Nixon's poker playing a little differently: "He played a quiet game, but he was not afraid of taking chances. He wasn't afraid of running a bluff."[15] Udall recalled how he once watched Nixon "bluff a lieutenant commander out of a 1,500-dollar pot with a pair of deuces."[16]

While some of these characterizations of Nixon's poker playing seem at odds with each other, they are probably all true. Poker is all about the art of the bluff. It is acting, and Richard Nixon was a great actor. Many of the details of exactly what Nixon won and how he ran the game are lost to history. He always downplayed his winnings when asked about them, but historians have estimated he won between five and ten thousand dollars while playing poker in the navy. Good money in 1945. How much he won will never be known for sure, but by the time he left the navy he was out of debt and soon to launch a campaign for Congress.

9

"Are you a registered voter in California?"

Richard Nixon left the South Pacific and was reunited with his wife in California in July 1944. He was stationed at Alameda Naval Station in a job he described to Pat as "chief janitor." But in January 1945 the navy found work for Nixon that more closely aligned with his training and experience. He was sent bouncing around the Northeast to work with a naval legal team terminating wartime contracts between private companies and the government. He was dining with Pat at a Philadelphia restaurant in April when the waiter informed them of FDR's death. He was working in a Manhattan skyscraper in May when he caught the first glimpse of his future. He looked down from the twentieth floor at a ticker tape parade on Church Street and saw Dwight D. Eisenhower, the star attraction, standing in the back of a car with both arms raised as throngs of New Yorkers cheered the victorious general.[1]

The postwar political climate of the United States in 1945 was turbulent. The country's unity in fighting the war had papered over deep divisions in society, and many of them came roaring back to the forefront once peace was at hand. The battle between labor and capital had been raging for half a century and never really disappeared during the war but took on new prominence in the postwar world. President Harry Truman endorsed wage increases and management refused. A conference was called that accomplished nothing and strikes ensued. Auto, steel, coal, and railroad workers all went on strike in 1946. Truman for the most part sided with the unions. He supported their demand for an 18-cent-an-hour raise but also threatened to draft union members into the army when they refused what he saw as a compromise. In the end, Truman received the blame from both sides. The public was angry at striking workers and blamed the White House even as the Congress of Industrial Organizations (CIO) was calling Truman "the number one strike breaker."

Meanwhile the cooperation between the Soviet Union and the United States was over. Without the common German enemy, the two sides found

9. "Are you a registered voter in California?"

themselves unable to move past their ideological differences. The Soviets' view of the postwar world was influenced by years of fending off invading armies. They saw a newly ascendant America occupying Japan on their west coast and Europe as a threat in the east. Stalin, in a betrayal of his agreement with Roosevelt at Yalta to hold free elections, installed communist governments in Romania and Poland. In March of 1946, Winston Churchill famously declared that an "iron curtain" had descended on Eastern Europe, and the Cold War was on.

The American public was anxious in the fall of 1946, and Truman and the Democrats took all the blame. Raw economic data shows unemployment was low and inflation moderate. Business profits, farm income and industrial production all reached new peaks in 1946. But none of that mattered. A marketing company in Boston devised the slogan Republicans would use in the midterms: "Had enough?" This simple phrase encapsulated the public's feelings. There had been nearly two decades of Democratic control and the country wanted a change. It was the perfect time for a man like Richard Nixon to get started in a career in politics.[2]

Herman Perry hated Jerry Voorhis. Perry had come to Whittier, California, in 1906 and came of age in the town. He rose through the ranks of the banking business as what a contemporary called "a true, shrewd banker" who was never shy about his politics. By the early forties he was the vice president of Bank of America in California and was known around Whittier as "Mr. Republican." His nemesis, Jerry Voorhis, represented California's 12th district and was one of the most liberal members of Congress. Voorhis had been elected in 1936 after changing his registration from Socialist to Democrat. He called himself a Progressive–Roosevelt Democrat, and he beat out a scandal-ridden incumbent to win the seat. He supported FDR's New Deal, backing even his controversial court-packing plan. Perry disagreed with Voorhis on almost everything. By 1945, Perry had enough power to do something. He said he wanted "to put an end to the socialist trend of the New Deal." He called the thirties and early forties a "communistic era."

Roy Day was the son of an orange rancher. He dropped out of high school to pitch semi-pro baseball before holding various jobs traversing Latin America for the United Fruit Company. He eventually made his way back to Southern California and found work as an advertising salesman in Pomona. Day fell in love with politics, at least the fight and competition of it all if not so much the cause. The Republicans were his team and he put together a group of businessmen, ranchers, bankers, and lawyers to find a consensus candidate to take on the Democrat. He called it the Committee of 100, and Herman Perry was one of the first members.

An ad was put in various district newspapers calling for conservative candidates. The committee met with a half dozen applicants, including a former registered socialist and a former Stanford football standout. None fit the bill. Frank Jorgensen, a San Marino insurance executive on the committee, was exasperated. "My God, if this is all we can get to run for Congress, let's not waste our time," he said.

Roy Day put forth the name of Walter Dexter. Dexter was the former president of Whittier College, and, while not everyone on the committee agreed, he seemed like the best choice. A meeting was scheduled. Several letters between Day and Dexter indicate that Day had convinced the group of wealthy kingmakers; Dexter just needed to come meet them and assure them he was up to the challenge. Four days before Dexter was to come meet the committee, he collapsed of a heart attack and died. Jerry Voorhis's longtime campaign manager wrote to him from Whittier about the committee's possible candidates. "None of them appear dangerous," he said.

Herman Perry had known Frank and Hannah Nixon the whole time they had lived in Whittier. He attended their wedding and loaned the family money for the grocery store. In late October of 1945, still searching for a candidate, he asked one of his employees at the bank who had attended Whittier College with Nixon, "What would you think of Dick Nixon running against Jerry Voorhis?"

"Well, I think it is an excellent idea, he can at least talk. That's something you haven't been able to find anyone to do yet," the former classmate told him.[3]

Perry floated the idea by other wealthy Republican contributors and the editor of the *Whittier Daily News*. All seemed to agree Nixon could work. Perry called the Nixon grocery, seeking to contact the potential candidate. Richard Nixon was living in Maryland, still terminating contracts in the Navy Reserve and eagerly looking for better prospects on the East Coast. Perry wrote him a life-changing letter:

> I am writing you this short note to ask if you would like to be a candidate for Congress on the Republican ticket in 1946.
> Jerry Voorhis expects to run—registration is about fifty-fifty. The Republicans are gaining.
> Please airmail me your response if you are interested.
> Yours Very Truly,
> H.L. Perry
>
> P.S. Are you a registered voter in California?

Nixon liked the idea but had some reservations. He and Pat were not super-keen on moving back to the small town they had left. There was also

9. "Are you a registered voter in California?" 47

the issue of money. They had ten thousand dollars in combined savings and poker money, with which they had planned to buy a house somewhere on the East Coast once Nixon found a job. Pat was already pregnant. Moving to California to run for Congress was a big departure from the plan they had made for their lives. It was a gamble, and Richard Nixon was a gambler. He called Herman Perry and said he was interested. Perry said he couldn't promise anything, but he would fly him out and he could meet the committee.

Nixon walked into the committee meeting in his Navy dress blues. He wowed the assembly with a speech about two opposing views of government in America. One idea, embodied by the New Deal and Democrats, called for government intervention in regulating the lives of Americans. The other advocated free markets and "all that initiative can produce." Nixon believed in the latter, he said. "I believe the returning veteran, and I have talked to many in the foxholes, will not be satisfied with a dole or government handout. They want a respectable job in private industry where they will be recognized for what they produce, or they want the opportunity to start their own business," Nixon said, embellishing his military service. He went on that he was prepared to wage "an aggressive and vigorous campaign ... and with your help I feel very strongly the present incumbent can be defeated."[4]

The committee was won over; they could not have said it better themselves. Roy Day was ecstatic. "That's salable merchandise," he told Frank Jorgensen. The committee voted unanimously to back Nixon for the Republican nomination. Nixon was discharged from the navy in January of 1946, and he and Pat moved back to Whittier. While gaining the committee's backing was an important step, he still had to win the election with everyday voters. He began studying the voting record of Jerry Voorhis, and he saw the weak spot.[5]

Voorhis was not a communist. But the Congress of Industrial Organizations did have quite a few avowed communists in its rank-and-file membership. The CIO had launched a political action committee in 1943 to help FDR's bid for a fourth term. CIO-PAC was the only PAC most Americans knew about. In 1944, with the CIO cooperating fully with industrial production to aid the war effort, the charge of being soft on communism made no impact. In fact, Voorhis's opponent in 1944 had tried it. But in 1946, more workers went on strike than at any other point in U.S. labor history. Russia consolidated Eastern Europe into satellite communist states and erected what Churchill called the iron curtain. Voters' views on communism changed.

Nixon started the campaign by harping on government price controls and Voorhis's continued support for them. But it was the charge that he was soft on communism that stuck. Roy Crocker, a Committee of 100 member, put out a press release saying, "Now that the Political Action Committee has publicly endorsed the candidacy of Jerry Voorhis for Congress, one of the real issues of the campaign is out in the open." A number of smaller newspapers in the district wrote editorials slamming Voorhis for his endorsement by a "radical" PAC. The CIO had in fact never endorsed him. In an arcane distinction few voters caught, it was a separate PAC, the National Citizens PAC, that endorsed him. It didn't matter, though. Nixon just kept saying "PAC" in his speeches and advertisements, and voters heard "communist."

Nixon told voters that communists were conspiring to slowly overthrow the government from within. He claimed the OPA where he had worked was "shot through with extreme left wingers" looking to "force private enterprise into bankruptcy, and thus bring about the socialization of America's basic institutions and industries." Nixon took out an ad in every paper in California's 12th district. "PAC looks after the interest of Russia," it said in a boldfaced headline. The meat of the argument was underneath: "REMEMBER, Voorhis is a former registered Socialist and his voting record in Congress is more Socialistic and Communistic than Democratic." Nixon was never one for nuance.

Voorhis had never faced an opponent like Richard Nixon, who well knew Voorhis was not a communist and admitted as much to a campaign aide years later. "Of course I knew Jerry Voorhis wasn't a communist," he said. "You know I know better than that: I know the processes of the legislature and Congress better than that. But … I had to win. That's the thing you don't understand. The important thing is to win." And win he did, by 15,000 votes out of the 117,000 cast. In January 1947, thirty-three-year-old Richard Nixon was sworn in as California's new congressman from the 12th district.[6]

Nixon arrived in Washington as part of the new majority in the 80th Congress. For fourteen years, Republicans had been in the minority, fuming at the New Deal and what they saw as a leftist takeover of institutions. Now they had their chance to enact some change. The first job was assigning committee positions to new members. Nixon was advised to seek a seat on the Agriculture Committee because of his district's large farming base. He knew that was no path to higher power and he angled for the Judiciary Committee, but was told that wasn't going to happen for a freshman. He settled for the Committee on Education and Labor, deciding that taking on labor unions would be a good way to make some headlines.

Then there was the committee he would always say he had not actually wanted to sit on. He would talk often in his future runs for office of anguishing over the decision to accept the assignment, the one he wrote

9. "Are you a registered voter in California?" 49

in his memoirs that he "accepted with considerable reluctance."[7] In reality, Nixon and his allies (Herman Perry was friends with the new Speaker of the House, Joe Martin) lobbied heavily to get him one of the three open seats on the House Un-American Activities Committee. "No one went on a committee of that kind who did not wish very much to be a member," Martin later said.[8]

HUAC, as the committee was popularly known, grew out of a 1919 ad hoc committee tasked with investigating communism after World War I. By 1946 it was a standing committee in the House. Its work was often dubious and attracted headlines. Nixon knew the committee was a prime way to get attention and that he just had to wait for the right moment to capitalize on. He found it on August 3, 1948.

The story of Alger Hiss and Whittaker Chambers has been told many times. It was the premier political story of the late forties and early fifties and one's opinion on the case could tell you quite a bit about their voting habits.[9] The story is complicated. It begins with a senior editor of *Time* magazine, Whittaker Chambers. Chambers was a confessed former communist and by the late forties was on a one-man campaign to rid the U.S. government of communist infiltration, which he claimed was rampant. He testified before the committee and named names. One of the men he accused of being a communist was Alger Hiss, a high-ranking State Department official.

Richard Nixon saw people as either "Franklins" or "Orthogonians." East Coast elites or real Americans.[10] Hiss was the very definition of a Franklin. Educated at Harvard, he had clerked for Supreme Court justice Oliver Wendell Holmes. He was friends with the current and soon to be secretaries of state Dean Acheson and John Foster Dulles. He had been on the committee to establish the United Nations and was an aide to President Roosevelt at Yalta. Chambers claimed that both he and Hiss had secretly been members of the Communist Party in the thirties. He claimed Hiss had allowed him to stay at his house and that Hiss had secretly passed him top-secret classified documents.

Hiss was enraged at the accusation. His friends advised him to stay quiet, just wait and let the whole thing blow over. Chambers was a drunk and probably a closeted homosexual; no one was going to take him seriously, they told him. If Alger Hiss had listened, it is highly probable his name would not be found in as many history books as it is today. But Hiss could not stay silent. He demanded an opportunity to clear his name in front of the committee.

Hiss sat indignantly before the committee and protested his innocence. He was not a communist and never had been, he said. He "had never heard the name Whittaker Chambers."[11] He had a sterling record of public service and was a proud patriot. He was outraged and would not stand for this libel. The committee was convinced. When his testimony was over, people applauded. Members came down to shake his hand and apologize. Not Richard Nixon, though. Nixon thought Hiss was condescending and insulting, and he thought he was hiding something. After all, Chambers and Hiss could not both be telling the truth. Nixon convinced the committee the allegations warranted further investigation, and they made him subcommittee chair to delve into them further. Nixon made a trip to Chambers's Maryland farm and coached him on how best to testify. He implored him to think back and remember every detail he could. And then he called Hiss back to Congress to testify again, this time in private.

In private questioning, Hiss was shown a photograph of Chambers and said he might have known him under a different name, George Crosley. He then admitted that he did know him as George Crosley. He had subleased an apartment to him and sold him a car sometime in the thirties. He claimed he had no knowledge of Crosley's communist activity and had never been a communist himself. The private round of questioning set up another public showdown on August 17. Hiss was allowed to cross-examine Chambers. He asked if he had ever gone by the name George Crosley; he had not. Had he ever sublet an apartment from Hiss on 29th Street in Washington, D.C.? He had not. Had he ever spent time alone in the 29th Street apartment in question? He had. How can you reconcile these answers? Hiss asked. "Very easily, Alger, I was a communist and you were a communist," Chambers said.[12]

There was an audible gasp in the committee room and the comment made national headlines. Having uttered this as part of congressional testimony, Chambers was protected from a defamation lawsuit. An enraged Hiss challenged Chambers to make the statements in public, without legal protection. The next week, Chambers went on the radio program *Meet the Press* and repeated the charge. Hiss sued him for libel.

The lawsuit led Chambers to expand his charge. Not only was Alger Hiss a secret communist, but he was also a spy, and Chambers had documents to prove it. Chambers produced retyped State Department cables and handwritten notes on State Department documents that he claimed were given to him by Hiss and his wife for transmission to Moscow. Chambers led investigators to his Maryland farm, where he had stashed a roll of microfilm in a hollowed-out pumpkin. The film contained classified documents he said were given to him by Alger Hiss.

The press went wild. Richard Nixon raced home from a Caribbean vacation with Pat to examine the new evidence. The Pumpkin Papers, as they came to be known, showed that Hiss's handwriting matched that of the handwritten notes Chambers produced. The typed documents were

9. "Are you a registered voter in California?"

consistent with the model of typewriter Hiss owned. The public turned against Hiss. The statute of limitations had expired on the espionage charge, but he was arrested and charged with perjury.

Nixon would always claim that he had just had a hunch. That there was something too "Franklin" in Alger Hiss's demeanor and he knew he was hiding something. Historians have since discovered that he had some help. Father John Cronin was one of the most influential Catholic priests in Baltimore and a vehement anti-communist. He had worked for the FBI in the thirties, infiltrating communist groups in the Baltimore area. He claimed in a 1945 report that Alger Hiss was the number one communist in the State Department. After Hiss's initial hearing, Father Cronin saw Nixon was skeptical and he met with the freshman congressman. The priest served as a "go-between, collecting information from the FBI and passing it to Nixon via the congressman's private phone line."[13] Nixon knew Hiss was hiding something and he orchestrated a public show to prove it. It worked. Alger Hiss went to prison and Richard Nixon became a household name.

10

"A time of pocket change"

Mel Crosby and Alma Conrow were high-school sweethearts. When Mel completed his stint in the army, he returned to his hometown of Oneonta, New York, and married Alma. They found a small house on East End Avenue which they purchased with the help of the G.I. Bill. Mel tended bar and refereed children's soccer and basketball games to make the $35 monthly payments. In mid–March of 1942, the young couple had a son and named him Ronald Clyde Crosby.

Ron Crosby's upbringing was typical for a white middle-class child of the postwar era. He attended school just six blocks from his home. He spent afternoons playing pickup games of baseball in the backyards of neighbors until suppertime came and, one by one, the voices of neighborhood mothers rang out from front porches up and down the streets calling the children in. He described it as "an Ozzie and Harriet" kind of life, a reference to the popular 1950s TV show that sold the idea of what the good life meant in mid-twentieth-century America.

On the weekends and in the summertime, Ron would head down the road to his grandparents' farm. His mother's parents, Clyde and Jessie Conrow, owned a small dairy farm with sixteen cows and a garden. It was a self-sufficient business built and maintained by hardworking people from a different time. Ron called his namesake Clyde "his first hero" in life. He was a big potbellied man with wire-rimmed glasses. He instilled his love of life into Ronald.

The Conrows held big family suppers almost every Sunday and afterwards Grandma Jessie would play the piano while everyone sang. The Conrows loved music and they formed a family band that played farmers' dances around the area. Jessie was the piano player and Clyde played the drums. Jessie's sisters would sing and sometimes they would bring in a guitar and banjo player for bigger gigs. The gigs would often go all the way to sunrise, with Clyde making it home and unloading his drum set just in time to milk the cows.

In 1954 Ron's family moved to an apartment in the middle of town.

10. "A time of pocket change"

A downstairs neighbor owned a Harmony guitar that he could not quite seem to get the hang of. He offered to let Ron borrow it and the boy began to teach himself what he could. For Christmas that year, Jessie paid the man eighty dollars, and the guitar officially became Ron's.

In the summer of 1957, Ron was working on his grandparents' farm, baling hay with one of his running buddies from school. They worked long, hard days and at the end Clyde told them they had worked like men and therefore could relax like men. They were allowed one Ballantine beer each as a reward for a job well done.

Ronald would write later in life that "what was left of my childhood ended on a sultry day when I was 15. That one last summer." On an especially hot August afternoon, Ron's friend, Mike Patton, loaded the last bale of hay on the wagon and hopped on the back. Clyde drove the tractor that pulled the wagon, and Ron was to follow in the Jeep. Ron checked the wagon gate and watched as the tractor and wagon disappeared over the hill; he never saw it happen. As he came over the hill in the Jeep, he saw the hay wagon jackknifed and the tractor upside down in a ditch, its wheels still spinning. Mike Patton had been thrown twenty feet but was essentially unharmed. Clyde Conrow was pinned under the tractor. He had died almost instantly in the violent chaos of the wreck.

From then on, Ronald Clyde Crosby's life was different. He looked old for his age and could buy beer. He began staying out late, disobeying his parents' curfew. Then he began not coming home at all. He and his father had a blowup over a nine o'clock curfew being imposed, and Ron moved out of the house and in with his friend. Eventually an agreement was made in which Ron would live at home until he finished high school and then he could be on his own.

Graduation came and Ron was one chemistry credit short. The school allowed him to participate in the ceremony, but he would have to attend summer school in 1960. Then he would be gone. But fall came around and Ronald Crosby was still in Oneonta, New York. He had no interest in going to college and no firm direction of any kind. He was ostensibly living on his grandmother Jessie's couch, staying out late drinking, sleeping until afternoon, and then repeating the process.

One day his father came to the farm and saw Ron lying on the couch. "Ron, you're going to lie around like a bum and break your mother's heart," he said. He told him he didn't have to go to school, but he had to get some kind of job. He said, "Son, if nothing else, why don't you join the National Guard?"

Ron took the advice to heart. He started delivering the Ballantine beer that he loved to drink to local stores and bars for spending money, and he joined the New York National Guard. In the spring of 1961, he reported for basic training. On weekend leaves, the soldiers would drive into New Jersey to drink, but the drinking age in New Jersey was twenty-one and Ron was only nineteen. He explained his predicament to one of his platoon buddies, who promptly pulled out a draft card and handed it to Ron. It read "Jerry Ferris." Jerry Ferris was twenty-one.

It wasn't long before the National Guard seemed like just one more thing trapping Ron in Oneonta. Once basic training was over, Ron continued to deliver beer during the week while spending his evenings drinking it and lamenting the sorry state of affairs in his life. He began running with some older guys. Listening to Miles Davis and Lord Buckley records, they would all talk about their big plans to blow town. Get out and see the world. But no one ever left.

It was after midnight and Ronald Clyde Crosby was sitting in a bar. He sat there drinking Ballantine beer and feeling sorry for himself. He pounded his fist on the bar and shouted, "How the hell do I get out of this town?"

"First you take Route 7," Howie Clark said in a calm voice.

Howie was a fixture at the local bars in Oneonta and Ronald knew of Howie, but didn't really know him. Howie had a fresh Ballantine beer in front of him and he raised his glass in a toast.

"That's the way I've always gone," he said. "You take 7, south. And get warm."

Ronald moved over to the barstool next to him. "But how?" he said.

"You just go," Howie replied.

"Right now?" Ron asked.

"As soon as I finish this beer." Howie looked at him with a mischievous smile and drained his glass. He slid off his barstool and Ron followed. They walked out the door and toward Route 7 and put their thumbs out, looking for anyone willing to take them south.

That first time Ron Crosby left Oneonta, he stayed gone about three months. He and Howie Clark found a ride somewhere along Route 7 and, through a series of Chevys and Fords, wound up in Fort Lauderdale Beach. It was the spring of 1962, and spring break, which was to become a national tradition for college students, was just beginning.

Glendon Swarthout published his novel *Where the Boys Are* in 1960. It was a coming-of-age novel about four girls who travel to Fort Lauderdale from their midwestern university. The book challenged conventional notions of adolescent sexuality and was an immediate hit. The novel and subsequent 1960 film inspired a generation of kids to head to Fort Lauderdale. The beaches were crowded with young kids throwing off convention and looking for a new way to live. It was a far cry from Woodstock, but it was the beginning of a cultural shift, a new generation of men and women coming of age in a nuclear world. The sons and daughters were now beyond their parents' command, as Bob Dylan would soon sing. Ronald Clyde Crosby fit right in. He worked odd jobs, parking cars at a hotel, flipping burgers, even running the limbo contest on the beach for two dollars a day at one point. He didn't have much money, but the party was never-ending, and he felt like he had escaped the life others had planned for him in New York. He spent his twentieth birthday playing songs on the beach for impromptu crowds.

Eventually the spring breakers returned to their respective college campuses and Ron Crosby began to feel anxious. He was due to report back to the National Guard soon and he owed his father money. He headed back to Oneonta and arrived on Easter weekend 1962, vowing that this return was only temporary. One thing led to another, though, and before he knew it he had a job and an apartment. He still had time left on his National Guard commitment and didn't know what to do. One afternoon, he decided he couldn't take it anymore. He told no one, including his family. He knew going AWOL meant the possibility of jail time if he ever returned. Still, he grabbed his duffle bag and guitar and headed for Route 7. His first ride was from the older brother of a co-worker on the beer trucks. Ron explained how he felt trapped by the small town and how he did not want to live the life others had planned for him. Ralph Goodrich listened as they rode along, and when he reached his destination, about twenty miles from town, he pulled over and let Ron Crosby out. He handed him twenty dollars and said, "Do what you think you have to do, son."

Goodrich pulled away and left Ron standing by the side of the highway, where he threw away all his identification except for the fake draft card. "Ron Crosby no longer existed," he later wrote. "It was Jerry Ferris who climbed into the next car and headed down the highway. This was not a road trip. This was the road."[1]

His first stop was Tampa, Florida, as he tried to re-create the party atmosphere from his first foray into life on the open road. But he found Tampa "grey and joyless," as he would describe it later in life, and it wasn't long before he drifted toward New Orleans. "I hitchhiked in from a little town that probably went to sleep every night at 10 o'clock and I walked down the streets of New Orleans, and its Dixieland music, people walking by with umbrellas in their drinks, kissing and hugging and it'd be Wednesday night! I thought, 'How long has this been going on?'"[2] Jerry Ferris felt he had found his destiny in the neon lights and vibrant street scene. All around him there were "skinny old black men tap dancing for change outside. Street singers on the corners, voices and guitars and tambourines chattering for some handout money."

Jerry met a man named Dick Westall on one of his first nights in town. Dick was a little older than Jerry and began to show him the ropes. The two split a room on Bourbon Street for two dollars a day and would spend the evenings playing their guitars on the street corners. Folk music was all the rage in the early 1960s. Bob Dylan had just released his second album and middle-class white kids everywhere were taking up the guitar and starting folk groups. One night a bartender gave Jerry and Dick some advice. He said they looked too preppy, like college kids from LSU, just drunk frat kids with guitars. He told them that if they wanted to make it as street performers, they had to look the part. So they went to the Salvation Army and bought some old shirts. Jerry began to realize the role image played in show business; "they were looking for color, wanting me to be different from them, so I became more colorful."

It wasn't long before Jerry was accepted into the informal fraternity of New Orleans street performers. He was performing every night on the corners of the French Quarter and at bars where owners would invite him in to "pick a few" and pass the hat. He started crashing at an old warehouse with army cots that cost fifty cents a night. It is where many of the street musicians wound up after a long night. Jerry began learning different fingerpicking styles and would spend the mornings practicing. He did not make much money, but he did not need much money. He would leave the old warehouse on Elysian Fields Avenue around lunchtime and start his day off with a po' boy and Pepsi from Minty's for 95 cents. He would spend the rest of the afternoon practicing his guitar and learning new songs, sometimes writing his own, and then head off to the street corners, bars, and coffeehouses to perform as the sun went down. "It was a time of pocket change," he would later recall. He began hanging out at the Ryder Coffee House and the Quorum, two New Orleans nightspots popular with the bohemian set. It was a mix of whites and Blacks who were "unconcerned with the politics of race," just "street musicians, sharing slugs of whiskey." This was the exception in segregated Louisiana, and in July of 1964 the police raided the Quorum, claiming it was the epicenter of "Communist propaganda, homosexual parties, and integration agitation." Seventy-three people were arrested, but not Jerry—he had just skipped town.

"You've got to go somewhere before you can be missed," Jerry used to say, and in between his stints of education as a street performer, he would take off. Jerry was constantly looking for adventure. He would spend a few months in New Orleans and then hit the highway with his duffle bag and guitar to experience life on the road. One night he wound up in Ohio, at Oberlin College. He saw Doc Watson and Ramblin' Jack Elliott perform, and he realized what he wanted to do. He wanted to "pick like Doc and tell stories like Jack and write songs all my own."

10. "A time of pocket change"

"Going where the weather suits my clothes" was a song line Jerry lived by throughout his life. After seeing Doc Watson and Ramblin' Jack, he could feel the beginnings of an Ohio winter setting in, so he headed back south to New Orleans. "Hitting the Quarter again felt like coming home," he said, and he soon met up with a man who would become one of his main influences, an old Black street performer named Babe Stovall.

Babe hailed from Tylertown, Mississippi, and had sold his pig to buy a guitar. He performed in the beer joints around Tylertown before eventually drifting south to New Orleans. He had been performing the night the cops raided the Quorum. Babe took Jerry under his wing and the two became inseparable friends. An odd couple at first sight for sure: a young middle-class white kid turned folk gypsy sitting around picking old blues songs and drinking jugs of whiskey with a Black ex-sharecropper-turned-street-performer more than twice his age. Still, in New Orleans this was not something that turned heads. New Orleans has long been a haven for free thinkers, artists, and pirates, and the cultural revolution of 1960s America found a distinctive expression in the Crescent City. "If you lived in the South in the '60s, and you were just a little bit different, New Orleans was where you belonged," Jerry wrote of his younger days.

One night in 1964 Jerry was playing in a French Quarter bar when Jack Baker walked in. Baker was the company clerk at Jerry's National Guard unit in Oneonta. Jerry saw him from across the bar and thought his adventure was over. He headed over to the booth where Jack was sitting.

"I surrender," he announced to the table. Jack looked over and almost spit his beer out of his mouth at the surprise of seeing his old friend.

"Did they send you down here to arrest me?" Jerry asked.

"Fuck no. I'm the last guy they'd send for anybody. I'm out of the Guard. Signed on with the navy again. I'm in port here. Just having a beer," Jack explained to him.

The two men laughed, shared a beer, and told each other stories from the past few years before Jack made a confession to Jerry. He said, "I don't think they even know you're gone." Jerry's eyes widened and an odd silence hung between them for a moment. "The last time you split, I just left your name on the records. You're probably still making roll call." Jerry sat in stunned silence as Jack, now whispering, continued, "What you ought to do is go back and get it all cleared up for good. If they screwed up your records, they're likely to make a deal with you. And your folks need to hear from you too."

The older brother-esque advice hit Jerry hard, and he knew his old friend was right. He had not spoken with his family in almost two years, and he knew that he would never be able to obtain a passport and travel outside the country without clearing up his status with the army. So Jerry headed for the highway and stuck his thumb out. He was back in Oneonta a couple days later. His parents saw him walking up the road in cowboy boots and an untucked shirt. A taller, full-grown man now, the prodigal son was welcomed home by Mel and Alma. Jerry met his kid sister for what was essentially the first time. She had been but a toddler when he took off and now she was in grade school and staring at him with inquisitive eyes.

The next day he combed his hair and exchanged his cowboy boots and Salvation Army shirt for some of his old clothes from high school, the kind the bartender had said made him look too preppy. He walked into the Oneonta National Guard office, prepared for the worst. The company commander was new to the post and he had the military file of PFC Ron Crosby in his hand. He thumbed through it and stared at him.

"Since I got in here, I've been cleaning up a lot of old business. We see you've had, well, a pretty much hit-and-miss deal with the U.S. military," he said, staring at Jerry Ferris, who had been cleaned up and transformed back into Ron Crosby.

"Yeah," was all Crosby could mumble in response.

"We saw that you'd been on our books long after you were gone. Looked bad for our records. So, what we did was put you on permanent standby reserve," the commander explained while closing the file.

He stared a hole through the young gypsy and said, "To tell the truth, we didn't expect to see your ass anymore."

The young man's voice cracked as he replied, "I believe you won't, sir."

"That'll be all, son, you're dismissed."

He walked out of the National Guard office that day in shock. He was free, truly free to do anything he wanted and be anyone he wanted. He could not believe it. He decided on the spot that he no longer wanted to be Jerry Ferris. Jerry Ferris was a man on the run, and he was no longer that. He did not want to be Ron Crosby either, though. Ron Crosby was the basketball player from Oneonta High. He was the man who played pickup baseball games and lived the Ozzie and Harriet life. He had bigger plans now, and decided that he would be Jeff Walker. "Walker" was a tribute to Kirby Walker, a jazz pianist in New Orleans who he loved, and he just liked the name Jeff. It seemed to fit his image of himself, and from now on he would be Jeff Walker.

Two weeks later he was back in New Orleans, playing on the street corners and in the bars and picking guitar with Babe over jugs of whiskey until early in the morning. When he came back to town, he proclaimed himself Jeff Walker. It wasn't taking, though. Too many people knew him as Jerry, and he could not seem to make his new name stick. One night, after a good bit of red wine, he was about to take his turn on a dimly lit stage when the bouncer announced to the crowd in a thick Louisiana accent:

"Ladies and gentlemen. Live. In New Awlins, Lews'yana. Jerry! Jeff! Walker!"[3]

PART 2

11

"Drifting, poor, and searching"

In the fall of 1964, Jerry Jeff Walker roamed the streets of the French Quarter like he owned the place. He knew all the bartenders, club owners and street singers. He had a solid repertoire of songs he could perform to make a living. He knew how to spot tourists and present himself as "a true street character," and they obliged with quarters, nickels and dimes. He and Babe Stovall were playing every Thursday at Cosimo's, a French Quarter club, making up to a hundred dollars a night in tips. He spent his days writing songs and street-corner philosophizing with other artists and writers. It was New Orleans in the mid–'60s, and it felt like a million miles from Oneonta.

On Thanksgiving 1964 some of Jerry Jeff's artist friends organized a dinner with Babe and some of his family. The party got underway early, and as night rolled around Jerry Jeff and Babe showed up at their weekly gig with a large interracial entourage. The club owner stopped them. "No niggers in my joint," he told Jerry Jeff. Babe was different; he would only be on stage, and he was performing. But his family? They could not come in, the owner said. Jerry Jeff pleaded with him, saying that the group would be guests of the band and stay in the band area. But the owner would not relent.

Jerry Jeff walked out and informed the group of the situation. He asked Babe what he wanted to do. Babe calmly looked at him and said, "Jer'uh. I makes money. Money don't make me." They both laughed and walked away with thirty-odd people in tow. They made their way through the Quarter to a spot they had heard was hosting a party. They set up in the corner and began to jam. They passed the hat and made as much as they would have made at Cosimo's.

Of course, when the following Thursday rolled around, they were out of a gig. But that didn't matter. Jerry Jeff wrote a song about it. Life was moving along and things were changing. Jerry Jeff met another free spirit named Barbara Lyons. She had also run away from New York with the intention of finding a less conformist life in New Orleans. The pair fell in love and were soon living together. At first, Jerry Jeff enjoyed the stability after his years of rambling. He still was playing street corners and bars and living the life a free man, but he had a hot shower and warm bed when he wanted it.

As 1964 turned to 1965, the soon to be twenty-three-year-old Jerry Jeff was concerned that New Orleans would tie him down like Oneonta if he didn't put his thumb in the wind soon. Later in life, writing of his hitchhiking adventures in the mid-sixties, he said, "I had seen enough of Texas to know I wanted to see more." He explained his predicament to Barbara, who understood. He told her he loved her and that he "had to do this." They kissed each other goodbye, and Jerry Jeff walked down the road with his guitar case.

He wound up in Dallas a few days later. Dallas was home to the Rubaiyat, a folk club where Jerry Jeff began playing. He made some friends and was soon living on McKinney Avenue and playing the Rubaiyat every week. He began focusing on writing every day. He soon wrote "Little Bird" about Barbara and young love. He wrote "Driftin' Way of Life," based on an old gospel melody he heard Michael Martin Murphey sing at the Rubaiyat. Both songs would become standards in his set for the next fifty years.

Jerry Jeff was living for music. It was all that mattered to him. Writing every day and at the Rubaiyat every night. If not performing himself, absorbing what others sang. He became friends with Andre Szucha, an artist who came to the U.S. as a refugee fleeing the 1956 Hungarian Revolution. Andre hung his paintings at the Rubaiyat, and he would have Jerry Jeff over to drink homemade wine and play songs.

One night, Ramblin' Jack Elliott came to town and played the Rubaiyat. Jerry Ferris had seen Ramblin' Jack at Oberlin College as a fan. It was a big reason why he had taken up songwriting. When Jerry Jeff saw Ramblin' Jack in Dallas, it was as a student. He watched how Elliott worked the crowd and spun songs into stories and stories back into songs. Watching Ramblin' Jack, Jerry Jeff learned how to "touch strangers in an audience" and "how to put magic and imagination into a song."

It wasn't long before Jerry Jeff started to feel the dust on his boots again. It was time to be moving. One of the Rubaiyat regulars suggested they drive down to Austin. Once there, Jerry Jeff found them a place to crash and a gig. He played around Austin and spent the spring of 1965 thumbing back and forth between Austin and Dallas, playing every club and roadhouse in between that would let him pass the hat. One night in Austin at a small folk club, the 11th Door, Jerry Jeff was booked to do a

11. "Drifting, poor, and searching"

set for twenty dollars. He sat in the spotlight, just him and his guitar, and played a set of all-original material. Everyone was dead silent, hanging on every word and applauding when he finished. He realized he was making something of this folk thing. It may have started out as a means of escaping conformity and buying a little wine, but he was good at it. He decided he wanted to have his songs published.

Back in New Orleans, a Tulane University graduate student named Jay Edwards was moonlighting as a folklorist. He hung around coffee shops and street corners, collecting and compiling folk songs. He had published a book with a couple of Jerry Ferris's songs included. Jerry Jeff reasoned that with all these new songs, maybe he could publish a book of only his compositions. He headed back to New Orleans to look up Jay Edwards.

He found Barbara Lyons living with a new boyfriend. "Within a few days I had pretty much discouraged him and fell in with Barbara like we had never been apart. The boyfriend left, bound for Big Sur," Jerry Jeff wrote in his autobiography. He went back to playing the streets and bars with Babe and it was like he had never left, but with one big difference. Now he considered himself a real songwriter. Years later, he would remember it this way: "I was writing from my own life knowledge, and always looking for an experience or an emotion that I could use as the starting point of a new song. Late one night—almost dawn during the Fourth of July weekend, '65—I hit the big bonanza."

"The big bonanza," as he put it, was the night Jerry Jeff fell in love outside the Café Du Monde. The night he put on a show about his belief in love at first sight for the all-night diner's patrons. The night he was arrested.

He was taken to the New Orleans First Precinct jail and logged in as a 42-22, drunk in public. Jerry Jeff told the story hundreds if not thousands of times over the next fifty years. There had been a murder in New Orleans a day or two before and with the holiday weekend approaching, the New Orleans police were sent out to arrest all the street people and put them in jail. The powers that be did not want scared tourists reporting back home that New Orleans was an unsafe place to visit. Jerry Jeff's early-morning show at the Café Du Monde landed him alongside them. They were stuck there three days until the court reopened after the holiday.

As he entered the cell, he saw unwelcoming eyes staring him down. One skinny and frail old man with clothes piled beside him told Jerry Jeff to come sit down. The old man had dirty, thinning, yellow-white hair. Jerry Jeff later wrote that "his face was peaceful. His clear eyes sparkled with kindness." The old man told him they were going to be there awhile, so they might as well talk and entertain themselves. The old man launched into a story about a girl he had loved. He then asked Jerry Jeff if he had ever been in love.

"Just tonight," Walker replied.

The old man laughed as he heard Jerry Jeff's tale of how he had wound up sitting next to him. The man called himself Bojangles. As with Jerry Jeff, Bojangles was not the man's real name. It was a common nickname for street performers and dancers. The origins of the name are hard to pin down, though they seem to have to do with minstrel and vaudeville characters of the nineteenth century. The most famous man to use the moniker was tap dancer Bill "Bojangles" Robinson, who claimed to have been given the nickname as a child. The current-day Bojangles went on to tell Jerry Jeff about marriages, divorces, and a life spent traveling. As Jerry Jeff would sing for years to come, "he looked ... to be the eyes of age as he spoke right out."

The old man had worked for minstrel shows in his youth and then spent time as a door-to-door salesman. Jerry Jeff later described it as "a life spent drifting, poor, and searching." It sounded a lot like where he found himself. Nowadays Bojangles was in New Orleans hustling for drinks and tips. Oftentimes more drinks than tips, which led him to be pretty well acquainted with the New Orleans jail. He would go into a bar and fire up the jukebox. He would start dancing and people would buy him drinks and throw him quarters.

"I had a dog. Great dog. Best friend for a lot of years. Part of my act," he told Jerry Jeff and his assorted other cellmates, who had all started listening to his tales. He said that he and the dog were making pretty good money traveling around as part of a show. He had bought a convertible car and life seemed to be going all right when one day in West Texas it all ended. He was at a filling station gassing up when the dog saw another canine across the road. The dog leaped from the convertible to go investigate his counterpart. Just then a truck came barreling down the road by the filling station.

"Wham. Car hit him. Killed him dead. Saddest day of my life," Bojangles recounted.

A silence hung in the air as the weight of the story settled on the concrete cell. Jerry Jeff recalled how his eyes welled up at the end of the story and remembered, "I realized he hadn't been this torn up telling me about any of his ex-wife's departures." One of the other street performers caught up in the sweep wanted to lighten the mood. He said, "Come on, Bojangles, give us a little dance." The old man jumped up and began doing the soft shoe while the men in the drunk tank clapped a rhythm.

Jerry Jeff Walker spent three days in the New Orleans jail with the man known as Bojangles. They talked of life and dreams and of what it all means. When the holiday was over and the court reopened, the drunks were lined up to see the judge. "Ten dollars or ten days," he told them. Jerry

11. "Drifting, poor, and searching" 65

Arrest record of Jerry Jeff Walker (aka Ronald Crosby, bottom entry) from the New Orleans First Precinct Jail, July 5, 1965 (courtesy of the City Archives and Special Collections, New Orleans Public Library).

Jeff paid his ten bucks and walked out of the courthouse a free man. As he left, he looked back at the line of men waiting for the judge and saw the top of the old man's head. It was the last time he ever saw him.[1]

This is the story Jerry Jeff Walker told countless times to interviewers over his half-century career. Arrest records from the New Orleans Public Library confirm most of the story. Ronald Clyde Crosby was booked in the first precinct jail at 5:20 a.m. on July 5, 1965. He was arrested at the corner of St. Ann and Decatur streets, where Café Du Monde still stands. But contrary to Jerry Jeff's story, the records indicate he posted bond about eight hours later, at 1:55 p.m.[2]

Regardless of how long he spent with the man he knew as Bojangles, a deep impression was left. As Jerry Jeff put his thumb in the wind to get out of New Orleans, he had a new idea for a song.[3]

12

"How can I follow this guy?"

Sammy was so excited on the train ride from Fort Warren to Los Angeles that he couldn't sleep. He was thrilled to be leaving the army and going back into show business. When he arrived at the LA train station, his father, in his trademark fedora, and his Uncle Will, with his gold-toothed smile, were there to greet him. After only ten months, their boy was back, and it couldn't have come sooner. The trio went to dinner and began catching up. Sammy told them about army life, though he spared many of the details about his race-related fights. He concentrated on his performances and the books he read. Will and Sam Sr. explained how they had been scraping by for the past ten months.[1]

When Sammy shipped off, the duo had begun looking for work around Los Angeles. Without young Sammy, though, bookings were harder to come by. Promoters did not believe that two aging vaudeville tap dancers could keep paying customers in their seats. Will put out an ad for a third dancer, and a young woman named Pudgy Barksdale applied. She was a small and graceful dancer, like Sammy. She dressed in a female tuxedo, and the show rolled along much as it had with Sammy. But there were tensions.

Pudgy was in her twenties and had her own life, yet Will often treated her like a minor who needed constant supervision. Pudgy liked to drink and occasionally was late to performances. Will Mastin was an old-school vaudevillian and found her unprofessional. To Barksdale, Mastin was the picture of "old-time show business," hanging on by a thread in the modern world. "I thought the routine he did was hokey," she would tell an interviewer years later. Eventually the tensions became too much, and she left the act for another in Las Vegas.

Years before, Mastin had traveled in a troupe with ten to twelve members, including a cyclist and a contortionist. When Barksdale left, he tried to bring back the circus element of the act by hiring a roller-skater. The aging hoofers and the man on roller skates did not impress audiences.

Bookings dried up. The two men hung around Los Angeles reading the theatrical publications and looking for work. They borrowed money to keep from starving, all the while scanning the skies for Japanese bombers. Waiting for word that the war had ended.[2]

By early summer 1945, life was back to what constituted normal. Sammy was home and the Trio went back to work. Sammy's time in the army had changed him in numerous ways and he came back more determined than ever to become a star. His idol, Frank Sinatra, had become a bona fide celebrity during the war years. While Sinatra did not serve in the army due to a perforated eardrum, his songs became the backdrop to a nation at war. "There was a great loneliness," he would explain about the mood of the country and his rise to stardom in the early forties. "I was the boy in every corner drugstore who had gone off, drafted to war."[3] Now Sammy pounded the pavement. He spent every evening in nightclubs looking for opportunities for the Trio. One of their first postwar bookings was at the Cricket Club in LA. Sammy was incredulous. "Who the hell is going to see us at the Cricket Club? My God, we played better places than that before I went in the army," he complained to his uncle.

Mastin did not fully understand Sammy's quest for stardom. He was thrilled just to be working again. He was hesitant as Sammy began improvising, doing the cakewalk and impersonating Edward G. Robinson and James Cagney. Sammy's talent as a mimic was undeniable, but Mastin did not want impressions of white people in the show.

"You just can't," he told him. "They'll think you're making fun of them. No colored performer ever did white people in front of white people," Will tried to explain.[4]

Sammy countered that the impersonations had been wildly popular in the army. The two did not see eye to eye, but, slowly, the impersonations became a standard in the act as audiences always laughed and cheered for them. Sammy's constant networking and magnetic performances began getting him attention. Recalling those days and his all-encompassing drive for stardom, he said he was "hungry and mad, baby."[5]

He met Abe Lastfogel of the William Morris Agency, who was taken with Sammy's talent. In late 1945, Abe took him to a party at the swanky Hillcrest Country Club in Los Angeles and introduced Sammy to his childhood heroes. He hobnobbed with Groucho Marx, Jack Benny, and Al Jolson. Sammy was blown away and wanted Lastfogel to represent the Trio. Will Mastin had other plans.

In early 1946, Mastin informed Sammy and Sam Sr. that Arthur Silber now represented the Trio. Silber ran a small-time booking agency and was an old vaudeville acquaintance of Mastin's. He did not have the connections of Abe Lastfogel. Still, Silber consistently put the Trio to work, and Sammy received a glowing review in *Metronome* magazine. The magazine profile led Silber to book the Trio on a tour with Mickey Rooney, who, having completed his wartime service, was trying to parlay his childhood stardom into a longer career in show business. Sammy and Mickey had a lot in common, both being children of the stage. Rooney was impressed by Sammy's talent and encouraged him to continue his impersonations. Rooney also introduced Sammy to guns. Sammy was impressed by Mickey's ability to quick-draw his Colt .45 and spin it around on his fingers. Sammy would soon buy his own gun and spend hours practicing his quick draw, eventually adding this talent to the show along with his dancing, impressions, singing, and trumpet and drum playing. Sammy was becoming a renaissance man of the theater, and people were taking notice.

Tracy McCleary was an LA musician who toured the country in various bands. He saw the Will Mastin Trio numerous times in the years immediately following the war. "Everybody was so taken with Sammy," he recalled. "He was just terrific. He would sing, dance, you name it. You couldn't help but notice this young guy was carrying these two older guys on his back." That seems to be the consensus among people who remembered the shows. Sam Sr. and Will Mastin understood what was happening. They were showbiz veterans, and as audiences and promoters took notice of Sammy, they went along for the ride, careful to always be in control of the main talent. The show went from being billed as the Will Mastin Trio to the Will Mastin Trio *featuring* Sammy Davis, Jr., to the Will Mastin Trio *starring* Sammy Davis, Jr. More work began coming their way.[6]

Will Mastin Trio (from left, Sam Davis, Sammy Davis, Jr., and Will Mastin) undated publicity photograph (courtesy University of Nevada, Las Vegas, Libraries Special Collections & Archives).

The Trio began playing better nightclubs in LA. Then they made their Las Vegas debut at El Rancho for $500 a week. Steve Allen booked Sammy on his LA radio show to do his impressions. They embarked on another tour of the Northeast and were booked to open a string of shows for Billie Holiday at the Apollo Theater in Harlem. Sammy made his first recordings, for Capitol Records. The Trio was backstage in Portland, Maine, when a telegram arrived. "Capitol Theater New York next month. Frank Sinatra Show. Three Weeks. 1250 per. Details follow." Sammy was ecstatic.[7]

Francis Albert Sinatra was the son of Italian immigrants. "I'll never forget how it hurt when the kids called me 'dago' when I was a boy," he would recall after his rise to stardom. "It's a scar that has lasted quite a long time and which I have never quite forgotten." Frank was taken with Sammy's talent, but he also understood the challenges a Black entertainer faced, and he wanted to help. He had personally played a role in having the Trio booked for the Capitol Theater engagement, though he did not let on about that. The first night of the engagement, Sinatra came out with the Trio and threw his arms around Sammy for all the cameras to see.[8] The Will Mastin Trio had the endorsement of Frank Sinatra, and that was a big deal. At the end of the run, as everyone was saying their goodbyes, Frank told Sammy he would help in any way he was needed. "You got a friend for life," he would say.[9]

Donna Mae Tjaden was a theatrical child always looking for a stage. After graduating high school, she moved to LA and was hired as a singer at the Hollywood Canteen. There, a Warner Brothers studio executive discovered her, and she changed her name to Janis Paige. For the next forty years she would be a staple in movies, television and on Broadway. In 1951 she was a rising star, most often playing the best friend or the villain in low-budget movies. She also had a nightclub act. She was booked to play Ciro's the night of the Academy Awards in 1951. It was one of the after-party spots, and the club was going to be filled with celebrities at the conclusion of the awards ceremony. Arthur Silber booked the Will Mastin Trio starring Sammy Davis, Jr., as the opening act.

Sammy knew this could be the big break. But when Silber informed Mastin that Herman Hover, the owner of Ciro's, would only pay $500 for an opening act, Mastin turned it down. The Trio had been regularly pulling in $550, and he was not about to take less. Sammy pleaded with Mastin to change his mind. Didn't he understand that this was Ciro's, the hottest club in the country? They would be performing for the who's who of Hollywood. Mastin wouldn't budge and neither would the owner. Silber, sensing Sammy's disappointment, and also probably understanding that

Sammy was right, kicked in the extra fifty bucks himself and told Will Mastin that Hover had relented.[10]

Fred Astaire hosted the Oscars that year and *All About Eve* swept the major categories. The film won six of its fourteen nominations, including Best Picture, Best Director and Best Supporting Actor. As the awards show wrapped up and the day's major movie stars began heading out to the Sunset Strip, the Will Mastin Trio was huddled in the attic of Ciro's, which doubled as the opening act's dressing room. Downstairs in the club's main room, waiters in tails brought French cuisine and champagne to table after table of movie stars. The three men were nervous as they left the attic and headed for the stage. When they hit the stage, though, all nerves evaporated, and they focused on the task at hand. They opened with "Dancing Shoes," a 1921 George and Ira Gershwin song. Will and Sam Sr. hit the stage first as the house band cranked up. Sammy then came out and took over the act with his magnetic and athletic dancing. "We probably started faster than any act this crowd had ever seen," Davis would recount in his autobiography.

After another dance number, Sammy went into his impressions. First Louis Armstrong, then Edward G. Robinson, for which Sammy brought out a giant cigar prop. The audience loved it. Next up, Sammy launched into a riotously funny impression of Humphrey Bogart, with Bogart seated just a few tables from the stage. The crowd ate it up.

By the time the Trio concluded their forty-minute set, the crowd was going wild. "They kept applauding and began beating on the tables with knives and forks and their fists, screaming for us to come back," Sammy recalled. They came back for an encore, something unheard of for an opening act. Sammy broke out his impression of Jerry Lewis. "The sight of a colored Jerry Lewis was an absolute topper," Davis recalled. After eight bows, the Trio left the stage. Ciro's was abuzz with talk about the Will Mastin Trio and its young star, Sammy Davis, Jr.[11]

Waiting in the wings, Janice Paige was furious. "That little son-of-a-bitch, he is killing me. How can I follow this guy?" she complained.[12] And she was right; there was no following that act. She had trouble keeping the crowd's attention and the next night insisted that owner Herman Hover reverse the order of the bill. She would open and Sammy and the Trio would close the show. The reviews in the press began coming in, and they were glowing. "Once in a long time an artist hits town and sends the place on its ear," the *Hollywood Reporter* said.[13]

The shows were so successful that Hover booked the Trio for eight straight weeks. At the end of the eight weeks, they landed a high-profile gig at the Flamingo in Las Vegas. Then back to New York and on to all the top nightclubs in the country. The Trio was working full-time and becoming full-fledged stars. They signed with the William Morris Agency for bookings, and Arthur Silber continued as the group's manager. At Sammy's insistence, they hired Morty Stevens as bandleader to help with musical arrangements and Jess Rand as press agent. It wasn't just the three of them anymore; they were now traveling with an entourage. In 1952 the Trio appeared on *The Colgate Comedy Hour*, one of television's first and most successful variety shows. By the end of 1952 they were regularly commanding a thousand dollars a week for performances and by the end of 1953 it was almost five thousand a week.

That year the Trio was playing the Fairmont Hotel in San Francisco when Sammy saw a performance by actress and singer Eartha Kitt. He had met her one other time in New York and was so taken with her that he showed up backstage in San Francisco to say hello. When he walked into her dressing room, she did not remember him and thought he was a stagehand. She sent him for coffee. Sammy didn't correct her; he went and got some coffee. When he came back, he explained who he was. "We all had a good laugh," she recalled. She caught his act and was impressed. The two began dating.

Eartha Kitt came from a very different world than Sammy. Both had been born in Harlem, but Kitt was a graduate of the High School of Performing Arts and had spent time in Europe. She was a critically acclaimed actress, touring the country in a smash Broadway play. Sammy was a rising star for sure, but he was still a nightclub act. There was more standing between them than their different social status, though. Eartha was refined and intelligent. Sammy could read and write, but his education was limited to what he had learned in the army and his experience on the road. They dated for a while, but Sammy was the more infatuated one. His high energy was too much for the laid-back Kitt. Sammy proposed marriage and she turned him down, yet it somehow leaked to the press that the Broadway star was soon to wed the rising nightclub crooner. "I like him, he's a sweet boy but he gets mixed up," she told her agent. The record was soon set straight and the two went their separate ways. Some recalled the incident years later as a publicity stunt to get Sammy more tabloid attention. Others close to him claimed he genuinely loved her, but that his lack of experience led to him handling the sensitive situation all wrong.[14] Regardless, as 1953 came to a close, Sammy was once again on his own, and the future looked nothing but bright for the Will Mastin Trio. But 1954 would change that.

13

"When your star is up"

Nixon cruised to reelection in 1948 and immediately turned his attention to the 1950 California Senate race. He wanted to capitalize on his newfound fame. Some members of the Committee of 100, which was so influential in Nixon's political rise, were skeptical. Herman Perry predicted they would "crucify this young man" when presented with the prospect. Frank Jorgensen urged him to stay in the House and gain some seniority. "You've got a good, safe district," he told him. However, Roy Day, the group's founder and one of Nixon's biggest supporters, endorsed the idea. "When your star is up, that is when you have to move," he told Perry. On November 3, 1949, Richard Nixon became a candidate for the U.S. Senate in California.[1]

By the time Nixon's campaign for the Senate kicked off, the international world order was undergoing unprecedented changes. India and the Philippines had gained independence. The nation of Israel had been established. Communist forces had taken power in China. And foremost on American minds was communist Russia and her detonating of an atomic bomb. The U.S. government began urging citizens to dig fallout shelters in their yards. Short films were produced explaining how to survive a nuclear attack at work and at school. Americans were on edge, and Richard Nixon had a keen ability to turn fear into votes.

Helen Gahagan Douglas was the thirty-third woman elected to the U.S. House of Representatives, and the first woman ever elected as a Democrat from California, when she succeeded Thomas Ford in 1944. She began her career as a Hollywood actress and found success in the movies. She became involved in politics in the late '30s and by 1950 had set her sights on becoming just the fourth woman ever to be elected to the U.S. Senate. She was an avid supporter of the New Deal and was labeled a leftist, but her foreign-policy views were a mixed bag. She was critical of China and Russia, but voted against appropriations for HUAC and against Truman's aid for Greece and Turkey. She thought the aid program should be run by the United Nations. (One of her biggest supporters at the time was registered Democrat Ronald Reagan.) 1950 was no time for nuance in dealing with communists, however.

Douglas ran an aggressive primary campaign against her fellow Democrats in early 1950, making more than a few enemies along the way. Her primary opponents formulated the attack lines that Nixon would perfect. She was a bleeding-heart liberal who ran around with Hollywood's "parlor pinks," they said. Her main primary opponent, Manchester Boddy, began attacking her by connecting her to Harlem congressman Vito Marcantonio. Marcantonio was an avowed socialist who made no equivocations about his leftist views in the '30s and '40s. Ironically, he also disliked Douglas, reportedly often calling her a "bitch" in private.

As the campaign began in earnest, a young John F. Kennedy walked into Nixon's office and handed him an envelope containing $1,000. "I obviously can't endorse you," he reportedly told his future rival, "but it isn't going to break my heart if you can turn the Senate's loss into Hollywood's gain."[2]

The campaign turned nasty as Nixon brought gender to center stage without ever explicitly bringing it up. He circulated half a million leaflets printed on pink paper that outlined Douglas's voting record and connected it to socialism. The leaflets claimed that Douglas had voted with Marcantonio 354 times. Never mind that Nixon himself had voted the same way on almost half of the votes listed. No one seemed to catch that. He called Douglas "the pink lady" in public. It was reported that he told an aide in private that she was "pink right down to her underwear."

The midterm election of 1950 came at the height of anti-communism in the United States. Made famous by Joseph McCarthy, the movement was in many ways perfected by Richard Nixon. Douglas had nuanced views on communism. She did not support communism, but did not see it as an existential threat. She did not believe communists were on the verge of taking over the U.S. government. Nixon was a more polished version of Joe McCarthy. Nixon acted as if there were subversives everywhere looking to overthrow the government, without actually saying it. Unlike McCarthy, Nixon did not name names. He didn't technically accuse Truman and Secretary of State Dean Acheson of treason; he just implied it. The male-dominated cabal that controlled Democratic politics resented Douglas, and she enraged conservatives with her policies. She never really stood a chance. On Election Day, she lost by almost 700,000 votes. Douglas and her campaign gave Richard Nixon something he could never shake, though: the nickname "Tricky Dick." On election night, Pat and the master trickster hopped from election party to election party, with Nixon playing "Happy Days Are Here Again" on every piano he encountered.[3]

13. "When your star is up"

As the election of 1952 approached, Republicans were divided on the best way to unseat twenty years of uninterrupted Democratic control of the presidency. Robert Taft, the son of former Republican president William Howard Taft, wanted to be president badly. Taft had broad control of the party machinery and by the start of 1952 was the favorite to win the nomination. But Taft's views on foreign policy created a rift in the Republican Party. To counter Taft in the spring of 1952, New York governor and former Republican nominee Thomas Dewey convinced one of the most popular men in America, Dwight D. Eisenhower, to run as a Republican.

The other complicating factor for Taft was the lack of any real leadership in the Republican Party structure in the South. No Southern state had voted for a Republican presidential candidate since 1876. What passed for the Republican Party in the old Confederacy was a much-divided group of loyalists to various individuals. In the summer of 1952, Georgia, Louisiana, and Texas each sent competing delegations, supporting different candidates, to the convention.

Earl Warren, the governor of California, also wanted to be president. He saw the chance of a divided convention and thought that was his "in." California's delegates were pledged to stay united on the first ballot and to vote for Warren. But Nixon had managed to stuff the delegation with members of his Committee of 100. Roy Day, Herman Perry, Frank Jorgensen, and others all boarded a train in Denver in early July and headed to the Chicago convention.

Historians would come to call it "The Great Train Robbery." As the locomotive rolled through the heartland, Nixon began a covert whisper campaign among the delegates. He said it was just too bad Warren couldn't win and that General Eisenhower should be the man to support.

Warren's plan was to keep the California delegation united so that if Eisenhower and Taft deadlocked, he could be the compromise candidate. But before the voting for candidates could start, some disputes needed to be settled, namely which of the competing Southern delegations would be seated. Some supported Taft and some supported Ike. Nixon's whisper campaign led to the California delegation voting 62–8 to seat the Eisenhower delegates.

When the nominating process formally got underway, the Californians stayed loyal and voted unanimously for Warren. But it didn't matter. The Southern delegations put Ike over the top. There would be no divided convention.

Earl Warren was furious with Nixon, but his gamble worked. The night after Eisenhower's nomination, the general met with Thomas Dewey and other Republican power brokers in a literally smoke-filled room at the

Chicago Hilton. They discussed possible vice-presidential picks. They settled on thirty-nine-year-old Richard Nixon.[4]

From 1946 to 1952, Nixon had been campaigning for higher office essentially nonstop. He had become a star in a Republican Party that had few. He gave speeches all over the country. He had offices in Washington and Whittier. The government provided him with $12,500 a year in salary and he made another $6,000 a year in speaking fees. He had a staff of thirteen, office space, and one free trip a year to California, all funded by the U.S. taxpayer. All told, the government provided Nixon about $70,000 a year. It wasn't enough. Nixon received a much larger volume of mail than most senators, partly from his fame and partly from the large population in his state. Replying to all this mail took time and money. He needed to travel to California more than once a year as well, and that cost money. To pay for all this, Nixon had set up a fund to which his supporters could donate that would reimburse him for his political expenses.

The fund was not illegal. Adlai Stevenson, the Democratic nominee he and Eisenhower were running against had a similar fund. Still, on September 18, 1952, the *New York Post* ran a headline that grabbed national attention: "SECRET RICH MEN'S TRUST FUND KEEPS NIXON IN STYLE FAR BEYOND HIS SALARY." At first Nixon brushed the story off as a partisan attack, but at every campaign stop questions kept coming. Eisenhower's advisors began to get nervous. Days went by and the national press was clamoring for answers. Eisenhower's staff voted 40–2 to dump Nixon. Eisenhower wanted to wait; he was worried about the optics of bailing on Nixon. He thought that if it was perceived that his first political decision had been to hire a crook as his running mate, he would surely lose. For a few days, Eisenhower did not speak to Nixon. Finally, on September 21, Eisenhower called. The two talked about what to do and Eisenhower suggested Nixon go on TV and lay out his financial situation to the American public. Eisenhower would not commit to keeping Nixon; he wanted to see the public's reaction.

Nixon went to Los Angeles and began to prepare. He wrote out a speech that included the lines that had received the best responses on the campaign trail. The morning of September 23, he went for a swim. A couple hours before he was set to go on live TV before the biggest audience in history to that point, he received a phone call from Thomas Dewey. Dewey informed him that a meeting of top Eisenhower advisors had just concluded, and they believed that at the end of the speech, Nixon should offer his resignation to the general. Nixon sat silent on the phone. Dewey asked what he should tell everyone to expect. Nixon screamed into the other end of the line, "Just tell them I haven't the slightest idea what I'm going to do,

13. "When your star is up"

and if they want to find out they'd better listen to the broadcast. And tell them I know a little something about politics too!"

All the clichés applied. Everything hung in the balance. His political career was riding on this one speech. At 6:30 p.m. Eastern Time on September 23, 1952, sixty million Americans heard Richard Nixon begin, "My fellow Americans, I come before you tonight as a candidate for the vice presidency ... and as a man whose honor and integrity have been questioned." He then proceeded to explain his and Pat's finances for the whole world to know. All their assets and liabilities. He said they had worked hard and earned every cent. He delivered the line about Pat not having a mink coat, only a "respectable Republican cloth coat," that had garnered so much applause on the campaign trail. The national TV audience found him honest and forthcoming. At the end, he endeared himself to the nation by explaining that there was one political gift he had received. A man in Texas had given the family a cocker spaniel puppy after he overheard Nixon's daughter talking about how she wanted one. Nixon said they had named him Checkers and that "regardless of what they say about it, we're going to keep it."

The speech led to over 300,000 telegrams and letters sent to the Republican National Committee headquarters in Washington advocating for Nixon to remain on the ticket. Eisenhower commended the speech once he knew the public's response. "When I get in a fight, I'd rather have a courageous and honest man by my side than a whole boxcar full of pussyfooters," the general told a raucous Cleveland crowd. And with that, it was settled. Nixon would remain his man. On November 4, 1952, the Eisenhower–Nixon ticket carried 55 percent of the vote and Richard Nixon became the youngest vice president in U.S. history.[5]

14

"A blind song-and-dance man"

The photograph is pure Sammy. He is suspended in midair, his arms outstretched to the sky and his legs kicking like a track star jumping hurdles. His shirt and tie are tucked in his pants and the expression on his face is a mix of joy and astonishment. It was the summer of 1954 and Will and Sam Sr. had just purchased their star a new car. Sammy had never driven a day in his life, and now he was the proud owner of a brand-new Cadillac convertible.[1]

Formed out of the remnants of the Henry Ford Company in 1902 after a business dispute between Ford and his two partners, Cadillac is one of the oldest car brands in the world. With Ford gone, the partners changed course and began producing a luxury vehicle they named after the founder of Detroit, Antoine Laumet de la Mothe, sieur de Cadillac. From the beginning, Cadillacs were the standard in luxury automobiles. They were the first cars to travel 65 miles per hour and the first to incorporate Phillips technology (Phillips-head screws). The U.S. government ordered 2,500 of them and shipped them to France for use by American officers in World War I. During the Depression years the auto industry suffered, with no market suffering more than the luxury car market. Making the problem worse, the Cadillac company had a policy that forbid sales to African Americans. Faced with a decline in sales of almost 80 percent, the policy was changed in the 1930s. In the postwar era, sales rebounded and Cadillac once again became a symbol of status for Americans. By 1954 owning a Cadillac meant more than just owning a car. It was proof of the American dream come true. Will Mastin owned a Cadillac, and now Sammy did too.

For the Will Mastin Trio starring Sammy Davis, Jr., dreams were indeed coming true; 1954 was a year like no other for the group. Looking to draw a younger crowd, the Last Frontier hotel and casino in Las Vegas hired the Trio to headline a week of shows for $7,500. It was the highest payday yet for the showbiz veterans, and it came with other perks.

14. "A blind song-and-dance man"

In years past, the Trio had stayed in segregated hotels and was often barred from entering the casinos they played at except for performing. With the permission of Will Mastin, Sammy negotiated directly with the management at Last Frontier. As a result, in addition to the higher pay, the Trio were given suites to stay in and access to the venue's restaurants, casino, and bars. This was not because of a liberal owner trying to do the right thing. Sammy knew he was getting hot. He wanted the perks that people like Frank Sinatra got. It also wasn't from a deep-seated political conviction on the Trio's part. The political upheaval over communism and subversion that was rampant in the culture of the time focused on the writers and poets, the actors and directors, not on old-time showbiz men like Will Mastin and Sam Davis. Regardless, it was Sammy's first foray into the burgeoning civil rights movement. On January 11, the Will Mastin Trio broke the color barrier for nightclub performers in Las Vegas, three months before the Supreme Court would overturn the separate-but-equal doctrine.

The next month, Sammy signed a recording contract with Decca Records. He recorded "Hey There," a song written by Jerry Ross and Richard Adler for the Broadway musical *The Pajama Game*. Sammy's version would reach number sixteen on the *Billboard* chart and number one in

Sam Davis, Sammy Davis, Jr., and Jerry Lewis on stage at the Copacabana in 1954 (courtesy Richard Nixon Presidential Library and Museum).

Cashbox. In March, the Trio headlined the Copacabana in New York City. In the darkest years of the Depression, Sammy and his father used to walk down to the nightclub just to watch the celebrities enter. They listened to the a popular radio program with the tagline "I'm at the Copa, where are you?" They had longed to be there, and now they were.

Soon after their headlining gig at the Copa, another offer came in. ABC wanted to develop a sitcom about the Trio. It was to be called "We Three" and would feature Sammy, Will and Sam Sr. as themselves, with an actress to play Sammy's girlfriend. The show was a fictionalized version of their real lives. Sammy's natural talent and love of the camera shine throughout the pilot episode. The show was groundbreaking by the standards of the time. Maybe too groundbreaking. In 1954 sitcoms were sponsored affairs. A corporate sponsor would pay for the show in return for hawking its product to viewers every week. As new shows went looking for corporations in the fall of 1954, none seemed very interested in backing a story about Black entertainers. The concept ended up on the cutting-room floor.[2]

Jess Rand had been traveling with the Trio for a little over a year as their press agent when he received a phone call backstage at the Copa. At first, he thought it was a prank. The vice president would like to come to the second show tonight, a voice said. Jess said no problem, still not really

The Will Mastin Trio with Vice President Nixon at the Copacabana in 1954. From left: Sam Davis, Sammy Davis, Jr., Richard Nixon, Will Mastin, and Jerry Lewis (courtesy Richard Nixon Presidential Library and Museum).

14. "A blind song-and-dance man" 81

believing it was true. A little before the second show was to begin that night, in walked Richard Nixon and his wife, Pat. The couple thoroughly enjoyed the Trio's performance, by all accounts. Afterwards the vice president and his wife went backstage to congratulate the Trio on a stunning performance. It was the first meeting between Nixon and Sammy. Jess Rand hastily found a camera and snapped a picture of the Trio with the vice president. This was public relations gold, he thought. He took the negatives to every paper in New York. No one would print them.[3]

As 1954 began to wind down, the Trio was far from a household name, but their stock was rising. Bookings were plentiful and they had a hit record. They had headlined the top nightclubs in the country. They had the endorsement of Frank Sinatra and the vice president of the United States. On November 19, after the late show at the Last Frontier, Sammy and his valet, Charlie Head (the entourage was growing), got in his new Cadillac to drive to LA. Sammy was booked to sing the title track to the new Tony Curtis film *Six Bridges to Cross*. Sammy sprawled out on the back seat and went to sleep. After a few hours, he awoke, and Charlie said he was getting tired. Sammy took over behind the wheel.

In the mid–1950s, Richard Nixon's boss had proposed a new idea. The Interstate Highway System was the brainchild of President Eisenhower. He had been impressed with the German Autobahn during his time there and believed America needed a similar network of high-speed roads to connect people and commerce as well as to aid in national defense. As Sammy took over behind the wheel, it was still just an idea, though; the law to create the modern American road system was still two years away. Sammy cruised that morning on a series of old two-lane roads. The sun was rising behind him as he drove through Cajon Pass in the San Gabriel Mountains. He was about an hour outside LA, near the farming town of San Bernardino. It was early and not many cars were on the road. A car with two women passed Sammy as he drove. A few minutes later Sammy saw the two women ahead of him, and they appeared to slow down. He then realized in the early morning light that they were trying to turn around. It was a dangerous move on a two-lane mountain-pass road. Sammy at first thought he could get around them to the left, but it quickly became apparent that would not work. He swerved to the right, never touching the brakes. The Cadillac slammed into the women's Chrysler Imperial.

Charlie Head's jaw was broken and most of his teeth were knocked out. The women in the Chrysler had been thrown into the back seat, with the front seat dislodged and lying on top of them. One broke her leg, but the other sustained only minor injuries. Sammy was in the worst shape by far. He was cut up from head to toe and his nose was broken. He had bitten through his lower lip and his left eye was dangling out of its socket, held on by a thin strand of muscle. He had impaled it on the cone-shaped decoration that sat in the middle of the Caddy's steering wheel. Charlie screamed at the sight, and Sammy felt the wound with his hand. He fell to the ground in shock, begging God for this all to be a dream.

Fortuitously a serviceman at a gas station just up the road from the crash site saw the whole thing and phoned for help. Sirens came wailing and loaded the men onto stretchers. They took them to County Hospital in San Bernardino. It was the "poor hospital" that catered to Blacks and the lower class. Word soon spread that this was not just any Black, this was Sammy Davis, Jr., the nightclub entertainer. He was moved to Community Hospital and specialist Dr. Fred Hull was brought in to look at Sammy's eye.

Jess Rand and Tony Curtis had been awaiting Sammy's arrival in LA, and they were the first to arrive at Community Hospital. The place was abuzz as the Hollywood movie star came in demanding to see Sammy Davis, Jr. He knew the quality of care was often substandard for African Americans and he was there to ensure that Sammy received top-notch treatment. Will and Sam Sr. left Vegas for San Bernardino as soon as they heard the news. They arrived at Community Hospital and rushed to find their partner. They found him on a gurney, bandaged and bloodied. Will saw it all disappearing. His years of working the vaudeville circuit and piecing together acts to stay afloat had all seemed to finally be paying off in 1954. He had come from sharecroppers in Alabama for whom slavery and the Civil War were not just chapters in a book but living memories. And yet here he was in the mid-twentieth century, a Black man with a Cadillac rubbing shoulders with the stars. Not for long now, he thought. His ticket to ride had just crashed. The seventy-five-year-old fell to his knees and began to pray. Jess Rand found a nurse to bring him a sedative. He told the typically teetotaling Mastin it was a vitamin.

The first doctors who had looked at Sammy's injuries thought they could save his left eye. Dr. Hull said it had to go. If they saved it, the right eye would always be trying to overcompensate for the bad eye, leading to total blindness over time. Sammy would be better off with one good eye and one plastic one. He was rushed to surgery and forty-five minutes later he was wheeled back into the room, with Rand, Mastin, Sam Sr., and Tony Curtis all waiting anxiously. The surgery had been a success. The skin around the missing eye would always droop a little bit, Dr. Hull said, but he gave Sammy exercises that would help with that. He said Sammy would need to wear a patch for a while until a plastic eye could be fitted. He might struggle with depth perception for a time, but he would not be blind. He would recover fully in time.

Meanwhile, word leaked out from the hospital to the press. The switchboard lit up with calls from Frank Sinatra and Eddie Cantor. Joey Bishop and Dean Martin called in to check on their friend. Someone phoned Eartha Kitt in Chicago, and she broke down screaming backstage. Strangers sent flowers and telegrams. Years later his friend Amy Greene remembered, "Everyone said his career is finished, it's over. Who ever heard of a blind song-and-dance man?"

The next day, Dr. Hull came into Sammy's room and began removing the bandages that engulfed his head. Slowly, the world came back into focus for Sammy. First lights and shapes, then people and their faces. He saw his father and Will. Tony Curtis and his wife, Janet Leigh, were there. After a few minutes, Jess Rand came in and lightened the mood by announcing that Sammy was "the hottest thing in the business." Sammy Davis, Jr., was front-page news in newspapers around the country. Those who were not aware of Sammy before the crash now knew his name and were pulling for him.

Eight days after the crash, the hospital staff loaded his fan mail into sacks and said their goodbyes. He was headed to Frank's place. Sinatra had insisted that Sammy come to his Palm Springs mansion to rest and recuperate after the crash. Sammy walked gingerly out of the hospital. He was still learning to use just one eye, and his muscles were still sore from the crash and the bed rest. As he waved goodbye to the hospital staff, he climbed into a brand-new, lime-green Cadillac convertible. The usually thrifty Mastin had bought him another. He wasn't letting this dream go down without a fight. They would return to the stage as good as new, as if nothing had ever happened.[4]

15

"The most dangerous man in America"

Drew Pearson made a name for himself with a syndicated newspaper column. By the mid-twentieth century, it was printed in hundreds of newspapers around the country and Pearson was a regular guest on political radio shows. Born to a wealthy Chicago family in 1897, he was educated at elite universities and began traveling the world in the 1920s. He sold articles about his various travels to newspapers. In the 1930s he co-authored a salacious book titled *Washington Merry-Go-Round*. The book was full of gossip and innuendo about politicians and the powerful. It was a bestseller. He parlayed that success into a syndicated column with the same name that became the longest running newspaper column in American history. Pearson's style of journalism was personal. He saw himself as tasked with taking down those he believed were working against the public interest. He saw journalism as a weapon, and in 1950 his sights were trained on Joseph McCarthy.

American history is full of boogeymen. Threats real and imagined are given a life of their own by prominent politicians warning Americans to be afraid, very afraid. In the middle part of the twentieth century, the boogeyman was the communist. They were everywhere and looking to forcibly change American life, according to many politicians and the partisan press. Senator McCarthy did not invent the issue, nor was he the movement's best spokesman. One journalist called him an "accidental demagogue." He gave a speech in February 1950 claiming to have a list of communists in the State Department. The charge made him a household name as the press corps followed him around like a loyal puppy for the next few years. How many names did he have? When would he reveal them? A sizable portion of the national press became enamored with McCarthy, and his name was in the papers almost daily.[1]

While much of the press were busy reprinting everything McCarthy said without fact-checking it, there was of course opposition. One member

15. "The most dangerous man in America"

of the opposition was Drew Pearson. Through his column, he began picking McCarthy apart, focusing on his taxes. McCarthy, it seemed, owed the federal government a large amount, and Pearson published scathing columns about him. McCarthy was furious at Pearson, and, one December night in 1950, things came to a head.

A Washington socialite and heiress to an Ohio newspaper fortune gave a holiday party at the swanky Sulgrave Club in Washington. She was a notorious practical joker and, apparently as a form of amusement, she sat Pearson and McCarthy at the same table. The night began awkwardly as McCarthy informed Pearson he planned to take to the Senate floor to denounce him the following day. McCarthy continued to heckle Pearson and, a few bourbons later, lunged across the table at him. The awkward move knocked Pearson off his seat and toppled an elderly Florida congressman who was crippled from childhood polio. McCarthy challenged Pearson to step outside and "settle this." At which point Pearson proclaimed the scene to be nonsense and got up to leave. To almost everyone's surprise, McCarthy got up and followed him.

As Pearson was getting his coat from the cloakroom, McCarthy grabbed him from behind and slapped him. He then kneed him in the groin twice. McCarthy began slapping him back and forth "movie villain style," according to trial testimony. As Pearson fell to the floor, in came Richard Nixon. "That one was for you, Dick," McCarthy claimed as he continued to pummel Pearson (who had written unflattering columns about Nixon as well). Nixon got between the two men, telling them to break it up. He told McCarthy to get out of there. McCarthy refused, saying, "I won't turn my back on the son of a bitch, he's got to go first." With Nixon still standing between the two men, Pearson hobbled away. Nixon then spent half an hour walking around Dupont Circle with McCarthy, helping him find his car. McCarthy was too drunk to remember where he had parked. He was sober enough to call friendly reporters later that evening, however, and make sure that the whole country woke up to the news that Joe McCarthy had kicked Drew Pearson "in the nuts." He took to the Senate floor the next day and claimed Pearson was "the voice of international communism."[2]

McCarthy's brand of anti-communism was useful to the Republican Party for a while. But once Republicans regained the White House with Eisenhower and Nixon, the wild and unsubstantiated charges were a problem for the new administration. It was one thing for the Truman government to be full of communists, but now that the Republicans had taken over, they claimed they had fixed the problem. But McCarthy was addicted to alcohol and attention. He became a headache for the new administration. Nixon was sent in to once again break things up.

In early 1953, Nixon took McCarthy to Key Biscayne, where he liked to vacation and would soon buy a house. There, he and his aides tried to quell McCarthy's fears and let him know it would be different now with the new administration. McCarthy played along, but his was more a game of headlines and press than genuinely finding communists. Once back in Washington, he quickly accused three of Eisenhower's nominees of being soft on the commies and unfit to hold their post. The game continued throughout 1953. Nixon genuinely liked McCarthy in some ways; the Wisconsin senator had come to his defense during the "Checkers" ordeal and the two men shared many policy positions. But as 1953 turned to 1954, McCarthy was becoming a political liability for the new administration and the Republican Party's chances in the November midterm elections. He was searching everywhere in government for subversives to call out and make headlines. He met his Waterloo when he went after the U.S. Army.

McCarthy held a series of hearings denouncing what he called the communist-infiltrated army. The best example he could come up with was an army dentist in Fort Monmouth, New Jersey, who had been ordered to be discharged for refusing to answer questions on a loyalty review form. The public wasn't quite buying that the dentist posed an existential threat to the republic. In February, McCarthy called in the dentist's superior officer, West Point graduate and D-Day veteran Gen. Ralph Zwicker. Zwicker was a Purple Heart recipient for his actions on Omaha Beach. But he had ignored McCarthy's demand to have the dentist court-martialed, granting him an honorable discharge instead. McCarthy called Zwicker "a disgrace to the army" and "not fit to wear that uniform." Outrage soon followed.

Nixon gave a speech attacking McCarthy, though not by name. Yet when he said that "reckless talk and questionable methods" are not the way to deal with the problem of communism, and that "when you go out to shoot rats, you have to shoot straight," everyone knew what he meant. The speech was soon followed by the Army–McCarthy hearings that spring. The hearings lasted fifty-seven days, thirty-six of which were televised. The new medium had people enthralled, and millions watched as McCarthy began to look more and more like a fool. The hearings culminated on June 9 when McCarthy accused a young lawyer with the firm representing the army of being a communist. The head counsel for the army took McCarthy to task, famously saying, "Let us not assassinate this lad further, Senator. You've done enough. Have you no sense of decency, sir, at long last? Have you left no sense of decency?" The public had seen enough and soon turned on McCarthy. He was censured by the Senate that December. He drifted further into alcoholism and died two and a half years later at age forty-eight.[3]

15. "The most dangerous man in America"

Nixon spent the fall of 1954 barnstorming the country for Republican congressional candidates. He campaigned in thirty states, pleading the case that he and the Eisenhower administration were making the country prosperous and keeping it safe. The Democrats argued the opposite, saying Nixon and the Republican Party were simply "McCarthyism in a white collar." In November the country voted overwhelmingly for the Democrats. The Republicans lost control of the Senate and the House. They would not regain the former for a quarter century and the latter for forty years. Many of the House members elected in 1946 with Richard Nixon were swept out of office. McCarthyism was dead. It had been the key to Nixon's rise and now the public mood had turned. Nixon decided it was over for him. He told his wife and top aides he would not seek re-election as vice president in 1956. A medical emergency would change his mind.

Ike was playing golf in Colorado on Friday, September 23, 1955, when he started experiencing chest pain and had to quit on the 27th hole. By Saturday evening, the headlines around the country had informed the people of the president's condition. It was serious but stable. Nixon was at home when he received the phone call. The gravity of the situation consumed the forty-two-year-old vice president. "Oh my god!" he exclaimed as Ike's press secretary broke the news. He was "numb" and in a "state of shock," he would write in his memoirs. He, along with everyone else, always knew this was a possibility. An old saying in American politics is that a vice president has two duties: to preside over the Senate and to check the papers for news of the president's health. Still, the gravity and shock Nixon felt were genuine. For a few weeks, it was touch and go, and the doctors were not sure Eisenhower would recover.[4]

For twenty-six days, Nixon played the part of president and won praise from critics and allies alike. He presided over cabinet meetings but would not sit in the president's chair. He was confident and in control without appearing to grab for power. Ike was eventually released from the hospital and returned to Washington, but many questions now arose. Was he healthy enough to run again? Should Nixon remain as VP?

Despite the good reviews Nixon received, Eisenhower was less than thrilled at the prospect of a Nixon presidency. He began to think of his own mortality and wondered if Nixon was really the man for the job. On the day after Christmas 1955, he summoned Nixon to the Oval Office. He wanted Nixon to accept a cabinet post in the next term and let someone else take the VP role. Eisenhower tried to convince him it would be good to get some executive experience. Nixon was not interested. He now had a taste of what it meant to be president and he was not interested in being a cabinet official. A back-and-forth game ensued in the press about whether Nixon would stay on the ticket or not. In the end, Eisenhower saw more political liability by kicking him off than keeping him. And so, as the 1956 election approached, it was once more Eisenhower and Nixon against Adlai Stevenson.

Stevenson was a seasoned politician; he was the grandson and namesake of a former vice president. He knew he could not win against Eisenhower. America loved the old general. He had a grandfatherly appeal, and he was the hero of World War II. So Stevenson and the Democrats ran against Nixon. Was this the man America could trust with the hydrogen bomb? Was this the man America wanted a heartbeat away from the presidency? Especially since no one knew how many ticks Ike's heart had left. It was a bruising campaign in which Stevenson developed a genuine dislike of Nixon, but his argument fell on deaf ears. The Eisenhower–Nixon ticket won forty-one states and the popular vote by a margin of almost ten million.[5]

As their second term began, the issue that would define the coming 1960s was first stirring in the white American consciousness. In 1955 the Supreme Court declared the doctrine of separate but equal unconstitutional and ordered that American public schools be integrated. Across the country, African Americans began decrying other aspects of segregated life. In Montgomery, Alabama, Rosa Parks refused to give up her seat on a city bus, sparking a boycott that would bring a young minister named Martin Luther King, Jr., to prominence. A year later the Supreme Court upheld Parks's right to sit where she pleased by outlawing segregation on public transit lines. Meanwhile, outrage grew in Black America after a fourteen-year-old boy from Chicago named Emmett Till was murdered in rural Mississippi, his killers allowed to go free.

Eisenhower was a reluctant civil rights warrior. He was a man of his times and had come of age in a segregated army. He did not believe you could "change the hearts of men with laws."[6] He was practical in his politics, though, and he could see the fissures opening in society. In 1957 he proposed the Civil Rights Act and sent it to Congress for debate. The Justice Department needed a law to prosecute cases like Emmett Till's when local authorities turned a blind eye. The version that ended up on Eisenhower's desk was watered down but still contained a few important new protections. It created a Civil Rights Commission to investigate discrimination and established a Civil Rights Division inside the Justice Department.

Five days before the act's passage, Orval Faubus, the governor of Arkansas, refused to let nine Black teenagers enroll in a Little Rock high school. The Arkansas National Guard prevented them from entering the school. Eisenhower federalized the state's national guard and sent a thousand soldiers into the streets of Little Rock to enforce the Supreme Court's

15. "The most dangerous man in America"

1954 *Brown v. Board of Education* decision. The country outside of the South by and large backed Eisenhower's move. The general consensus was that there must be law and order and if rifles and soldiers were once again needed in the South, the American people were behind the administration. Nixon told a group of reporters that Eisenhower had almost certainly saved the children from a lynching. He called Black Americans' civil rights "a very real moral issue."

Earlier, when the U.S. Senate convened in 1957 and Richard Nixon gaveled it to order, the first thing he did was propose a rule change. As vice president, he was the head of the Senate, and he proposed a rule that would eliminate the filibuster and remove the Southern hold on Congress that prevented the Civil Rights Act from going forward. The move failed but was seen as audacious and won praise from civil rights advocates. Martin Luther King, Jr., admitted he had not thought much of Nixon before but was coming to believe he was genuine. King was impressed with Nixon when they met, saying he had a "magnetic personality" and a "genius for winning people." Nixon fought hard for the Civil Rights Act of 1957. He was at his core a Quaker's son who believed in equality. He had befriended Jackie Robinson and dined with the sports star at his home. In his first campaign for Congress, in 1946, he spoke on civil rights and was awarded honorary membership in a local NAACP. One of his earliest celebrity supporters was Kenny Washington, a star running back at UCLA who later became the first African American in the NFL. The society Nixon founded at Whittier College was the only one there to admit a Black student.

But there was the "tricky" side to Nixon as well. He always had his eye on the next election. African Americans were leaving the South and heading north in droves in the 1950s. Their voting power in crucial states could swing the Electoral College. While Martin Luther King came to like Nixon and believe in him during the course of the struggle to pass the Civil Rights Act of 1957, he also saw the politician and showman, the carnival barker in Prescott trying to get his grandmother to win a ham. He wrote to a journalist shortly after the passage of the bill that "if Richard Nixon is not sincere, he is the most dangerous man in America."[7]

16

Don't You Have Enough Problems?

January 11, 1955. Ciro's nightclub in Los Angeles.

"There was a line down the Strip," Jess Rand remembered. Stars pulled up in limos; Humphrey Bogart and Marilyn Monroe were whisked away to reserved tables. *Life* magazine ran a full spread on the event. The room was filled with smoke and dry martinis as Hollywood's elite mingled.

Backstage, two aging hoofers and their young one-eyed partner sat in their underwear. They wore stocking caps to keep their pomaded hair perfectly in place. They smoked cigarettes and talked about women. Just as they had thousands of times before. Finally, as the club owner was checking his watch, they slipped on their tuxedos and looked each other over. Will Mastin brushed his suit and polished his cane. Sammy adjusted his eye patch and then down the hall they went to be introduced by Frank Sinatra.

Sammy opened with a thirty-foot knee slide onto the stage and the audience roared. He sang "Glad to Be Home" and went right into "The Birth of the Blues." He was twisting and doing axels. He played the trumpet and the drums. He spotted Gary Cooper in the audience and broke out an improv impression. Dean Martin flashed his million-dollar smile and Jerry Lewis howled with laughter. It was an astonishing performance for a man a mere seven weeks removed from losing his eye.

The Trio did forty minutes of encores. Judy Garland was weeping. Sammy's father and uncle hugged him. As the band was winding down and the applause was just about over, Sammy reached up and took the eye patch off his head. He threw it into the crowd.[1] One last flare of dramatics, the final exclamation point. Sammy Davis, Jr., was back.[2]

Sammy had arrived in Palm Springs several weeks earlier worried about his future and still a little sore from the accident. He lounged by the pool and listened to records while being waited on by Sinatra's staff. He began to learn to function with only one eye and began wearing the patch.

16. Don't You Have Enough Problems?

Frank assured him it would all be OK and Sammy's awe for the man only grew. After two weeks at the desert resort, he returned to Los Angeles and began rehearsals for the comeback show.

"I'd reach out for something and miss it [by] two, three inches. The first time I tried dancing again, I kept kicking myself in the other leg and tripping," Sammy would recall. He holed up in a studio in Los Angeles and tried to maintain anonymity. He did not want anyone other than Will and Sam Sr. around.[3]

His exuberance and his drive had returned. They had never really left, just sidetracked by the physical limitations of having been in a car crash. Once the bumps and bruises healed, he was back to his old self. A constant ball of energy waiting to explode, but now with only half his vision. He spent hours every day laser-focused on learning to dance with only one eye. Will and Sam Sr. watched and encouraged.

In late December he went back to see Dr. Hull for an assessment of his progress. Hull said his right eye was compensating for the left just as he had hoped. He gave Sammy a pair of thick glasses, a style that he would take to wearing often in years to come, their thickness masking the artificial left eye. But recently the eye patch had been getting him press, and there was little Sammy loved more than seeing his name in the paper.

His stay in the hospital and his recovery time at Frank's brought up existential questions in Sammy's mind. A twenty-nine-year-old kid, he had very little education and was raised with no religion. His father had been brought up Baptist but had long since given up any pretense of reverence. His mother was a Catholic but likewise was not devout, and besides he had only seen her a handful of times in his life to that point. The absence of any formal understanding of how man explains his presence on earth and the good and bad that come with it left Sammy looking for something. As one biographer explained, "Sammy had always been a fervent searcher. And where his mind was not intellectual, his heart was always vulnerable."

During his hospital stay Eddie Cantor brought him a Star of David. The next day he saw a young rabbi making rounds at the hospital. He flagged him down and began asking questions. Why me? he asked. Why had he been chosen to live this life that most African Americans of the time could not begin to fathom? Why had God spared his life from the twisted wreckage on that California roadside?

The rabbi had few direct answers but gave Sammy some reading recommendations. He told him not to view circumstances in life as direct reward or punishment from God but that certain events could be seen as wake-up calls of sorts. Was Sammy living the life God intended for him?

Once back in Los Angeles and relearning to dance, Sammy was introduced to Rabbi Max Nussbaum. Nussbaum was one of the most famous rabbis in Germany before fleeing Hitler's pogroms in 1942. He wound up in Hollywood, where he fit right in. Nussbaum became rabbi to the stars. He was hired by Temple Israel, where some of the founding members were leading Hollywood moguls. Sammy was taken with Rabbi Nussbaum and began going everywhere with the copy of *Everyman's Talmud* the rabbi had given him.

He announced his conversion to the bewilderment of his friends and the press, Jerry Lewis comically asking him, "You don't have enough problems already?"

Many of his friends believed it was a publicity stunt. With Sammy, the need for publicity was as deep-rooted a conviction as he had. So, it isn't out of the question that a desire to be more accepted in Hollywood's inner circle and see his name in the papers may have played a role in his conversion. After all, Louis B. Mayer and Samuel Goldwyn, both Jews, ran the biggest studios in Hollywood. It is not conceivable that this fact escaped Sammy. That said, he was also a young person with no formal understanding of the myths man had developed to explain his existence. Judaism, while a convenient choice, may also have been felt deeply at such a confusing and life-altering time.

Will Mastin reacted with confused indifference, while Sammy's father began wearing a Star of David as well in solidarity. Just another piece of flashy jewelry for the old hoofer. Regardless of his intentions or piety, Sammy Davis, Jr., would claim Judaism as his own for the rest of his life. As his star rose higher and higher, it became a unique part of his identity.[4]

And his star was indeed rising higher. The Will Mastin Trio starring Sammy Davis, Jr., was in demand nationwide at all the biggest nightclubs. But Sammy now looked at the marquee and wanted to see only his name. He was almost thirty years old and eager to have his own act. But he was under contract with Will Mastin through 1965. His father believed he and Sammy owed everything in life to Mastin and must remain loyal.

The contract was not generous to Sammy. Will took 20 percent off the top and the remaining money was split three ways. The net result was that Sammy's take was a little over 26 percent of the act's earnings. Not the typical haul for the star of the show. In 1956, Will signed over the Trio's bookings to the William Morris Agency. The agency now took 10 percent off the top and the rest of the deal remained in place.

Sammy liked to spend money. He always spent more than he made. He spent money on clothes and flashy jewelry and women. He wanted to be like Sinatra, and Sinatra had plenty of money. Jess Rand remembered that one night Sammy took a $3,000 advance on a $5,000 gig. His father was enraged and slapped him around, telling him, "You want to blow your money, fine, but don't blow mine."

16. Don't You Have Enough Problems?

Sammy began borrowing money from nightclub owners and committing the act to future engagements. The nightclubs of the forties and fifties were run by the Mob. The Riviera and the 500 Club in New Jersey. The Chez Paree in Chicago and Cocoanut Grove in Miami. All across the country, crime families had their hands in the business of nightclubs. As Sammy's star rose, he found himself further and further in debt to people like Sam Giancana in Chicago and Skinny D'Amato in Atlantic City.

Before the accident, Broadway composer Jule Styne had seen the Trio perform and approached Sammy about starring in a Broadway musical. In 1956 he offered Sammy the starring role in his new musical, *Mr. Wonderful*. He had even worked a nightclub scene in to appease Will Mastin and make the whole Trio part of the process. There was a hitch, though. Sammy would need to be in New York all the time to star on Broadway and the act had nightclub commitments, and debts.

Paul "Skinny" D'Amato lost both his parents at a young age. He became a pimp on the streets of Atlantic City and ended up in a federal penitentiary during the Depression. When he was released, he started booking acts at the 500 Club. He ended up running the place. He was in many ways the classic caricature of a mid-twentieth-century mobster: six feet tall, sunglasses, nice dark suit and coiffed hair. He would walk around the club telling people, "Need anything? Remember, if you do, come see me first—all right?"

Sammy often did need something and Skinny was happy to provide. But now Sammy wanted out. He wanted to go to Broadway and prove himself in a new medium. Sammy invited Jule Styne and his writing partner, lyricist George Weiss, to the 500 Club. Sammy thought they could convince Skinny this was a good idea.

The two Broadway men walked into the 500 Club and headed toward the back. There were Sammy and Skinny D'Amato and what Weiss recalled as "five or six of his henchmen. You can see they are all carrying weapons.... I was personally scared to death."

Weiss and Styne began to sell D'Amato on the proposal to take Sammy away to Broadway. Sammy became animated and excited in explaining his role in the production. All the while Skinny just sat there "without as much as a smile on his face." Weiss, Styne, and Sammy sang some lines from the show in the making. An awkward silence hung in the air until someone finally asked D'Amato what he thought. "You got six months," he said.[5]

Sammy was headed to Broadway.

Mr. Wonderful: A New Musical Comedy with The Will Mastin Trio starring Sammy Davis Jr. was Jule Styne's semi-biographical creation. The story centered around a young nightclub performer facing prejudice and hardship who overcomes the odds to make it big. The story was not all that different from the real-life experience of Sammy. The first act focused on his younger down-and-out days until he is discovered. In the second act he breaks out and takes the world by storm.

Aside from having one the longest titles in the history of Broadway, the show lacked much originality. In February of 1956 the show traveled to Philadelphia to begin a four-week run before its Broadway debut. The reviews were not good. "Shoddy and tasteless," wrote the *New York Daily Mirror*.[6] The *Philadelphia Daily News* called it "a tedious two-hour build-up for a half-hour night club act." Years later, one of the show's own cast members would critique the play as "trite."[7]

A meeting was called, and some changes were made before the Broadway debut. Not the least of which was reducing the role of Mastin and Sam Sr. The show opened on Broadway in March of 1956, in the same week as *My Fair Lady*, a show destined to become one of the all-time Broadway greats. The reviews on Broadway after the plot changes were not much better, but Sammy was undeterred. He took to promoting the show himself in every avenue he could find. After performances he would head to nightclubs, making impromptu appearances and plugging the show. He sought out every radio microphone in New York that would have him, urging listeners to come see the musical. Ticket sales began to increase. Early in the show's run a woman called from the audience, "The critics are crazy, Sammy, we love you." Sammy blew her a kiss and said, "Tell your friends." The audience roared in approval and Sammy did a thirty-minute encore.[8]

While the critics were not impressed, ticket sales were strong. Sammy was a one-man promotion machine and seemed to enjoy the role. Things were going so well that Jule Styne went back to Skinny D'Amato and asked for more time, as they had a bona fide hit on their hands. Skinny relented, saying, "You can have Sammy 365 days, but on the 365th day he opens at the Chez Paree in Chicago."

Sammy was relishing his role on Broadway. He was living in a high-end Manhattan hotel and would have all-night parties with the cast. He would sometimes take everyone out to the Copa or across the river to the 500 Club. He began drinking whiskey in his Cokes. He rarely slept; he was just too full of energy. He took to doing breakfast shows at the 500 Club as a means of preparing for a solo career, and to begin paying off debts.[9]

While Sammy was living it up, Will and Sam Sr. began to see the writing on the wall. Sammy was thirty years old; he wanted to go solo. Will knew but refused to accept it. Will Mastin had come from a family of sharecroppers in Alabama to running the top African American

16. Don't You Have Enough Problems?

entertainment act in the country. All those years traveling the vaudeville circuit. All the nights in rundown hotels and boarding houses. Now the Trio headlined the biggest nightclubs in the country. He was not ready to give it up.

On February 23, 1957, *Mr. Wonderful* closed its run on Broadway after having grossed over one million dollars. The final night was a star-studded event, with celebrities surprising Sammy during the show. He did twelve curtain calls. The show could have gone on, as it was wildly popular at the time of its closing, but Skinny D'Amato wasn't giving any more extensions. He needed Sammy's drawing power back in the nightclub world.

There was some talk at the end of the Broadway run about Sam and Will retiring. Will decided it would be best if Sammy eased gradually into a solo career. Sammy was ready to go solo, but Will had the contract. On February 24, the Will Mastin Trio starring Sammy Davis, Jr., headlined the Chez Paree in Chicago, keeping their commitment to Skinny. In the audience that night was a woman who would soon change Sammy's life: Kim Novak, one of the top stars of Columbia Pictures.

17

"A call from Chicago"

Marilyn Pauline "Kim" Novak was born in 1933 to a family of Slavic descent in Chicago. She grew into a stunningly beautiful woman. After working as an elevator operator and salesclerk in her teens, she was taken by her mother to a modeling audition. The advertising agency hired her and through a series of fortunate events she was seen by Harry Cohn. Cohn was the head of Columbia Pictures and was looking for a new star since his falling-out with the studio's leading lady Rita Hayworth. By 1957 he had turned Novak into one of America's top box-office attractions.

Kim Novak was not quite ready for the limelight, however. She never really embraced her fame. She felt constrained by the publicity and studio control. Unlike many stars of the day, she did not actively court stardom. Her mother had gotten her into modeling because it paid better than operating elevators. Harry Cohn saw an ad with her standing in front of a refrigerator, and she was making movies a few months later. She craved privacy while at the same time working her best at being an actress, understanding that many would kill for her position.[1]

She first saw Sammy at the Chez Paree gig in Chicago after the closing of *Mr. Wonderful*. A few months later, the two met at a party in Los Angeles. Tony Curtis would recall that they "spent the evening together—deep in thought, deep in talk. I could see right in the beginning they were getting along in an intense way." Someone at the party told the tabloids. The next week, gossip columnists were writing about the budding romance. Columbia's white leading lady gallivanting around with a Black nightclub entertainer was juicy news in 1957. Sammy phoned Kim with his apologies, telling her, "We can handle this any way you think is best, I understand the situation you're in with the studio." She seemed amused and unconcerned. She told him she was cooking spaghetti and meatballs and asked if he would like to join her for dinner.

Novak had been signed by Columbia at age twenty, barely a year into her modeling career. She was sent to live at the Studio Club, an all-girls dormitory of would-be starlets. They put her on a diet and dyed her hair three shades of blonde. By the time of her performance in Alfred Hitchcock's *Vertigo*, she had come to resent the studio and Harry Cohn's influence on her life. *Vanity Fair* wrote in 1999 that "Kim Novak was Harry Cohn's revenge on Rita Hayworth. Sammy Davis Jr. was Kim Novak's revenge on Harry Cohn."[2] The two began a clandestine relationship. Sammy would have Arthur Silber, Jr., the son of his manager and a main member of his entourage—a bodyguard of sorts—drive him to Kim's house. Sammy would hide under a rug in the back seat to avoid anyone seeing. Sammy eventually used a third party to rent a house in Malibu specifically for their rendezvous.

Their friends all said they were crazy, that they were going to ruin their careers. Interracial marriage was illegal in thirty-one states in 1957 and still a decade away from being ruled constitutional. They understood the situation and tried to keep their relationship under wraps. But word leaked out. The tabloids called it "the biggest Hollywood scandal in twenty years." When questioned by studio executives, Novak would deny everything. It was just gossip, she said.[3]

Later that year on a return engagement in Chicago, Sammy reserved one of the best tables for Novak and her family. By all accounts, they loved the show. Harry Cohn's spies caught wind of this. Not long after, Jess Rand, Sammy's press agent, received a call asking him to come meet Harry Cohn. Cohn began screaming about Kim and Sammy. He threw a lit cigar at Rand's head and threatened, "I know the right people, I'll see he never works in a nightclub again." Cohn kept a framed picture of Benito Mussolini on his desk. Rand believed him when he said he knew people. He boarded a plane to Chicago to warn Sammy.

When he arrived and walked in the hotel room, Sammy was deep in conversation with a man Rand had never seen. The man made a comment about Sammy's eye.

"If you fuck with my right eye, I'll kill you," Sammy told the man, doing an almost Bogart–like voice.

The man pulled back his jacket, revealing a pistol. "Don't ever say that, kid, unless you mean it," he said as he slowly walked out of the room.

Rand and Davis were scared and wondering exactly what to make of the scene they had just witnessed, when things took a turn for the worse.[4]

On New Year's Day 1958, Irv Kupcinet published his "Kup's Column" in the *Chicago Sun-Times*. He was starting the new year out with some extra-juicy news. A marriage license had been taken out in Aurora, a suburb of Chicago, for Sammy Davis, Jr., and Kim Novak. Cohn called Kupcinet, fuming. "Who's going to go see a movie star who's married to a black man?" he ranted to Irv, to no avail.

"Harry, we've been friends for a long time. But I have to print what I think is news," Kupcinet told him.

"'Fuck you,'" Cohn replied and slammed the phone down.

It was the final straw. Harry Cohn was a man accustomed to getting what he wanted and controlling what he believed was his. He had made Rita Hayworth and now he had made Kim Novak. He believed she belonged to him. He was not going to have some one-eyed Black nightclub performer destroy his main investment. This time the message would not come from a random goon with a gun.

Sam Davis, Sr., frequented the Hollywood Park racetrack. So did Mickey Cohen. Cohen was one of the most famous gangsters in America. He was the understudy of Bugsy Siegel, and had spent time in Alcatraz. He would be played by movie stars Harvey Keitel and Sean Penn in films about the Mob. One magazine profile called him "a hothead thug with a taste for beautifully tailored suits." He had a warning for Sam Sr.

"Listen. I got some terrible news for you. I just got a call from Chicago to hurt Sammy." Sam Sr. knew this was trouble. "I tell you what, there's one chance," Cohen told him. "I'll give him 24 hours. Sammy has to get married—to a colored girl."

Sam Sr. relayed the news to his son, who had moved on from Chicago to the Sands in Las Vegas. Sammy was terrified. His first reaction was to call some of his nightclub contacts for protection. He finally got through to Sam Giancana. His answer to Sammy's plea was not reassuring.

Arthur Silber, Jr., was in the room as Sammy talked to the Mob boss. He recalled the conversation a half century later. "We can protect you here in Chicago, or when you're in Vegas, but we can't do anything about Hollywood," Giancana warned Sammy. "Don't go back home unless you straighten things out with Harry Cohn." Silber claimed he and Sammy began carrying loaded guns because they did not know who was sleeping in the next suite.

Silber shared Sammy's suite at the Sands and was sitting on the bed polishing his shoes. Sammy was frantically pacing around in his white terry-cloth robe, rummaging through his address book and looking agitated.

"Sammy, what are you doing?" Arthur asked.

"I'm looking for someone to marry," he replied.

Loray White was born in Houston in the mid–1930s. She was married with a child shortly after dropping out of high school. Domestic life was not for her, though, and she left her family in Texas to pursue a career in show business. She had met Sammy in 1955 and the two had dated for a time. She had scored a bit part in Cecil B. DeMille's movie epic *The Ten Commandments* in 1956 and by early 1958 she was working at the Silver Slipper as a dancer. The Silver Slipper happened to be right across the

17. "A call from Chicago" 99

street from the Sands, where Sammy was performing. Most importantly, Loray White was Black.

Sammy would claim in his autobiographies that he saw Loray perform at the Silver Slipper while drunk, having just lost $39,000 at blackjack. The memories of their time dating came flooding back. She was a catch, he decided. She knew the business and was beautiful. He decided on the spot that they should get married. He proposed and she accepted.

Arthur Silber, Jr., remembered it slightly differently years later. He claimed Davis found Loray's name in his address book and gave her a call, as related above. He invited her over to the suite. "He sat her down—he was sitting in a chair and I was sitting on the bed—and he made her a proposition, to marry him for a certain sum of money. She would have all the rights that Mrs. Sammy Davis Jr. would have, but at the end of the year they would dissolve the marriage. She agreed to that, and that's what took the heat off."

The circumstances of the proposal may differ, but there is no question about what came next. On January 10, 1958, Sammy and Loray married in

Sammy Davis, Jr., and his first wife, Loray White, at their wedding on January 10, 1958, at the Sands Hotel in Las Vegas (courtesy University of Nevada, Las Vegas, Libraries Special Collections & Archives).

Las Vegas. The ceremony was conducted by a justice of the peace. Harry Belafonte was the best man. After the ceremony Sammy proceeded to do his usual show at the Sands, singing love songs to his new bride, who sat in the front row. Following the show, everyone got drunk.

The next day, the wedding made all the papers and Arthur received a phone call from Giancana. "You can tell him that Mickey says the pressure is off. You can relax."[5]

Loray White played the most convincing Mrs. Sammy Davis, Jr., she could. Sammy rented her a big house in the Hollywood Hills and bought her a ten-diamond ring and mink coat. She was given a shopping allowance and used it indulgently. But Sammy was nowhere to be found. He was on the road performing or out at parties while Loray stayed home in her Hollywood mansion. Silber would always claim that while Loray was in on the deal, she secretly hoped Sammy would settle down and the marriage might work. Others claimed she was hoping that being Mrs. Sammy Davis would open up career opportunities for her. Neither happened. By June, Sammy offered her $25,000 to divorce him. Of the whole affair Sammy would later say, "It's not a pretty story. I'm not proud of it."[6]

For her part, Kim Novak would always claim that their affair was innocent and nonsexual. In 1997 she explained to an interviewer, "I didn't really have an affair with him. I was a gentile raised in a Jewish neighborhood—always being shoved in the snow or having rotten pies pushed in my face—so I identified with him as a minority. I could tell he was in love with me as he was so nervous taking pictures of me that he forgot to take the lens cap off. It was sweet, you know. 'Oh, you're a white girl and you talk to me.'—I knew how he felt."[7]

That is hard to believe, given the evidence. Many of Sammy's friends backed up Novak's assertion while others disagreed. Regardless of whether the relationship was sexual or platonic, it had a major impact on Sammy's life.

Harry Cohn died of a heart attack about a month after Sammy's marriage to Loray White. Kim Novak's career never recovered. Cohn had been her big supporter and her acting skills were limited, as she readily admitted. She virtually retired from filmmaking several years later.

Sammy was still at the top of his game, though. His father had bowed out gracefully after the Chicago shows. He claimed he had health problems but in reality, he knew his time was up. Will Mastin not so much. Mastin continued to travel with Sammy and open the show. He would come out and do the soft shoe before introducing Sammy. The marquee continued to say "The Will Mastin Trio starring Sammy Davis, Jr." Sammy would complain that the old man still thought it was 1938. Why wouldn't he just realize it was time to pack it in? Even as his role in the show dwindled to nothing, Will insisted on his own dressing room. Every night he would lay out his makeup and suit like he was getting ready to perform. Just in case Sammy needed him, he said, but he would rarely go on stage. "It was so sad," Silber recalled.[8]

By mid–1958 Sammy was once again single and in high demand at nightclubs around the country. He was also drinking more than ever. He was depressed about his love prospects and America's systemic racism. He felt like no matter how famous he became, he would never shake the stigma of being a "Negro act." And yet recording and acting offers kept coming.

He was cast as Spider, a soldier, in a World War II drama on NBC's *General Electric Theater*, hosted by Ronald Reagan. He played Danny Johnson, a sailor, in a film version of the play *Anna Lucasta*. Between 1956 and 1958 Sammy released seven albums and had several songs on the charts.

He rented an office in Hollywood. At nightclubs and high-end department stores, Sammy loved telling waiters and clerks to send the bill to the office. Sammy was the first African American entertainer to have an office in Hollywood, and he relished it. So did Will Mastin in some ways. As his role in the shows dwindled, he would spend more time at the office reminiscing on all his show-business accomplishments to anyone who would listen.

In 1925, DuBose Heyward wrote a novel (*Porgy*) about down-and-out African Americans living on Catfish Row in Charleston, South Carolina. All the main characters are deeply flawed. Porgy is a crippled beggar and Bess is a drug addict. In 1935, George Gershwin turned the novel into an opera that toured the world to wide critical acclaim. By the late '50s, Samuel Goldwyn had bought the rights for a feature film.

Casting began and controversy immediately followed. The NAACP disavowed the movie and called on Black actors not to participate because of the opera's portrayal of African Americans. Harry Belafonte was first offered the lead role and turned it down. "DuBose Heyward wrote a very racist story," he said. "The leading man was on his knees. The second leading man was a cocaine pusher.... The leading lady was a prostitute.... [T]he images were highly distasteful."

Still, Samuel Goldwyn was one of the most powerful men in Hollywood and he believed the story worthy of being told. He cast Sidney Poitier as the lead. Reportedly Poitier turned down the role for the same reasons as Belafonte but was convinced by his manager that Goldwyn could ruin his career if he refused, so he reluctantly accepted.

In the late 1950s Sammy was craving more acting work. He was not worried about Harry Belafonte's or the NAACP's concerns. He saw a massively popular work about to be turned into a movie by one of Hollywood's leading producers, and he wanted in. He knew Sam Goldwyn was having trouble casting the role of Sportin' Life, Catfish Row's cocaine dealer. He begged Judy Garland to invite him to a party that he knew Goldwyn would attend. Once there, he proceeded to take charge of the piano and sing the entire songbook from the opera.

Goldwyn's wife whispered to her husband, "Swear on your life you'll never use him."

"Him?" the studio head asked. "That monkey?"

But there were not many African American actors willing to play the part. The William Morris Agency came around to Sammy's way of thinking and began to pressure Goldwyn. They reserved a private box and Goldwyn went to see Sammy's nightclub show with Abe Lastfogel, Sammy's William Morris manager. He had asked that no one tell Sammy he was coming, but word got around. Sammy spent the whole show essentially auditioning for the part. Toward the end, he told the audience, "Ladies and gentlemen, you can't see them, I can't either, but Sam Goldwyn and his wife are up there. Mr. Goldwyn, I'll do the role of Sportin' Life for nothing." The crowd cheered. Goldwyn looked at Lastfogel and said, "He's a vaudevillian, I need an actor." But Goldwyn could find no actors, so in the end, the vaudevillian got the part.[9]

The problems with casting spilled over into production. The elaborately designed set made to resemble the poor waterfront section of Charleston looked fake and unconvincing to many moviegoers. It burned down in the middle of production and had to be remade, costing millions. Unhappy with production early on, Goldwyn fired his director and brought in another.

The film finally premiered in the summer of 1959 to mixed reviews. The *New York Times* called it "a stunning, exciting, and moving film,"[10] while *Time* magazine considered it "a sometimes-ponderous failure."[11] The film's ticket sales were strong, though, and it won a Golden Globe. The mixed reviews did all have one thing in common, praise for Sammy Davis, Jr.'s, performance.

Samuel Goldwyn came to view the film as one of his biggest failures. After its theatrical release, it aired one time on television in 1967 and was never released on home video. Goldwyn left the rights to the film to his estate, along with the wish that it would never be commercially released again. And it never has. In 2017 the *Hollywood Reporter* called it "the holy grail of missing films."[12]

The film contributed to the continuing raising of the profile of Sammy Davis, Jr. The 1950s had been his breakout decade and the future looked nothing but bright as the 1960s dawned.

17. "A call from Chicago"

As for Will Mastin, he finally came to understand his time was up. As the seventy-nine-year-old hoofer gazed upon the movie posters for *Porgy and Bess*, he saw a contractually obligated phrase under Sammy's name, "under the personal management of Will Mastin." He knew it was no longer true. Sammy was his own star now and Mastin's time was done. He took his final bow and retired in Los Angeles. In the coming decade, marquees around the country would have just one name: Sammy's.[13]

18

"God is on our side"

The glass shattered and hit the Venezuelan foreign minister in the eye. Protesters were rocking the limousine back and forth. A Secret Service officer pulled his revolver. "I think we will have to get some of the sons of bitches," he told Nixon. Nixon instructed him to stand down. He said if they tried pulling anyone from the car, he could shoot, but not until then. "If it got that bad, I knew it would all be lost anyway," he would later recall. The Venezuelan police showed up and fired tear gas at the protesters. It dispersed the crowd enough to open a lane for the limo to speed away. They made it inside the gates of the American embassy.[1]

A few days before, Pat and Dick's arrival on the South American continent had been met with protesters holding signs that read "Nixon—Merchant of War" and "Nixon Dog." They had been spat on and forced to dodge rock throwers in Lima, Peru. One of the stones knocked out an aide's tooth and hit Nixon's shoulder. Eisenhower dispatched marines and navy ships to the South American coast to ensure the vice president's safety. The trip was not going as planned.

The president had sent Nixon to Latin America on a goodwill junket to shore up waning Cold War alliances. The United States had for years been treating its southern neighbors as nothing more than a repository of cheap labor and raw materials for American companies. The anger among the Latin American population had reached a boiling point by 1958.

The American public didn't read any of this background in newspapers, however. Press accounts of Nixon's coolness under pressure were glowing. He made the cover of *Life* magazine. He returned home to a hero's welcome. Eisenhower met him and Pat at the airport, and they rode in a motorcade past thousands of cheering citizens, proud of the way the vice president had stood up to the communist agitators. Many saw the young VP as just the man needed to lead the country into the new decade.[2]

As the sun rose on New Year's Day 1960, the nation was still a long way from the turbulence that would define the decade. But the rumblings were there. The Montgomery bus boycotts and the emergence of rock 'n'

18. "God is on our side"

roll were harbingers of the world to come. Uneasiness about the postwar homogenization of American life was boiling beneath the surface.

It was amid this rising boil that Richard Nixon would make his first of three runs at the presidency. His performance in Latin America and subsequent tour of Moscow with the Soviet premier cemented Americans' view of him as an able steward of foreign affairs. His skill at intraparty politics secured him the Republican nomination over Sen. Nelson Rockefeller. Nixon had never lost a political race, but in 1960 he would face an opponent unlike any other. The sheer antithesis of Richard Nixon, John F. Kennedy was a "Franklin" through and through.

Jack, as he was called by friends, was born to wealth. His father, Joe, was a second-generation immigrant with a drive to make it big in America. By any measure, he succeeded. He made millions on Wall Street and according to some by bootlegging whiskey in the 1920s and became a major player in the movie industry in the 1930s. By the 1940s his wealth had made it possible for him to cajole an ambassadorship out of FDR. The dream of his life was to have one of his sons become president.

The eldest and favorite son, Joe Jr., died in the latter days of World War II. That meant it was up to young Jack to fulfill his father's dream, and he took to the task dutifully. After graduating from Harvard in 1940 he enrolled in business school at Stanford. He traveled with his father throughout South America as part of the elder Kennedy's position in the Roosevelt administration, and when war came he joined the Navy Reserve. He earned a Purple Heart after saving his comrades from a Japanese torpedo strike. When the war ended, he moved back to Massachusetts and ran for Congress.

His rise from congressman to senator to presidential candidate was greased with money and connections. He had written a book, with considerable help from an aide, that won a Pulitzer, but he had done little to distinguish himself in government. His record on civil rights and other progressive causes was weak. And yet he had movie-star looks, a beautiful wife and adorable young children. His intelligence poured through his thick New England accent and much of America fell under the spell of the Kennedy mystique.

Nixon was a proud Orthogonian, and he had been beating Franklins all his life. This would be no different, he surmised. He took over his own campaign. "You could have taken the key to the Republican National Committee and locked up the office and thrown the key in the Potomac and shipped all 175 employees off to the Virgin Islands and saved money for all the good we did the campaign, for all Nixon listened," a staffer recalled. By 1960, Nixon had been through seven national campaigns either as a candidate or lead surrogate for the party. He decided where to campaign and when. How the money was allocated and why. "I know the answer," longtime backer Frank Jorgensen said his attitude seemed to say, adding, "This is the arrogance that the position breeds, that power breeds." He began taking what aides called "jolly pills" to stay awake and get through his grueling schedule. Campaign aide Don Hughes recalled finding the candidate asleep on his feet one night. As Hughes put Nixon to bed, he opened one eye and told Don not to worry. "It will be all right.... God is on our side."[3]

One of his first decisions was a pledge to campaign in all fifty states. Aides advised him against it. It was impractical to try to cover all fifty states before the election and it was completely unnecessary, they said. Still, Nixon decided it was the way to go. He had some bad luck, too; he banged his knee on a car door in North Carolina and ended up with a staph infection that put him in the hospital for twelve days. He felt like he was falling behind.

All through the spring Kennedy's name had been in the headlines as he battled Hubert Humphrey for the Democratic nomination. Nixon, through his own political acumen, had wrapped up the Republican nomination early, and while that was advantageous in many ways, it left a lot of space for Kennedy to draw headlines and garner name recognition.

More bad luck followed Nixon via the economy. Unemployment rose in the weeks leading up to the election. Nixon pleaded with Eisenhower to order some aircraft and military equipment to grease the wheels of the economy. Ike refused.

One of his biggest strategic mistakes of the campaign was agreeing to debate his less experienced and lesser known opponent on TV. It was to be the first televised presidential debate in history. "Television is not as effective as it was in 1952, the novelty has worn off," Nixon told a reporter. But he was wrong; the share of American households with TV sets had risen from 11 percent to 88 percent in the years since Nixon first entered public life.

The first debate took place on September 26, 1960, in Chicago. Nixon arrived at the studio looking haggard. After acquiring the staph infection in late August, he had lost eight pounds during his hospital stay. Once released, he had hit the ground running harder than before, trying to make up for lost time and keep his fifty-state pledge. He had caught a cold and fever. Still wincing in pain from his bad knee, he made it to the dressing room. He had done no real preparation. He was running as the candidate of experience. While it is true Nixon had plenty of experience debating and with television, the two had never been combined.

While Nixon had been running himself ragged, Kennedy had spent the four days before the debate at his family's compound on the Massachusetts coast. He was tan and rested. He had been studying up on the issues and had attack lines prepared.

18. "God is on our side"

Commercials preceded a notice that regularly scheduled programming would not be seen. Instead, the three networks would be televising the first-ever presidential debate. The debate opened with a question about domestic affairs that Kennedy immediately turned into an attack on the administration's dealings with the Russians. For almost an hour the two sparred back and forth, the camera catching Dick Nixon's darting eyes and fidgety movements in contrast with the confident Kennedy and his perfectly coiffed hair. In a nation of 107 million adults, an estimated 70–80 million watched the event. Almost all the rest listened on the radio. Radio listeners thought Nixon won, but the verdict on television was hands down for Kennedy. He had gone toe to toe with the vice president and appeared every bit his equal. The first one is the most remembered, but the two men held four televised debates between September 26 and October 21. When the debates were over, Kennedy had closed a six-point gap in Gallup survey polls. The race was tied going into the home stretch.[4]

Nixon ran on his experience and his success in keeping the communist menace at bay. But that also meant he was charged with defending the status quo. Kennedy claimed that he was prepared to lead a new generation into what he called the "New Frontier." America was firmly divided. In the end, the issue that would decide matters was not experience, but race.

The Civil Rights Act of 1957 that Nixon had been instrumental in shepherding through Congress had been reauthorized in 1960 at the behest of Nixon and the Eisenhower administration. Many of the loopholes that existed in the earlier version were closed but massive problems still remained, especially concerning voting rights in the South. Over the prior forty years, African Americans left the South in droves and headed north, where they formed a powerful voting contingency. Like the rest of America, the African American community was divided on who would better serve their cause.

On October 19, Martin Luther King, Jr., was arrested during a sit-in at an Atlanta restaurant. The judge found an unpaid parking ticket on King's record and sentenced him to six months of hard labor at a rural Georgia prison. His pregnant wife, Coretta, was distraught, fearing he would be murdered, like so many other Black men in the South sentenced to prison for petty crimes only to never return to their families. Murdered either by racist officers or racist inmates. She pleaded with everyone she could. Nixon, in a rather baffling move, did nothing more than mention it to the attorney general, who explained he could not intervene. Nixon's public line was simply "no comment."

Kennedy was not a civil-rights ideologue by any means and his first reaction was likewise to ignore the situation. But his brother-in-law Sargent Shriver convinced him to phone Coretta. The conversation led to a change of heart, or at least a change of political calculation. Kennedy then phoned the Democratic governor of Georgia and pleaded King's case. This laid the groundwork for his brother Bobby to call the judge, who relented. On October 27, King was released from prison.

The Kennedy team played up their accomplishment to the hilt with the African American press. They circulated flyers in heavily populated Black areas that read "No Comment—Nixon versus a candidate with a heart, Senator Kennedy." While King would never formally endorse either candidate, his father, also a prominent Southern minister, came out as all in for Kennedy. "It took courage to call my daughter-in-law at a time like this," he said. "He has the moral courage to stand up for what he knows is right. I've got all my votes and I've got a suitcase and I'm going to take them up there and dump them in his lap." Explaining his thoughts on Nixon later, the younger King said, "I had known Nixon longer. He had been supposedly close to me.... And yet when this moment came, it was like he never had heard of me.... I really considered him a moral coward."

The weekend before the election Nixon flew to Alaska for a campaign rally, completing his fifty-state promise. From there he flew to Chicago for an election-eve telecast with Eisenhower and his running mate, Henry Cabot Lodge, Jr. On Election Day he and Pat took a pre-dawn flight back to Whittier to vote. Afterwards he sent Pat home and took off in a convertible, along with Don Hughes and a secret service officer. He wanted no talk of politics; the polls were tied, and he had done all that could be done. Right now, he wanted to go to the beach. They sped along the side streets of Whittier, the press finally losing their trail. They laughed as motorists did double takes when they pulled up next to Nixon at stoplights. "Let's go to Mexico! Let's go down to Tijuana and have some Mexican food," Nixon proposed. As the rest of the nation was voting, Richard Nixon left the country for lunch.[5]

19

"We gotta have laughs"

Sammy was always hustling. His nightclub draw was strong, but he wanted more acting jobs. When he was not touring, he would sometimes just hang around the studios in Hollywood. He was having lunch at the Fox Studios commissary with his old friend Barbara Luna one day in 1959 as she explained he had no chance with the woman he had just spotted.

"She is a nice girl, but she doesn't do anything but work. She goes nowhere with nobody!" she said.[1]

The girl she was referring to was May (pronounced "My") Britt, the star of the movie Barbara was working on. Britt had taken a winding road to Hollywood. She was born in Switzerland in 1933 and was working in a photography studio at the age of nineteen when an Italian director saw her and cast her in his newest movie. He wanted an unknown leading lady with shoulder-length blonde hair and light freckles. May was the perfect fit and she accepted his offer to go to Rome and make a movie.

She found minor success in Italy as a young actress and in 1958, 20th Century–Fox brought her to the United States, where she starred opposite Marlon Brando in *The Young Lions*. The reviews were good, and Fox signed her to a seven-year contract. Sammy had seen her in films but never in person. After she walked into the Fox commissary that day, Sammy was a man on a mission.[2]

He began calling Luna, asking her to invite Britt to the get-togethers Sammy was always hosting at his house. She refused, partly out of fear that as a Filipino actress she might encounter trouble herself by playing matchmaker to an interracial relationship. He tried other showbiz friends and they all told him he was crazy for going down this road again. Another blonde darling of the studio, had he not learned his lesson? Finally, one night at a party he was introduced to Britt. He turned on his charm and she fell for him right away. May had no sense of what it meant to be in an interracial relationship in America in 1960. She was young and completely unaware of America's violent racial past and its burgeoning civil rights movement. They were falling for each other fast when, in early 1960, Sammy took off for Vegas.[3]

The actor Peter Lawford came to Frank Sinatra with a movie idea, a story about a gang that rips off a Las Vegas casino. Frank loved it and he pitched it to Warner Brothers, who gave him the green light. He called up Dean Martin, Sammy, and his old buddy Joey Bishop. He told them, "The idea is to hang out together, find fun with the broads, and have a great time. We gotta make pictures people enjoy. Entertainment, period. We gotta have laughs."

Sinatra owned a 6 percent stake in the Sands Hotel and Casino in Las Vegas. The hotel did big business when he was in town. Filming for the movie would take place all over Las Vegas. He and the boys should perform at the Sands every night too, he thought. All through January and February of 1960 the gang would perform shows at night and film during the day. The supergroup of performers drew huge crowds to the Las Vegas Strip, including some of Hollywood's elite like Jack Benny and Lucille Ball. Sinatra called it the Summit; Sammy would often refer to the group as the Clan. But the press started calling the five men the Rat Pack.

The Rat Pack had initially begun as a group of friends led by Hollywood power couple Humphrey Bogart and Lauren Bacall. The gossip columns claimed that when Bogart and his pals returned home from a Las Vegas trip, Bacall said they looked like "a goddamn rat pack." After Bogart's death, the press anointed Sinatra the leader. With the 1960 Vegas shows and the filming of *Ocean's 11*, he took it from an informal moniker used to describe a social circle to a profession of sorts.

The Rat Pack would make other films as well as television appearances and tours over the years. While never any of the men's main source of income or star power, the group became a symbol of a particular time and place in American history. Sporting skinny black ties with a swinging attitude, they drank Jack Daniel's and called men "Charley" and women "broads." The group consisted of Frank, Sammy, Dean Martin, Joey Bishop, and Peter Lawford. Others, like Shirley MacLaine and Don Rickles, were honorary members of sorts at certain times. But it was Frank, Sammy and Dean who were the main stars of the act and the three most often remembered as the central members.

The Vegas shows the men did together are legendary. They would sing songs and crack jokes, some of it scripted, some of it improvised. The dynamics of the men, who were personal friends as well, left audiences reeling. Sammy was often the butt of the jokes. "Hurry up, Sam, the watermelon's getting warm," or, when the stage lights would dim, "Smile, Sam, so the folks can see you." Frank's nickname for Sammy was "Smokey."

Davis would admit years later that some if it did bother him. "I loved

19. "We gotta have laughs" 111

The marquee of the Sands Hotel in Las Vegas, circa 1960 (courtesy University of Nevada, Las Vegas, Libraries Special Collections & Archives).

those guys and I knew they loved me," he said. "But yeah, it wasn't right.... Sometimes I had to wonder, Are these cats for real or what? I had to bite my tongue a lot."[4]

Still, it was Sammy who would light up the stage with his dancing. He was the youngest member of the Rat Pack and by far the most athletic. He gave the shows an energy that the others never could. Some nights he had to subdue his instincts so as not to steal the show and anger Frank.

The film they made, *Ocean's 11*, became a classic of the buddy-comedy genre. The movie's plot centers around a gang of World War II vets who plan to cut power to Las Vegas and steal millions from the casinos. It is an elaborate operation in which the bagmen drop the cash in the hotel garbage cans. Sammy plays the garbage man who smuggles the money out. In one scene, Frank, Dean and Peter are dressed as garbage men as well and rubbing burnt cork on their faces as they prepare to retrieve the money from the landfill. Sammy laughs and Frank asks, "What's so funny?" "I knew this color would come in handy someday," Sammy responds. The three white men look comically aggrieved as Peter Lawford asks, "How do you get this stuff off?"[5]

The film was a huge success, as were the shows that accompanied the filming. People were sleeping in their cars in Vegas during the early months of 1960, hoping to get a glimpse of the Rat Pack.

Sammy took May on a cruise after filming wrapped. They sailed from LA to Mexico, falling more in love along the way. When they returned, Sammy flew to Miami for a week of Rat Pack shows. May headed to New York and began filming a new project. The two were no longer hiding their relationship from the press and during a late-night call Sammy proposed marriage. May accepted. Responding to critics who claimed the marriage would ruin her career, she said, "I just married the man I love."[6]

May had grown up sheltered in a middle-class, postwar European world. She had no idea what it meant to be a white woman married to the most famous African American entertainer in 1960. She would soon find out.

Sammy announced the engagement in London, where he was performing, on June 6, 1960. Nazis picketed his show the next night. The couple returned to America to much of the same. The press was going wild, claiming Sammy Davis, Jr.'s, lifelong quest for a white woman was fulfilled. A few months later, while he was performing at the Lotus Club in Washington, D.C., the Nazis showed up again. They marched outside the club holding signs that said, "Go Back to Congo You Kosher Coon" and "Sammy Davis, Jew-noir." A fight broke out before police could disperse the crowd. A few weeks after the engagement, it was announced that May's contract would not be renewed by Fox. By all accounts, the two had fallen deeply in love. No amount of protest or nasty magazine articles was going to keep them apart. A wedding was planned for the fall.

As 1960 rolled on, the Rat Pack was becoming more of a cultural phenomenon. Peter Lawford, one of the group's main members, was a brother-in-law of John F. Kennedy. Kennedy was running for president. Sammy was partial to his opponent, the man who had come to see him in New York in 1954. But Frank and Peter convinced Sammy that Jack Kennedy was the man to help the cause of civil rights. And Sammy knew that being part of the Rat Pack was good for the business of Sammy Davis, Jr., so he threw his support in with Kennedy.

Kennedy came to see the Rat Pack at the Sands in February, shortly after declaring himself a candidate. FBI files tell of showgirls and late-night parties. Kennedy seemed to enjoy the Hollywood glamor and hanging out with Frank. It is through Frank that he met Judith Campbell, with whom he would have an eighteen-month affair. She would claim later in life to have carried messages between Mafia boss Sam Giancana and the president. It is also through Sinatra that JFK would eventually meet Marilyn Monroe.[7]

19. "We gotta have laughs"

Sinatra re-recorded his hit "High Hopes" with lyrics supporting Kennedy's bid. "Everyone is voting for Jack / 'Cause he's got what all the rest lack," the song claimed. In the lead-up to the West Virginia primary, there were rumors that Kennedy aides drove through the state paying restaurant and tavern owners to put the new version on their jukeboxes.

In July, Sammy and the gang were in LA as the Democratic National Convention came to town. Sammy, Frank and Peter were invited to sing "The Star-Spangled Banner." As they came on stage, the Mississippi delegation booed. Sinatra rolled his eyes and whispered to Sammy not to worry about the bigots. But it hurt Sammy. They were not booing Frank or Peter. They were booing the Black man who would dare to be engaged to a white woman. He cried as he performed the national anthem. Afterwards he ducked reporters and headed straight to the airport.[8]

Sammy began getting hate mail. "Dear Nigger Bastard, I see Frank Sinatra is going to be best man at your abortion. Well, it's good to know the kind of people supporting Kennedy before it's too late.—An ex-Kennedy voter."[9]

John F. Kennedy was not the natural choice of most African American voters in 1960. The Democratic Party was still the realm of South Carolina senator Strom Thurmond and Southerners who opposed civil rights. African Americans had by and large voted Republican since the Civil War. Sammy worked for Kennedy all through the fall of 1960, trying to garner support from the African American community. Wherever his performance schedule took him that fall, he coordinated with the Kennedy campaign. He would drop by the cocktail parties and fundraisers, lending his star power to the affairs and helping raise more money.

As the election approached, many in the Kennedy camp grew wary of the Rat Pack, and of Frank Sinatra in particular. Rumors about Frank's involvement with the Mob, specifically Chicago's Sam Giancana, were running rampant. People inside the campaign began distancing themselves. On top of that, Frank was scheduled to be the best man at Sammy's wedding, scheduled for late October. Kennedy and his men worried about the optics of the interracial marriage. Word was sent to Frank to ask Sammy to postpone the marriage until after the election.

Frank was furious and embarrassed. He did not know how to tell Sammy. But Sammy caught wind of the whole thing on his own. He called Frank and offered to postpone the marriage without being asked.

On November 8, 1960, John Kennedy defeated Richard Nixon by 100,000 votes in one of the closest elections in American history. On November 13, Sammy married May Britt in a Las Vegas ceremony.[10]

20

"Too many words ... strange words"

Jerry Jeff Walker left New Orleans in the summer of 1965 and headed to New York City. Someone had told him they wanted to publish his songbook. He wrote his mother a letter to prove he was alive and well. He met up with some old friends and played the clubs in the Village for a few weeks before realizing the book deal was not going to come through. So, he stuck his thumb in the wind again and headed back to Texas.

All along the trip back, he was reading Dylan Thomas's poetry and thinking of the man he had met in the New Orleans jail cell. A guy, who like him, was drifting, poor, and searching. When he arrived in Austin, he stayed up late one night picking on his guitar and working out ideas that might turn into new songs. He began to strum a 6/8 waltz pattern with a yellow legal pad in front of him. Dylan Thomas's internal rhyme schemes were in his head as he began to put in words his experiences of the last few years. "I knew a man Bojangles and he danced for you," one song began.

Years later he would write, "It came, just sorta tumbling out. One night while the rest of the country was listening to the Beatles, I was writing a six-eight waltz about an old man and hope. It was a love song."

He began performing the song and people would often let him know it was his best. One night in 1967, he played it for his idol, Ramblin' Jack Elliott. "Too many words. Strange words," he said. In time the song would become Jerry Jeff's best known and be covered by other artists over a hundred times.

But ahead of that, America's musical tides were changing. Dylan had gone electric and psychedelic rock was all the rage. Jerry Jeff was living with musician Pete Troutner and the two of them fell in with an older jazz-centered musician named Bob Bruno. The trio talked of starting a band. Music was evolving and they wanted to ride the wave, Jerry Jeff with his traditional folk storytelling and Bruno with his improvisational jazz.

Jerry Jeff would write of Bruno years later, "He never wanted to play the same thing twice and I couldn't."

The trio worked up some of Jerry Jeff's and Bruno's songs, they learned a few Buddy Holly tunes and then they were out playing shows. They called themselves the Lost Sea Dreamers. The LSD reference was intentional. Before long, they headed to Houston to find steadier work playing gigs. They lived and practiced above Guy Clark's guitar shop, years before Clark would become a hit songwriter in his own right. They decided that if they wanted to break out, they needed to head to the coast, either San Francisco or New York. They chose New York, but on their first night in town all their instruments were stolen out of their car, which barely ran. They had nothing—no money, no instruments, and no gigs. They split, vowing to return to New York soon.

Bob Bruno had family and friends in Washington, D.C., and so the trio retreated there. They found a cinder-block house in the Maryland countryside to rent; they acquired new instruments and began the band anew. For six months they gigged and planned their return trip. One night they were playing, in Jerry Jeff's words, "one of those basement dungeon clubs of stone and wood that had been made popular earlier in the '60s," and Janet Forbes was in the audience. Janet was twenty years old and longed for adventure the way Ronald Crosby had. She and Jerry Jeff hit it off immediately and married five days later. Bob Bruno thought it was a bad idea, but Jerry Jeff did not care.

With the help of some of Janet's money, they returned to New York with new instruments, better prepared for the city. They all shared an apartment on Thompson Street. They began playing at Cafe Wha? and all around the Village. They were playing loud psychedelic rock, Bruno's wild and improvisational style mixing with Jerry Jeff's traditional sensibilities. They became the house band at the Electric Circus. James Taylor, Mama Cass, and Emmylou Harris all had regular gigs there. They ended up with a record deal with Vanguard Records.

The suits at Vanguard were worried about the obvious drug reference in their name and asked them to change it. They obliged and became Circus Maximus. Vanguard released the first of the band's records in 1967 but it did not gain much traction. Bob Bruno wrote seven of the album's songs and Jerry Jeff four. The sound was improvisational psychedelic rock and was very much in line with what was all over the radio at the time. But Circus Maximus never found its way to any mainstream success. They recorded a second album, but two weeks before its release the band had a knock-down drag-out fight during rehearsal one night and that was that. The band broke up and the men went their separate ways.

Jerry Jeff had played "Mr. Bojangles" for Circus Maximus, but it didn't fit their sound and the band had never worked it up. The executives at Vanguard Records agreed and didn't think the song was a good fit. Jerry Jeff continued to play it on his own, though. He had met David Bromberg in 1966 and the two hit it off immediately. Bromberg was a prodigy on stringed instruments and provided the perfect accompaniment to Jerry Jeff's folk sound. Even before Circus Maximus was officially done, the two began performing together often.

One November night in 1966, Bromberg and Jerry Jeff were walking around the Village and drinking rather heavily. Bromberg suggested the pair drop in on Bob Fass at WBAI. Fass ran a local radio show on a Pacifica Foundation station that aired from midnight until dawn. Jerry Jeff described the show as "[l]ive music, new music, poetry, Pacifica's left of left political harangues ... a musical reference point for the entire city." The two drank a bottle of Seagram's Gin mixed with 7-Up, and they talked with Bob and played songs from two until five in the morning.[1]

One of the songs they played was "Mr. Bojangles." Fass was floored, asking Jerry Jeff almost skeptically, "That is a beautiful song. You wrote that?"[2] The two left the studio that night and went home with no idea how important that impromptu jam session was. Fass had recorded them playing "Mr. Bojangles." He began to play it on his show every night. People began asking for the song in record stores around town. Astonishingly, Vanguard still wanted nothing to do with the song. They gave Jerry Jeff permission to record it with Atlantic Records and in 1968 his first solo album came out.

"Mr. Bojangles" was released as a single and peaked at number 77. The song was not a huge success at first, but critics loved it. Twenty-six-year-old Jerry Jeff Walker had glowing reviews in the *New York Times*, *Variety* and *Billboard* in the summer of 1968. He played the Newport Folk Festival that year. Harry Belafonte came to the Bitter End one night to see him perform and wound up cutting the song. He was the first big name to try a rendition, but would certainly not be the last.

Jerry Jeff had a problem, though. He started getting checks made out to Jerry Jeff Walker. His legal name was still Ronald Crosby. He hired a lawyer and by the end of 1968, Ronald Crosby, the basketball player from upstate New York, no longer existed. There was only Jerry Jeff Walker, the songwriter.

The Nitty Gritty Dirt Band's version of "Mr. Bojangles" would make it to the Top 10 in 1970, but the song was already becoming a cult hit in 1968. Jerry Jeff had found a little fame and a little money in New York; now it was time to leave, he decided. He and Janet took a train upstate and bought a Corvette convertible. They put the top down and headed out to see America.

PART 3

21

"The folk process"

Jerry Jeff and Janet took I-95 south out of New York. Somewhere along the way they turned west. Jerry Jeff wanted to head back to Austin. In Texas, he said, "they always thought of me as one of them." They arrived around the Fourth of July 1969. Upon his return, his newfound cult status as the writer of "Mr. Bojangles" got him working almost immediately. He played a Hill Country folk festival for almost six thousand people shortly after arriving and had opening slots for Gordon Lightfoot and Jimmy Driftwood at the Municipal Auditorium by fall. But he wanted to keep moving. "Pisces always return to the sea," he wrote in his autobiography, so he and Janet left Texas for Florida.

"Mr. Bojangles" was a cult hit and Atlantic Records had a contract for another Jerry Jeff Walker album. He convinced them to let him cut his new record in Miami. Atlantic had found some success at Criteria Studios in Miami with the Bee Gees, so they set up Jerry Jeff with a house band to record his new project. He and Janet rented a place on Summerland Key and Jerry Jeff would drive back and forth to record, leaving Janet alone for days at a time.

Janet began going a little stir-crazy in the islands. She "always liked to work, and the Florida Keys are for people who stop working," Jerry Jeff would say. He bought Janet a motorcycle to get around on while he was gone recording in Miami. Still, this wasn't the spot for her. She decided she wanted to go to California. She left Jerry Jeff the motorcycle, bought a VW bus and headed to San Francisco. It was an easy come, easy go kind of time, and Jerry Jeff wished her luck.

"Looking back ... the three years I spent with Janet were wonderful. She gave me stability and a sense of place I'm sure I needed," he recalled. But it was 1969 and Jerry Jeff had another record in the can for Atlantic and royalty checks for his unlikely hit coming in every quarter. He had a booking agent, and gig offers were plentiful. He was ready for whatever life might bring.

He got arrested in Key West one night trying to drive the convertible back up US 1. He had been drinking on Duval Street all night and never made it off the island. His driver's license was suspended. The next week, he flew to a gig in Washington State. Before flying home, he went to the DMV and applied for a motorcycle license. There were no computer databases to run his name through. He passed the test, and he was street-legal again.

Back in the Keys he decided he wanted to go on tour on his motorcycle. He told his agent to book him across Canada. His friend Ray Carter was a sculptor and a bike mechanic. They loaded their bikes in a U-Haul trailer and headed for upstate New York. They stopped in Woodstock, where Ray stayed. Jerry Jeff rode his Harley back to Oneonta, where he took his mother on her first motorcycle ride. He then wrapped his guitar in a rain poncho and headed across the border.

He did a TV show in Ottawa and then came back through Montreal for a couple nights of gigs. There he fell in with a woman named Cindy who invited him to Paris. He was about to blow off the rest of his tour and join her in Paris when, he said, "I woke up in her bed, looked out the window and found a blue-sky morning. I thought, what a great day to hit the road with my bike, she saw that look and kicked my ass out of the house and down the street, and I was gone."

He continued his tour through Rivière-du-Loup and New Brunswick. He hopped a boat to Nova Scotia, then back to the U.S. He rode through New Hampshire and Massachusetts before landing back in Woodstock in the fall of 1970. He jammed with The Band at Big Pink, their famous pink house, and played a couple gigs with one of his songwriting heroes, Fred Neil. Atlantic Records had released *Bein' Free*, the album he had recorded in Miami earlier that summer. It wasn't getting much traction on the charts, though, and Woodstock was turning cold. He and Ray Carter loaded their bikes in the U-Haul and headed back to the Keys.

On the long drive, Ray was behind the wheel and Jerry Jeff got drunk, lamenting Cindy and how he should have just gone to Paris. He finally fell asleep. Somewhere between Virginia and North Carolina, Ray woke him up.

"Didn't you tell me you wrote 'Mr. Bojangles'?"

"Yeah, I did," Jerry Jeff replied while wiping the sleep from his eyes.

"I don't know, but the last two or three hours I've been driving this car, every station on the radio keeps playing a song called 'Mr. Bojangles' by some group called the Dirt Band," Ray told him.[1]

The Nitty Gritty Dirt Band was formed by Jeff Hanna and John McEuen in 1966 and would undergo more than a dozen lineup changes over the years. In 1969 multi-instrumentalist Jimmy Ibbotson joined. A few years before, as Ibbotson was packing his car to leave Indiana for the cross-country trip to California, he was approached by "a good witch." This was a 1960s euphemism for a female drug dealer. She wore a

21. "The folk process"

wide-brimmed hat with "purple granny glasses" and long dyed-black hair. Typically, when she came around, her purse was full of weed, mescaline, LSD, or cocaine. On this day, she came to Jimmy with something different: a 45-rpm single of Jerry Jeff's song.

"I know this will mean a lot to you," she told him.

Ibbotson took the 45, put it in his trunk with the rest of his belongings and headed west for LA. A few years later he hooked up with Hanna and McEuen and the band was in the process of recording their fourth album. They were looking for songs to record. In 2017, Jeff Hanna told the story to the Nashville *Tennessean* this way:

> Well, we were recording an album, this was like late '69, early '70, in Los Angeles.... I'm driving home late one night. I'm flipping through the dial and I hear this song that just blew my mind, it was so beautiful, and poignant. Pulled the car over to the side of the road so I could hear better, and cranked it up, of course FM radio late night, no back announcing. I had no idea who it was. I just knew that I was tearing up hearing this tune about this old guy and a dog, you know, and this beautiful story. So, I come into rehearsal the next day, "Guys, I heard this tune, it's like, it's a perfect fit for what we're doing! I know how to do it! You know, we'll use a mandolin, we'll use the accordion, and it'll work, it'll be great, and uh, but I don't know the name of the song." And I'm describing the tune and Jimmy Ibbotson jumps up and says, "I know the song! I know the song!" We run outside to the parking lot; he pops the trunk on his [car]. Under the spare tire in his trunk, in a rusty pool of water, is a 45. Jerry Jeff Walker, "Mr. Bojangles."

The 45 was so scratched they could barely make out the lyrics, but the band was in agreement that the song was a classic. In fact, they thought it was "too good" to be a single. They did not think radio would take to a waltz about a drifting dancer and his dead dog. But they wanted it on their record anyway. They listened to the scratched single in the control room of the studio, then went into the main room and began recording. As they did not understand the lyrics completely, "he spoke right out" became "the smoke ran out," among a few other lyrical improvisations. The song had been recorded and shipped to radio stations before anyone even noticed the variations.

Jerry Jeff laughed when he heard the story. "It's just the folk process," he said.[2]

Back in 1970, as he and Ray drove, they changed the stations, looking for the song. It kept coming on both country and rock stations all the way to Florida. The Nitty Gritty Dirt Band had a genuine crossover hit. The song would enter the Top 10 a few weeks later. Jerry Jeff Walker's royalty checks were about to get a lot bigger.

22

"Would you buy a used car from this man?"

No one knows exactly how the fire started. It was ruled an accident in the end. On November 5, 1961, the Santa Ana winds picked up from the south and caught a spark somewhere along the way. The spark found some brush and within hours the community of Bel Air was engulfed. A photographer for the *Los Angeles Times* found Richard Nixon on top of his house with a garden hose. He was wetting his roof in hopes of saving his abode from the fate of the movie stars' homes surrounding him. A few hours later, cameras would catch him and Pat, suitcases in hand, evacuating the area.

He had come west after his election loss with no clear objective, though he had no shortage of prospects, including an offer to become the commissioner of Major League Baseball. He rented a house from a Hollywood director on Bundy Drive and wound up taking a position at a prestigious West Coast law firm for $350,000 a year. He signed a book deal and wrote his first book. But for the most part, Nixon spent the first year after the 1960 election fuming and full of regret. "We won but they stole it from us," he would privately confide to an Eisenhower speechwriter.

He had good reason to be suspicious. He lost by only 100,000 votes and many commentators at the time believed there had been irregularities. Lyndon Johnson, JFK's running mate, controlled the voting precincts in South Texas, where the votes were recorded as nearly 80 percent for Kennedy. Precinct 13, near the border, went 1,145 to 45 for Kennedy, almost certainly the result of Johnson's alliance with George Parr, the area's foremost political operative. Then there was Chicago, where election fraud has been called a work of art. The notoriously corrupt mayor, Richard Daley, halted ballot counting on election night in Cook County. He wanted to see how much Nixon won by in the rural areas. When counting resumed, Kennedy won Chicago by almost 40,000 more votes than expected, more than enough to overcome Nixon's margins downstate. An

22. "Would you buy a used car from this man?"

Illinois Republican House member wrote to Nixon shortly after the election, "I sincerely believe in my heart that you were elected, but the votes weren't counted that way."

Recount committees were set up in disputed states. In Illinois, a teenager named Hillary Rodham, who would soon lead the Wellesley Young Republicans Club (and later become Hillary Rodham Clinton), went door to door looking for evidence of fraud. Theodore White, who wrote the most popular contemporary account of the election, a pro–Kennedy book titled *The Making of the President 1960*, would admit fifteen years later that "vote stealing had definitely taken place on a massive scale."

In the end, it cut both ways. Unlike the election of 2000, in which the dispute centered on one state, the 1960 race was close in eighteen states. If Nixon had challenged the count in Texas and Illinois, Kennedy could point to California, where Nixon had prevailed by only 36,000 votes. There were other irregularities in Hawaii and Alabama. Nixon thought that to contest the election would be wrong. "Our country cannot afford the agony of a constitutional crisis," he told a sympathetic journalist. Still, he believed in his heart that the Kennedys, with their money and East Coast connections, had stolen the presidency from him.

In mid–January he presided over the counting of Electoral College ballots, as is the ceremonial duty of the vice president. On his last night in Washington, the night before the inauguration, he went out on his balcony. Snow was falling as he gazed out at the Lincoln Memorial. He told an interviewer in 1962 that a thought came and it "seemed to overwhelm me.... I'll be back."

So, he and Pat rented the house in Bel Air and Nixon contemplated his next move. Pat wanted a return to normalcy. Their girls were entering their teenage years and Pat thought a nice quiet life in California would be best. Richard Nixon was far too ambitious for that. But what should he do next? The GOP was fractured. The party was split between the moderates and the burgeoning ultraconservative movement. The far right was gaining momentum, with the John Birch Society leading the way. Barry Goldwater and George Romney could duke it out for who would lose to Kennedy in 1964, he thought. There was no need to be involved in that fight. Maybe he could clean up the GOP mess in 1968. But what to do now?

He wrote his first memoir, *Six Crises*, in which he relived six times in his life that had tried him. He had persevered, he said, and come out stronger because of them. He used the book to further his feud with the Kennedys. He was critical of JFK's disastrous Bay of Pigs operation. The operation had been planned under the Eisenhower administration, but was not supposed to be enacted until a series of preconditions were met on the ground. Kennedy gave the covert operation a green light in the spring of '61 without any of Eisenhower's conditions being met. The result was a disaster, as Cuban exiles rushed the beaches and were gunned down and taken prisoner en masse by Castro's better equipped revolutionary forces. Kennedy explained that he did not want to send in air cover for fear of Soviet reprisals. Nixon saw this as a lack of backbone and said as much.

Richard Nixon may have lost the election in 1960, but he was still a highly regarded figure in national and international affairs. Which is what made his next move a little confusing. He didn't want to do it. His wife and family did not want him to do it. Close friends and associates told him it wasn't a smart idea. But the Republican hierarchy from Eisenhower on down was trying to convince him to run for governor of California in 1962.

In response to a letter written by Eisenhower to convince him to run for the Golden State's top job, he wrote, "My entire experience in government has been in national and international affairs. I think the problems which governors have to handle are immensely important but my interests simply are in other fields."[1]

This was a logical view. Nixon had spent his career fighting international communism. He had dodged rocks from protesters in Latin America and gone toe to toe with Khrushchev in Moscow. Now he was going to argue about school funding in Los Angeles or bridge repair in the Anderson Valley? It didn't make sense then or now. But for whatever reason, Nixon went along with the idea and decided to run.

The campaign encountered problems from the beginning. The political landscape of California had changed immensely over Nixon's fourteen years in Washington. The *Los Angeles Times*, a paper that fawned over Nixon with glowing coverage in the early days of his political career, had been sold. The new owners and reporters were less sympathetic to the Republican cause. And then there was the John Birch Society.

The society was founded in 1958 by Robert Welch and he named it after John Birch, a soldier who was killed by hostile actions in China a few days after World War II formally concluded. Birch was a Baptist missionary as well as an intelligence officer in the U.S. Army, and Welch claimed he was the first casualty of the Cold War. By the early 1960s the society had over 100,000 registered members. They held views that were ultraconservative for the times. Extremely anti-communism and anti–New Deal, the John Birch Society's platform was a far cry from the Eisenhower–Nixon conservatism of the era.

One of the society's members was Joe Shell. Shell was a USC football star turned wealthy oil baron turned state legislator. He ran against Nixon in the California Republican primary. Nixon denounced the society as a bunch of "nuts and kooks." The problem was that about a third of Republican primary voters in California did not believe that. Welch claimed that if the John Birch Society was extremist, it was because they were "extremely American." In his campaign against Nixon, Shell said the former VP was too centrist and that the "middle of the road is seventy-five percent socialism." In the end Nixon prevailed, but the scars remained. Shell wanted concessions in return for his support. Nixon would not offer them, and Shell never did endorse Nixon in the general election.[2]

Democrat Pat Brown was born in 1905 in San Francisco. He earned a law degree by age twenty-two and by 1943 had been elected as district attorney of San Francisco. Fifteen years later, in 1958, he became the thirty-second governor of California. He seemed a weak incumbent to the national Republicans who encouraged Nixon to run. They convinced him it would be an easy race and a means of staying "politically viable." But Pat Brown proved much more formidable than the Republican influencers understood.[3]

Nixon had always been an aggressive candidate, but in 1962 he began to refine the political tactics that would come to define his legacy. Bob Haldeman, a man whose name all of America would know in a decade's time, was brought in as campaign manager. "We cannot allow a situation where they are stirring up trouble all the time and we are not," Nixon instructed Haldeman. He wanted a covert organization, financed by but operating outside the campaign, to conduct "everything from getting information surreptitiously to heckling," Nixon told his aides.

Brown gave as good as he got. He claimed Nixon was only in the race as a steppingstone to the run for president again. Nixon denied the charge, but no one believed him. Brown convinced the Justice Department, which was being run by the president's brother Robert Kennedy, to investigate Nixon's brother Don. Don Nixon had found himself in financial trouble in recent years over a failed fast-food concept he called Nixon Burger. He ended up with a quarter-million-dollar loan from the eccentric billionaire Howard Hughes. No evidence of any wrongdoing was ever uncovered; Don Nixon was just not cut out for the hamburger business. But Brown sent people to Nixon rallies with signs that read "What about the Hughes loan?"[4] The implication was that Nixon had used his power as vice president to facilitate something crooked. Brown supporters mailed out postcards with a picture of Nixon that asked the question, "Would you buy a used car from this man?"[5]

Nixon went to his old standby move, calling Brown a communist sympathizer. He surged ahead in the polls but then fell behind again. "He was always talking too much about national issues, not about the streets of Shasta," campaign aide Herb Klein remembered. Then all of a sudden national issues took Nixon by surprise. On October 22, he watched from an Oakland hotel room as JFK told the American television audience that the Soviets had placed missiles in Cuba capable of reaching the U.S. "I just lost the election," Nixon confided to an aide after the speech.[6]

For the final two weeks of the campaign, the Cuban Missile Crisis dominated the headlines. Brown flew to Washington to consult with Kennedy on civil defense. For years Nixon believed the timing of the crisis was intended to hurt him. The crisis was genuine, but the Kennedy camp realized it was bad for Nixon and used it as much as they could to help Brown.

Nixon blamed many things for his rapid downfall from national prominence. There was of course the Kennedys and their Franklin allies, the type of men Nixon had seen himself as fighting against his whole life. There were the nuts and kooks of the fringe right, who never did support Nixon. But most of all, it was the press. In the 1962 gubernatorial election the California journalistic establishment turned on Nixon. He began keeping a list of enemies that would grow over time, but it began as a list of unfriendly California reporters. The feeling was mutual. The California press corps was for the most part full of men ideologically opposed to Nixon. They felt that as a former vice president he presented a haughtiness and expected glowing coverage.

On election night Nixon rented a suite at the Beverly Hilton to monitor the returns. It didn't go well. He began drinking heavily. By late that evening it was clear he had lost. Brown had received almost a quarter million more votes than Nixon. It wasn't just a loss; it was a humiliating loss. Brown was as surprised as anyone. "I must confess I was dismayed [to learn who his opponent would be].... I can't tell you today why I defeated Richard Nixon," he told the *LA Times* thirty years later.[7]

As night turned to early morning, reporters gathered at the Hilton, waiting on a Nixon concession speech. He wasn't going to give them the satisfaction, he said. Herb Klein was sent to read a statement on Nixon's behalf. Halfway through, Nixon changed his mind and headed for the microphones.

"I congratulate Governor Brown.... I believe [he] has a heart, even though he believes I do not," Nixon said in his opening remarks. What followed is a landmark moment in American political history. Nixon railed against enemies real and perceived in a fifteen-minute struggle with his own mind. The different sides of him were on display for all the world to see, his idealistic vision battling a deep cynicism within. His cousin Jessamyn West would remark that it was as if Frank and Hannah were having an argument. The two parents' influence on their son seesawed back and forth in a public display.

He ended with an admonishment of the press: "I leave you gentlemen now and you now write it. You will interpret it. That's your right. But

22. "Would you buy a used car from this man?" 125

as I leave you, I want you to know—just think how much you're going to be missing. You won't have Nixon to kick around anymore because, gentlemen, this is my last press conference…"

It appeared to be the end of the line for Richard Nixon. No one in American politics had gone so publicly off the rails and come back. Kennedy and Brown, discussing the election a few days later, were recorded on the White House taping system. "I'll tell you this, you reduced him to the nuthouse," JFK told the newly reelected governor. Brown responded, "I don't see how he can ever recover…. I really think he's psychotic. He's an able man, but he's nuts."[8]

Richard Nixon had been a stone's throw away from becoming president of the United States just two years prior. Now, he was an unemployed lawyer in Los Angeles. ABC ran a prime-time special, *The Political Obituary of Richard Nixon*. One of the guest commentators was Alger Hiss, recently released from prison. Hiss opined that this was thankfully the end of the line for the menace to society known as Richard Nixon. Alger Hiss was very bad at political predictions.

23

"Get Sammy"

In late 1960 an invitation arrived at the home of the newlywed Davises. It was a large flat envelope with a piece of cardboard that kept the invitation from bending. "How is this for a sense of history?" Sammy asked May. The couple were headed to John F. Kennedy's inauguration gala in Washington. Sammy couldn't believe it. He thought, "It really can happen in America ... an uneducated kid from Harlem could work hard and be invited to the White House."

The next day Sammy and May went shopping. A new evening gown and Chanel suit for her. A new perfectly tailored tuxedo for him. May protested briefly, telling Sammy he already had fifteen tuxedos in a closet. Sammy responded, "Would I be so crass as to wear a previously worn tuxedo to entertain the president?" Sammy was so ecstatic about the invite that he canceled his show at the Latin Casino in New Jersey and told everyone he knew.[1]

Frank Sinatra was organizing the gala to be held the night before the inauguration. The event was in many ways a pioneering moment at the cross-section of entertainment and politics. The star-studded gala would take place at the D.C. Armory, near the Capitol. All the country's biggest stars were to perform. Six of the two dozen performers scheduled were African Americans. "The environment itself was as charged as any I've ever known," Harry Belafonte recalled. "The expectations were so great with Kennedy, and what he represented to us." The night had a purpose aside from celebrating the election of the youngest man to hold the presidency: $2 million was needed to retire the Democratic campaign debt. The gala accomplished that goal and then some.[2]

On January 16, three days before the big show, Sammy woke up to a telephone call. Evelyn Lincoln, the president-elect's personal secretary, was on the phone. "Mr. Davis ... the president has asked me to tell you that he does not want you present at his inauguration. There is a situation into which he is being forced and to fight it would be counterproductive to the goals he has set. He very much hopes you understand."

23. "Get Sammy"

Sammy was crushed but simply told Mrs. Lincoln that he understood. Peter Lawford called a bit later with more explanation and an apology. They talked him into it, Lawford told Sammy. They told him it was their "first time out. Let's not do anything to fuck it up. We've got Southern senators, bigoted congressmen. They see you as too liberal to begin with," Lawford said, quoting JFK's advisors. Lawford told Sammy that Bobby Kennedy had stood up for him and said it was crazy to disinvite him, claiming the younger Kennedy had walked out of the room in protest. Sammy would write that while he was "pleased to hear about Bobby ... it didn't help much."

Sammy told the press that he was choosing not to perform at the gala. He said the Latin Casino could not afford to give him the night off and he did not want to disappoint his fans. It was an obvious lie. He held to this line in his first autobiography in 1965 but by the time of his second in 1989, he expressed how he really felt:

> I could handle it from the idiot in the street who pickets or calls me a name or writes a letter. But when the President of the United States does it? To someone he knows. Someone he shook hands with and told, "I won't forget your help..." My God, if he'll do this to me, then what hope have the millions of invisible people got?[3]

To Frank and the other performers, the Kennedys' father, Joe, was to blame for Sammy's absence. The old ambassador and patriarch would not stand for Sammy and his white wife to be there. It would just cause too big a headache for the new administration, they were told. Harry Belafonte did his best to rationalize the disappointment fifty years later:

> It was one of those moments where not only was Frank not happy about it, the rest of us were put up against a moment where [we thought], How do we let this slide? And since we were not really and truly in command of what the total facts were, because the fact that it was the ambassador ... we didn't know that until after. And Sammy not being there was a loss.

The show rolled on without Sammy, but five of the nation's other biggest African American entertainers—Belafonte, Sidney Poitier, Nat King Cole, Ella Fitzgerald, and Mahalia Jackson—all performed. In what must have felt like a knife twist in one of the greatest ironies in presidential inauguration history, Kennedy became the first president to dance with a Black woman at an inaugural ball, the next evening.[4]

Sammy hid his pain. He performed at the Latin Casino in Camden, New Jersey, on the night of the big show, pretending nothing was wrong. But something had changed. Before the inauguration, Sammy was a somewhat reluctant civil rights warrior. He believed in the cause, but much of his support was centered on fundraising. He refused to go South, other than to perform in Miami Beach, fearing the death threats he received. Bobby Kennedy had warned him that he was on the White Citizens' Councils' "Ten Most Wanted" list.[5]

As a child traveling the Chitlin' Circuit with his father and Mastin and then again in the army, Sammy experienced America's systemic racism firsthand. His love life had been dissected in the press and he had been forced into marrying a Black woman by white organized crime. Meanwhile his father and Mastin cautioned all through his early years that this was just how it was, and nothing could be done.

At first Sammy accepted this as fact even as he desperately longed for acceptance in a white world. Critics pointed to his convenient conversion to Judaism as a ploy to integrate himself into white Hollywood. They claimed Davis was unapologetically playing up what they saw as an "Uncle Tom"–type deference to whites. In his early TV appearances on *What's My Line?* he was careful to modulate his speech and answered the moderator's questions with "sir" and "ma'am." In his first autobiography he recounted a joke Mastin overheard about his "trying to be white." In the joke, Sammy is sitting in Danny's Hideaway, a bar in New York, when a guy looks at him and calls out, "Nigger, nigger, nigger!" Sammy jumps up and yells, "Where? Where? Where?"[6]

While Sammy certainly accepted some of the conventions of the time as a means of getting ahead, equality of the races was a deeply held conviction for him. He desperately wanted to be seen as a talented performer, not just a talented Black performer. Like many other Black pioneers, Sammy capitalized on racist tropes at times as a means of advancing an anti-racist agenda.

By the late 1950s Sammy began to realize his power as a celebrity could be an enormous benefit for the civil rights movement. Once the Trio became a headlining act, Davis would no longer perform for segregated audiences. He got into a public spat with Louis Armstrong over the issue after the 1957 Little Rock crisis. Later that year he brought the cast of *Mr. Wonderful* to Madison Square Garden for an NAACP benefit that raised $7,000. In 1958 he headlined a week of shows for the organization and raised another $4,000. He led a membership drive for the NAACP that sparked such interest that the national office was "bombarded with requests" for Davis. "We must put our time, our money, our whole-hearted efforts on the line with our conscience," he said.

He rode a "Freedom Train" with Belafonte and Sidney Poitier to the Prayer Pilgrimage for Freedom held on the steps of the Lincoln Memorial in 1957, where he met Martin Luther King, Jr., for the first time. Sammy saw in King a real possibility for social gains. His inspiring oratory and message of nonviolence gave Sammy hope, as it did to millions of others.

23. "Get Sammy"

Sammy had something King needed as well: he was loved by white people.

In early 1960, despite the increasing national profile of their leader, the Southern Christian Leadership Conference (SCLC) was still in its infancy financially. "A blueprint for an organization" was how one historian put it. The group needed more cash to effectively continue its efforts, which were being met with increasing legal challenges.

Sammy became the biggest early fundraiser for King and the SCLC. When looking to raise cash, King would tell Belafonte, "Get Sammy." Davis could sell out a fundraiser in no time, and when he brought his Rat Pack buddies money came in at levels the nascent organization could only have dreamed of before. Sammy Davis, Jr.'s, fundraising was arguably one of the most instrumental factors in the rise of Martin Luther King, Jr., as a national leader.

One week after Kennedy's inauguration, Sammy organized a Carnegie Hall benefit for King and the SCLC. Frank and Dean came and performed, and the show sold out. The concert raised $22,000 for the organization, a quarter of its operating budget for 1961. At the time, it was the most money ever raised at a Carnegie Hall fundraiser. It was Sammy's most public support of the movement to date, but it would be far from his last.[7]

Life continued to move at a frantic pace for Davis throughout the early '60s. In 1961, his first child, Tracey, was born. He rushed from the studio to the hospital in time to hold the child for some publicity photos. Then he was off again. He toured Europe and performed for the Queen. The UK press said, "He is more than a mere star. He is unique. He is a troupe of acrobats. He is a team of dancers. He is a one-man band. He is a hit parade of singers. He is show business." From 1961 to '62, Davis released five record albums, guest-starred on six television shows, and starred in two films. In 1962 he earned two Grammy nominations for his LP *What Kind of Fool Am I*. *Variety* dubbed him "one of the superior performers of the era."

The best remembered aspect of his work at this time is probably the second Rat Pack film, *Sergeants 3*. The film was directed by John Sturges and was a remake of the 1939 film *Gunga Din*, starring Cary Grant, which was based on a Rudyard Kipling poem of the same name. The 1962 version transports the action from colonial India to the American Old West. Frank, Dean, and Lawford play three U.S. Cavalrymen stationed in Indian Territory in 1870. Sammy's role is that of a trumpet-playing ex-slave. He is the punchline to many of the jokes in the film.[8]

Despite the harsh racism Sammy faced, the majority of fans who packed his nightclub shows, bought his records, and saw his movies were white. He turned the pain into part of his act. He was self-deprecating almost to a fault about his race. He played off the jokes of his Rat Pack buddies with a smile. Writer Alex Haley asked him about it in a 1966 interview:

> **HALEY:** Your nightclub and theater audiences are predominantly white. Do you think there may be some element of race consciousness in your compulsion to win their approval?
>
> **DAVIS:** No question about it. I always go on stage anticipating what people out there may be feeling against me emotionally. I want to rob them of what they're sitting there thinking: Negro. With all the accompanying clichés. Ever since I recognized what prejudice is, I've tried to fight it away, and the only weapon I could use is my talent. Away back, when I was learning the business, I had no education, no influence; entertainment was the only way I had to change prejudiced thinking. I could see it happen every time Will Mastin, my dad and I did our act. For as long as we were on stage our skin had no color: people were just seeing us as entertainers.[9]

In late 1962, another White House invitation arrived. For the first time in history African Americans held jobs in the White House other than those of cook, maid, or butler. Most notably, Andrew Hatcher was deputy press secretary. But the streets were beginning to come alive with student protests and sit-ins. A few jobs here and there no longer felt like enough.

Louis Martin was a prominent African American journalist who had been recruited by the Kennedy campaign as an advisor. He served as advisor to three presidents over the course of his career and would come to be known as the Godfather of Black Politics. He sent a letter to Kennedy on January 31, 1963. "American Negros through sit-ins, kneel-ins, wade-ins, etc. will continue to create situations which involve the local, state, and Federal government," he told the president. He wanted Kennedy to introduce strong civil rights legislation. He told him African Americans were tired of being told to wait their turn. Kennedy offered to throw a party.

The president announced he would hold a reception on Lincoln's birthday, February 12, for 800 of the country's most well-known African Americans. It would be a grand party to celebrate the centennial of the Emancipation Proclamation. Louis Martin oversaw the guest list.

Martin invited Langston Hughes and Duke Ellington along with numerous NAACP leaders. He invited Mahalia Jackson, Martin Luther King, and James Baldwin. And he invited Sammy Davis, Jr., and his white wife. He submitted the guest list four times and each time it came back with Davis's name struck off. And each time, Martin would add it again. It somehow made it through the final edit, and the invitation was sent.

23. "Get Sammy"   131

```
162 & 163.   Davis, Eddie (Mr. & Mrs.)
             2447 W. Jefferson
             Philadelphia, Pennsylvania

164 & 165.   Davis, Edward (Mr. & Mrs.)
             303 Euclid Avenue
             Akron, Ohio

166 & 167.   Davis, Sammy Jr. (Mr. & Mrs.)
             136 W. 55th Street
             New York City, New York

      168.   Dawson, William L. (Congressman) Honorable
             New House Office Building
             Washington 25, D. C.

169 & 170.   Day, J. Edward (Hon. & Mrs.)
             Postmaster General
             Washington 25, D. C.

171 & 172.   DeBow, Russell (Mr. & Mrs.) (Attorney)
             8008 South Rhodes Avenue
             Chicago, Illinois

      173.   Denniston, Arabella (Mrs.)
             1824 Belmont Road, N. W.
             Washington, D. C.
```

Internal White House document showing the potential guest list for the 1962 celebration of the Emancipation Proclamation's centennial. Sammy's name was removed four different times before sneaking through in the final edit. When Kennedy realized Davis and his white wife, May Britt, were at the ceremony, he ordered them removed before allowing photographers in the ballroom (John F. Kennedy Presidential Library and Museum).

On the night of the big event, Martin marveled at his accomplishment. "I'm the man who got Langston Hughes into the White House. It looks like Uncle Tom's cabin around here," he joked with the poet. Walking down the stairs to the reception, Kennedy spotted Davis and his wife. "What is he doing here?" he whispered to an aide, furious. He feared that photographs of Davis with a white woman in the White House would be a political disaster. "Get them out of there!" he ordered. It was decided the situation must be handled delicately but quickly before any photographers caught a glimpse of the Davises. An aide asked Kennedy's wife, Jackie, who was still upstairs getting ready, to discreetly pull May aside before photos could be taken of the couple together. Jackie was so incensed at the idea and angry at her husband for the suggestion that she refused to come down. She would eventually show up late to the reception.

Finally, a low-level aide asked the Davises to step into another room as photographers came into the main ballroom. No photos of the couple were taken that night. When the photographers left, the couple was brought back to the gala. They knew what had just happened, though. Sammy and May left the White House that night hurt by the awkward treatment they had received.

Whatever illusions Sammy had about Jack Kennedy and his commitment to civil rights were gone. And so were Louis Martin's and Martin Luther King's. And James Baldwin's and Duke Ellington's. A party was no substitute for meaningful legislation. Kennedy had campaigned in 1960 in support of civil rights. But once in office, he had delayed any meaningful action in deference to the segregationist Southern senators and congressmen in his party. It was decided that African Americans should take to the streets with a march on Washington.

Philip Randolph secured the permit two weeks later. Randolph was in his seventies and had been fighting for equal rights for Blacks since 1925, when he founded the Brotherhood of Sleeping Car Porters. He was the grandfather of the civil rights movement in many ways. He brought together the different factions of the movement, and the March on Washington for Jobs and Freedom was scheduled for August 28.

In June, Kennedy announced a new civil rights bill, one that went further in addressing the problems of segregation than the 1957 bill, which then–Senator Kennedy had voted against. He was hoping to placate Blacks and head off the need for a public demonstration at the National Mall. Civil rights leaders for the most part applauded the legislation, but it still had to pass Congress. The March was still needed. Kennedy was worried that violence might erupt. *Life* magazine claimed Washington had "its worst case of invasion jitters since the First Battle of Bull Run."[10]

In early August, Martin Luther King, Jr., held a fundraiser in Birmingham, Alabama, to raise money for marchers to travel to Washington later that month. "Get Sammy," he told planners. Davis had told King explicitly over the years that he would raise money all he could, but that he would not go to the South for fear of being murdered. King had told him, "We'll get you down there." On August 5, he did. The money raised brought hundreds of people to Washington.[11]

The March became the seminal moment most often associated with the civil rights movement. Over a quarter million people marched from the Washington Monument to the steps of the Lincoln Memorial. The event was broadcast on national television as Martin Luther King looked over a sea of people and declared that he had a dream. Standing behind him in the group on the steps of the Lincoln Memorial was Sammy Davis, Jr.

23. "Get Sammy" 133

Sammy Davis, Jr., on the steps of the Lincoln Memorial, August 28, 1963 (National Archives).

Three months later Sammy was back to work in Hollywood on the newest Rat Pack film. *Robin and the 7 Hoods* was another one of the comedy-musicals for which the crew had become known. A Sinatra–controlled production, the film took the classic Robin Hood story and put it in Prohibition–era Chicago. Sammy's role in the final Rat Pack film was that of the driver of Frank's character. His roles in the films were token and his skin color the implied if not direct butt of jokes, but it was Sammy's association with the Pack that truly brought him into the Hollywood mainstream for the first time, and he relished it. He invited May to visit him on the set, but she refused. "I can't stand your relationship with Frank," she said, "the way he treats you, the jokes, the way you kowtow to him."[12]

Barbara Rush played the female lead, and she recalled how the whole cast was preparing for a funeral scene. Edward G. Robinson's character in the film is killed, and the crew was gathered around a Hollywood soundstage designed as a cemetery when Howard W. Koch, the executive producer, rushed in. President Kennedy had been shot, he told the cast. Sinatra shut down filming for the next two weeks.

24

"A real clown's act"

In the early weeks of 1963, Richard Nixon and an informal group of advisors met at the Waldorf Astoria in New York to strategize what Nixon should do next. Nixon had told the assembled group of reporters in Beverly Hills two months prior that he was done. ABC had run the prime-time special eulogizing the former vice president's career. Everyone who knew Richard Nixon knew it wasn't true. ABC had received 80,000 telegrams after the broadcast, almost all of them from disgusted viewers who still thought highly of the former vice president and did not like the network kicking the man while he was down.

The group at the Waldorf was eclectic, to say the least. From Eisenhower's former ambassador in Mexico to a producer from *The Jack Paar Show*, the group tossed out different ideas. Nixon listened intently. The group advised Nixon to remain a political free agent. The problem, they said, was that this was impossible in California. He would end up in protracted intraparty state fights that would diminish his stature. The group advised a move east and a job at a law firm that would allow him financial freedom while at the same time keeping him involved in international affairs. As one advisor put it, "There was no foreign policy angle in California. It had to be the East. He had to have his cake [money] and eat it too [pursuing his interest in foreign policy]."

For a variety of reasons, this was a hard sell. "There just weren't too many places he could get two hundred and fifty thousand dollars and all his time," a fellow lawyer would remark later. "A lot of lawyers didn't want a tiger in their midst," said another associate; they were afraid they would be reduced to co-stars in the evolving national drama of Richard Nixon's ambition.[1]

Back in 1959, fresh off of almost being killed in Venezuela, Nixon, along with a group of about thirty-five other American officials, had flown to Moscow for the opening of the American National Exhibition. *Time* magazine called what followed "peacetime diplomacy's most amazing 24 hours."[2]

Nixon and Soviet premier Nikita Khrushchev toured the exhibition, bickering all the way. They argued over a multitude of things big and small, but it all came around to the merits of communism versus capitalism. Though the pair did seem to agree on the usefulness of washing machines. The tour was filmed by American media and broadcast nationwide a few days later. In one of the more ballyhooed moments of the so-called "kitchen debate," Nixon stopped by a booth featuring the newly rebranded American product Pepsi Cola. Khrushchev took a "skeptical sip"[3] and furrowed his brow. Khrushchev's opinion of the soda notwithstanding, Nixon had just gained a powerful ally.

Four years later as Nixon went looking for a high-profile East Coast law job, he was helped immensely by Donald Kendall, CEO of Pepsi Cola. Pepsi was looking to aggressively expand into overseas markets and Kendall let it be known that the soda maker's giant legal contracts would follow the former vice president.[4]

On May 2, 1963, Nixon announced he would be moving from California to New York. He was taking a position as senior advisor to Mudge, Stern, Baldwin and Todd. Once he was admitted to the New York State bar, the firm's name would change to include Nixon's. One associate called it a "backwater" firm[5] in which Nixon would quickly become top dog. The Nixons left their house in Bel Air and bought a Fifth Avenue apartment. On June 1, Richard Nixon said goodbye to his neighbor Groucho Marx and moved in next door to Nelson Rockefeller.

Before settling into law practice in New York, Nixon took his family on vacation, traveling through Europe and the Middle East. While taking in the sights, he found time to meet, and be photographed with, world leaders like Charles de Gaulle and Pope Paul VI. The wire reports carried the news and pictures of Nixon looking every bit the statesman to the papers back home. Richard Nixon was far from running for any political office, but was also clearly not through with politics as he claimed.

In March of 1963 he made his first television appearance since the disastrous press conference in Beverly Hills. He was the featured guest on the prime-time *Jack Paar Program*. Paar's previous show, *Tonight Starring Jack Paar*, was a precursor to what would become a staple of American entertainment, the late-night talk show. Both Kennedy and Nixon had appeared on the show during the 1960 race. Paar's new show was mostly humorous but would veer into news and politics in a genial way.

Paar was a family friend of the Nixons. He spent most of the interview quizzing Nixon on foreign affairs and allowing him ample time for long, unchallenged answers, all the while breaking up the seriousness with wisecracks. Along with giving Nixon space to opine on everything from the Bay of Pigs to Khrushchev's drinking, he humanized the politician by telling stories of his family.

Paar explained how the two families had vacationed together recently in the Bahamas. The children grew tired of island life and wanted some adventure. So, Paar convinced Nixon to let him take the kids to a club in Nassau. He said:

> It's the native quarter and it's wild. Oh, it's fun, jumping and the limbo and the twist, it's crazy. So, I walk in and it's an outdoor nightclub and it's about a thousand people there.... The Negro drummer, he's pounding on the drums and so he walks over and grabs the little blonde girl next to me and suddenly he gets this little girl out there and it's Trish [Nixon's daughter] ... she's a very prim and proper little girl, but let me tell you she went into the wildest twist I'd ever seen! But I mean wild and crazy and a limbo.

Paar continued to explain that Trish won the top prize, a "great big kind of heathen statue." The next morning Nixon saw the statue and asked what kind of trouble they had found the night before. Paar said he felt like a pimply teenager asking for an apology from a scolding father whose daughter he had taken out. He ended by saying, "To tell you the truth, Mr. Nixon, if she had done that in Mississippi in '60 you'd be the president by now!"

The audience ate it up.

The interview ended in a lighthearted manner as Paar introduced America to Nixon the musician:

> Listen, Mr. Nixon plays the piano. See, anyhow, I heard some time ago, from a friend of his, he wrote a selection, wrote a composition. And we had—can you bring the piano out here? ... but the funny thing is we have hired about fifteen Democratic violinists [laughter] to fill out—we are spending more money for this orchestra than we ever spent in our life. And José [Melis, Paar's music director] has made a concerto arrangement of this hinky-dinky song that you wrote [laughter]. Would you play it for us?

Nixon smiles and responds, "Now, Jack, let me say this. You asked me a moment ago whether I had any future political plans to run for anything and if last November did not finish it, this will! Believe me, the Republicans don't want another piano player in the White House."

The last line was a reference to Harry Truman and drew huge laughs. Nixon walked over to the piano and played a mid-tempo number in a classical style. The audience loved it and cheered wildly as he waved and exited the stage.[6]

There had been talk of a "new Nixon" before, and now the press started talking about a "new, new Nixon." "It's a Nixon most people never saw, a Nixon who is relaxed and quick with a wisecrack," according to a 1963 Associated Press profile.[7]

Richard Nixon playing piano for Harry Truman, Pat Nixon (left) and Bess Truman, March 21, 1969 (courtesy Richard Nixon Presidential Library and Museum).

Nixon's image as a sore loser was receding in many Americans' minds. His move to New York had been a success. He was making more money than he ever had. He was traveling on a diplomatic passport all over the world, furthering his image as a premier American statesman. On November 21, 1963, he was in Dallas, Texas, speaking to a group of Pepsi Cola manufacturers and bottlers. When he arrived at the airport the next morning, crowds were already gathering to greet President Kennedy and the First Lady. He boarded American Airlines flight 82 and flew home to New York. When the flight landed, he got in a cab and learned that the world had changed.

"My cab was stopped at a light in Queens and a guy ran over and said, 'Have you got a radio? The president has been wounded'... A half hour later I got to my apartment and the doorman told me he was dead," Nixon told an interviewer, adding that he immediately dialed the head of the FBI, J. Edgar Hoover, and asked what happened. "It was a communist," Hoover told him.[8]

Lyndon B. Johnson took the oath of office aboard Air Force One just over two hours after Kennedy was shot. Beside him stood the newly widowed Jackie Kennedy, a look of shock on her face, her husband's blood still visible on her dress. The plane flew back to Washington in haste. Johnson was concerned there could be a broader conspiracy afoot and that he might be a target. In an address to Congress a week after Kennedy's death, Johnson said, "No memorial oration or eulogy could more eloquently honor President Kennedy's memory than the earliest passage of the Civil Rights Act for which he fought so long."[9]

The 1964 act went further in addressing systemic discrimination than the 1957 act. It banned discrimination in public places and in federal jobs, among many other provisions. No longer could there legally be whites-only hotels or theaters or water fountains. While it would take years to fully implement the bill, in March 1964 the historic legislation was passed. It remains one of the largest legislatively mandated societal changes ever undertaken by the federal government.

Barry Goldwater opposed the Civil Rights Act and he was the leading candidate for the Republican nomination in 1964. The Arizona senator was a leading voice in the conservative wing of the Republican Party, but he was seen as an extremist by many. He famously defended his views by saying that "extremism in the defense of liberty is no vice."[10] Many in the party wanted a more middle-of-the-road nominee to take on the popular Johnson.

Nixon had no plans to run in 1964 before Kennedy was shot. Contrary to what Brown had claimed in the gubernatorial race two years prior, Nixon had not sought the governorship as a steppingstone to run for president. Not in 1964, at least. He saw the Governor's Mansion in Sacramento as a hideout to avoid another contest with Kennedy. But once Kennedy was dead, things changed. He saw Johnson as suddenly vulnerable and believed he could take him on and win. Behind the scenes, he began an attempt to position himself as a compromise candidate.

All through the spring and summer, he worked both sides, saying things that appealed to Goldwater supporters like "planning an economy eventually ends in planning men's lives." He told the press before the California primary that he supported Goldwater. Behind the scenes, he was in constant conversation with the "stop Goldwater" movement, made up mostly of the more liberal East Coast element of the party. At a conference of Republican governors, Nixon gave a speech saying that a Goldwater nomination would be "a tragedy." He then opened the floor to questions. An awkward fifteen-second silence hung in the air as the attendees slowly came to realize he was waiting for someone to ask him to run for president.

As the convention drew closer, it became apparent that Goldwater would receive the nomination. Nixon was initially scheduled to speak on the Tuesday night of the convention. He was still hoping for a backroom deal that could make him the nominee. It became clear that was not going to happen, and he switched tactics. He asked to change his speaking slot and be allowed to introduce the nominee. "Most people climb on a bandwagon. Nixon threw himself in front of it," was how one Republican National Committee state chair put it. A political cartoon ran in papers across the country portraying Nixon as a hitchhiker trying to flag down both a pro- and anti–Goldwater car at the same time.

Nixon was a political animal, and in the weeks before the convention he came to understand something very important. The battle for the 1964 nomination had not been won in the press or even in the states with direct primaries. It had been won by conservative activists at caucuses and at county and district conventions. The John Birch Society and its followers had effectively played a game of inside baseball, and he knew they would be significantly stronger in 1968 even if Goldwater was trounced in the election.

Thus, Nixon threw his unwavering support behind a man who, only weeks before, he said would be "a tragedy" for the nation. He campaigned all fall, as had become his bi-yearly tradition over the past two decades. He traveled the country and gave 156 speeches on Goldwater's behalf. He went on national television the week before the election, urging his countrymen to vote Republican. Goldwater was far behind in the polls. Almost all other prominent national Republicans had abandoned ship. They saw the looming disaster and did not want to be associated with it.

In November, Goldwater lost in one of the largest landslides in American political history. He carried just six states, five from the former Confederacy and his home state of Arizona. *Esquire* magazine ran a long profile of Nixon's behind-the-scenes campaign, declaring that "each of his carefully calculated moves in 1964 was followed only by his own further political destruction." Nixon knew better, though. In January, at an RNC meeting called to take stock and prepare for the future, Goldwater praised Nixon's tireless efforts, saying he "worked harder than any one person for the ticket." Nixon knew that he needed the hardcore conservative wing that had backed Goldwater so enthusiastically. In 1962 they were "nuts and kooks"; in 1964 he realized they held the key to his future. Nixon walked to the podium at the January meeting to a standing ovation. He offered his thanks and said the party should focus on gains in the midterms. There should be no presidential campaigning until after 1966.[11]

A few months later Nixon found himself in Finland on behalf of an oil company. He finished business early and, "on impulse—it was said," took off on a twenty-hour train ride to Moscow to look up his old debate opponent Nikita Khrushchev. He arrived at the former Soviet leader's home a little after 11 p.m. and knocked on the door. He was told that Khrushchev was not home. He left a handwritten note expressing his hope that they would meet again.

24. "A real clown's act"

Before he left Moscow, he found his way into the office of the government newspaper, *Pravda*. "Conceited by the fact that his person still means something" was how the paper described him. "On the street, Nixon for some reason accosted a policeman with stupid questions," the report went on. "He tried to start arguments with strangers ... a real clown's act, he tried to provide sensational material for the foreign newspapermen who followed on his heels." Regardless of the official Soviet paper's take on the situation, the incident was met with glowing coverage in the U.S. Nixon, the old communist fighter, was once again standing up for American principles abroad. No politicking until after 1966, he had said. And he wondered why they called him tricky.[12]

25

"I'll buy the night"

Martin Luther King called Harry Belafonte in mid–March 1965 with a familiar request: "Get Sammy." The preacher explained to the famous singer and actor that they needed more star power. This was going to be a big one.

Dallas County, Alabama, had 15,000 African American residents in March of 1965. Only 350 of them were registered to vote. The Student Nonviolent Coordinating Committee (SNCC) had been in the county seat of Selma attempting to register Blacks for months. They planned a march to Montgomery to deliver a petition to Alabama's governor, George Wallace. On March 7, six hundred nonviolent protesters were met on the Edmund Pettis Bridge by the sheriff of Dallas County, Jim Clark, and his troopers as well as a deputized band of white nationalists waving the Confederate flag. The ensuing melee left seventeen marchers hospitalized and twenty-eight others critically injured. Over a hundred marchers were treated for some type of injury. The group's leader was beaten unconscious and left for dead on the bridge. The ensuing photograph made national headlines.

ABC was showing *Judgment at Nuremberg* in prime time, the *Sunday Movie of the Week*. Forty-eight million Americans were tuned in, watching Spencer Tracy and Burt Lancaster in a fictionalized account of America's quest for justice against Nazi racial ideology. ABC interrupted the broadcast for a special report on the violence in Selma. The irony was not lost on the television audience, and public support was overwhelmingly with the marchers.

When a second march also failed, a third march was planned for March 21. Belafonte called Hilly Elkins, who was producing Sammy's newest project, a return to Broadway in a musical version of Clifford Odets's *Golden Boy*.

"Hilly, I'm calling on behalf of Dr. King," he said. "King would like Sammy and you to come with us."

Elkins said he was honored and could not wait to tell Sammy. He walked into Sammy's dressing room at the Majestic Theatre and broke the news.

25. "I'll buy the night"

"I ain't going to Selma," Sammy replied.

"Why?" Hilly asked, astonished.

"They're going to kill me."

Elkins understood Sammy's concern. He had seen the mail Sammy sometimes received. The letters were full of vile remarks about his interracial marriage and peppered with both subtle and overt threats on his life.

But Sammy did not want his producer calling one of his peers and telling him he was scared. "Tell him you can't afford to close the show," he said.

Elkins did not want to do that. He felt they should go. But he called Belafonte back and told him anyway.

"I'll buy the night," Belafonte responded.

Elkins was flabbergasted and ecstatic. Sammy now had no reason to say no. When the big day arrived, Belafonte came personally to the Gotham Hotel to pick Sammy up. Murphy Bennett, Sammy's personal assistant, told him he didn't know where Sammy was. He said Sammy had never come back the night before. But then Murphy gave Belafonte a sly wink and said he should maybe go upstairs, use some of his acting ability and knock on the door.

Belafonte walked to the room and knocked on the door, pretending to be a bellhop. A young blonde who was not May answered the door. Sammy was hiding under the covers. Belafonte came in and began guilt-tripping him like a disappointed father. Sammy got dressed and headed to the airport.[1]

On the flight down, Sammy started drinking brandy. He truly believed he might be heading to his death, and he began musing on his life. The women he'd known and the places he had seen. "He was reflective," recalled *Golden Boy* composer Charles Strouse. The plane landed in Birmingham and the press snapped photos as Bull Connor, the city's former commissioner of public safety, looked on. Charles Evers, the brother of slain civil rights hero Medgar Evers, picked them up. They drove from Birmingham to meet the marchers at their campsite. They passed a billboard urging motorists to "Help Keep the US Out of the UN." The DJ on the car radio said his station was "the white news" before recounting the headlines. Hilly Elkins told an interviewer later, "It was not conducive to relaxing. For any of us."[2]

The marchers left Selma under the nominal protection of a federalized Alabama National Guard and FBI agents sent for the purpose. The order allowing the new march to go forward limited participation to three hundred people on the two-lane road. When U.S. Highway 80 opened up to four lanes outside Montgomery, thousands of people from all over the country joined the march, swelling the numbers that would descend on the Alabama state capitol the next day.

Coleman Woodson, Jr., was a teenager from Selma who marched the whole way. He remembered the marchers were all nervous, fearing violence when they reached Montgomery. They were thrilled at the sight of the newcomers. "It was really, really a lot of people everywhere," Woodson said. "There was excitement in the air because we were coming into the city. There were so many people already there to greet us. I was relieved."[3]

They arrived at the City of St. Jude, a Roman Catholic campus on the west side of Montgomery, on March 24. That evening, the celebrities on hand organized a show for the now almost 10,000 marchers camped out on the campus. While Belafonte had been focusing on the logistics of getting all the performers to Montgomery, he had thought little of the actual show they were to perform. "I thought the crowd would be much smaller, that we'd set up on some nearby hillside," he would recall years later.

The spring rains came early to Alabama that year and the field was muddy. There was no stage, so they borrowed empty coffin shipping crates from a local African American mortician and held them together with pieces of plywood overlaid to create a makeshift platform. Shelley Winters called the commander at nearby Maxwell Air Force Base and demanded lights for the show. When he balked, the famous actress threatened to call President Johnson, for whom she had campaigned.

"The Southern colonel was so angry he almost came through the telephone at my throat," she would remember.[4]

But the lights were delivered, and the show would go on. Hilly Elkins became the show's impromptu producer. Tony Bennett and Joan Baez sang. James Baldwin and Martin Luther King, Jr., gave speeches. Dick Gregory lightened the mood with jokes like this one: "I read in the paper a week ago that Sheriff Jim Clark said, 'They'll make that march to Montgomery over my dead body!' And I thought that wouldn't be a bad route."[5]

Sammy kicked the whole thing off with "The Star-Spangled Banner."

The next day the marchers, now 25,000 strong, rose with the sun, locked arms, and sang as they strode the three miles from St. Jude to the capitol. Barricades lined the streets as citizens looked on. "Glaring at us ... there were no jeers, no insults, they watched us in silence, despising us," Sammy wrote in his 1989 autobiography.[6] He said the Alabama National Guard was "of little comfort." Hilly Elkins remembered it more bluntly: "He was scared shitless."

The civil rights activists made it to the steps of the Alabama capitol by mid-morning and attempted to deliver their petition to George Wallace. They were refused and the petition wasn't delivered. But a speech by Martin Luther King on the county courthouse steps about the need for voting rights was delivered to millions of households via newscasts that evening.

25. "I'll buy the night" 145

Sammy had been scared to come South, and with good reason. After the march, a white housewife from Detroit drove an African American woman back to Selma. As she attempted to drop her off, she was murdered by a Klansman. Her passenger only survived by playing dead. The courage and determination Sammy saw in the marchers would remain a guiding source of inspiration for him over the years. He left for the airport almost immediately after the march concluded, but before he left, he hugged Harry Belafonte. With tears in his eyes, he said simply, "Thank you."[7]

Back in New York on April 4, Sammy hosted a "Broadway Answers Selma" fundraiser at the Majestic Theatre. He brought together sixty actors, singers, and writers for an evening of entertainment. The event raised $150,000. Sammy deposited half the proceeds in the newly formed Freedom National Bank in Harlem. The press coverage of the concert kept the Selma events from fading in public memory.

Sammy wanted more roles in Hollywood films. He wanted to be a full-fledged movie star like Frank Sinatra. But in the mid-sixties Hollywood still adhered to many of the racial norms that pervaded in the rest of the country. What roles Sammy could get were few and far between, and when they did come, they often were not the type that would bring stardom. He was the garbage man in *Ocean's 11*. But Hilly Elkins had had a vision of Sammy Davis, Jr., on Broadway.

Elkins wanted to update Clifford Odets's 1937 play about an Italian American who gives up his dream of becoming a concert violinist to become a professional boxer. Elkins envisioned making the protagonist into an African American boxer rising from an impoverished youth in Harlem. He intended to keep the hero's love interest white, though, thus bringing the real-life controversies in Sammy's life to the Broadway stage.

Sammy's financial situation had improved considerably since his association with the Rat Pack. He still spent more than he made, as he would his whole life. He still netted only 30 percent of his earnings because of his contract with Will Mastin. But he was no longer in debt to Mob-run nightclub owners. He liked the idea of returning to Broadway in a more substantive vehicle than his previous foray a decade before. And he liked the idea of getting off the road and settling down a bit. In addition to their first child, Tracey, Sammy and May adopted two biracial boys, Mark and Jeff, in 1961 and 1963, respectively.

He agreed to undertake the ambitious project, but with some conditions. He wanted a fully integrated cast, insisting that at least 50 percent of the performers be African American. Elkins said of course. He wanted to be the highest-paid performer on Broadway. Elkins gave him $10,000 a week.

Odets took to the task of updating the script for a 1960s audience, but died of cancer in 1963 before he was finished. The book then went through several incarnations and revisions. Extended rehearsals in Philadelphia, Boston, and Detroit took place before the opening at the Majestic Theatre in New York in 1964.

The final product featured a modern jazz score and incorporated references to civil rights issues throughout. The show mirrored Sammy's life with its Harlem backstory and interracial love interest. There were fight scenes and comedy routines, dance numbers and songs. Davis explained how his character "can't survive in the ghetto because he is repulsed by it. He resents his dad, who he considers an Uncle Tom, and resents his brother, a civil rights worker, because he sees the fight as useless. I thought it [was] important showing this kind of frustration within the American Negro."[8]

He "dredged up so much of his own being and infused it into the story, that it was impossible to divorce the role from the man," mused *Life* magazine.

A week before the big opening, Sammy told a friend about the first performance, "I'm doing this show for only two people. Walter Kerr and Howard Taubman." They were the *Herald Tribune*'s and *New York Times*'s respective theater critics. "If they knock me, I'll be destroyed."[9]

On opening night Sammy came out a little flat, according to his own critique, but he dug deep. He danced and sang his heart out, and the night ended with a standing ovation. But Sammy knew that most of the audience was friends and industry professionals. What mattered was the critics' reaction. Backstage after the show, he received congratulatory telegrams from Laurence Olivier and Bobby Kennedy. He then "slipped into a tux," according to *Life*, and headed for a nightclub bar. There, he and his entourage partied and waited for the reviews. Finally, the phone at the nightclub rang. Walter Kerr's review was in. The show was a hit. The critic called Sammy's performance "serious, expert, affecting."[10]

The *Times*'s Taubman was more critical but still opened his review by saying the play was "as crisp as a left jab and as jolting as a right uppercut. One can have nothing but admiration for the snap, speed and professionalism of this musical."[11]

Life ran a picture of Sammy receiving the news at Danny's Hideaway. He had a cigarette in hand and his head tilted back as "he let out a joyous cry to spread the news to everybody."

"I'm ten feet tall! I'm a Broadway star! We've got a hit," he yelled.[12] The show was indeed a hit. It ran for 568 performances, toured the world and received four Tony nominations. The show established Davis as a mainstream star independent of the Rat Pack.

He moved with May and the kids into a two-story brownstone off

Fifth Avenue. May had hoped for a family life in New York. She envisioned Sammy coming home from the theater and the couple watching TV on the couch together. But Sammy had too much restless energy. Sammy did eight shows a week and still somehow found time to record two LPs, appear on the *Tonight Show* eight times, and guest-host the program once during the musical's first year. A journalist for the *Herald Tribune* wrote that "some people think Davis has a God complex, but this is absurd. On the seventh day he works."[13]

During the rare times Sammy was not working, he was partying. In the early days of the show's run, May asked him for a quiet Friday night at home after the show and Sammy agreed. When Friday came that week, he called and told her to get ready, they had to go down to the 21 Club with Hilly. He promised they would have a night at home next Friday. When the next week came, their quiet night at home was joined by photographers from *Life*, which was running a profile on Sammy and the show. The article talked up Sammy's newfound domesticity. May was furious. She did not want pictures of their children and their home going out to the world via one of the most widely read periodicals of the time. But in the second week of November 1964, that is exactly what happened.

Sammy's good friend Burt Boyar explained the unraveling of Sammy's second marriage this way:

> Sammy openly wanted a movie-star wife. He wanted people to say, "Hey, there's May and Sammy!" He wanted to step out of a limo at an opening and have everybody scream. He wanted it to be two movie stars.... May, to her credit, wanted to be a housewife. She began resisting what Sammy wanted. She wanted to have the kids in the back of the station wagon and take the kids off to school.[14]

There was no final fight scene. Sammy lived his life in theatrics but when it came to the unraveling of his relationship with May, there was only an eventual sad realization. May came to understand that Sammy was never going to change. She loved him and he loved her, but after seven years it became clear they were not compatible. They had different visions of what the good life was.

The *New York Daily News* broke the news first, on November 25, 1967. On December 19, May walked into the Santa Monica courthouse and told the judge "there was no family life to speak of." He granted her the divorce and $3,000 a month in alimony. Sammy told a London newspaper in 1968, "I have loved twice in my life and both times have failed. Now I no longer want to love or be loved ... Life ain't pretty all the time. You can't always be the winner. I know I am not a winner any more. A winner is a man who can walk tall with his head held high. Unashamed, unafraid and unsupported. I walk haltingly with each step."[15]

26

"As long as you win"

The story of how America became entangled in the decades-long conflict known as the Vietnam War is complicated, punctuated at each turn by a cascade of reactionary policy missteps and failures of imagination.

French missionaries and traders came to Vietnam in the early seventeenth century and by the late nineteenth century the entire country was under French rule. Revolutionary leader Ho Chi Minh spent years traveling the world and when he returned home to Vietnam in the 1940s he began calling for independence. He formed a nationalist army and quoted Thomas Jefferson in his speeches. He appealed to U.S. president Harry Truman for recognition of his movement. Truman ignored him.

The Marshall Plan was underway to help rebuild Europe, and America was perfectly happy to support France in maintaining what was left of her overseas colonies. Especially the ones that were vital sources of rubber, tin, aluminum, and other raw materials needed to create the postwar American consumer economy. For the first ten years of Ho Chi Minh's independence movement, he was opposed by French troops that were supplied and financed by American taxpayers. That all ended in 1954 when Ho's army surrounded what was left of the French resistance in the town of Dien Bien Phu. The French knew they were outgunned, outnumbered and trapped. They called for American air support. It was the only way out. Eisenhower refused and the French surrendered.

A peace conference was held in Geneva that summer, with the Soviets and Chinese exerting considerable political pressure during the talks. The result was a settlement that divided Vietnam at the 17th parallel but called for unifying elections within two years. The U.S. never gave explicit endorsement of the settlement and set out on a clandestine course to build up a non-communist South Vietnam. With the backing of the CIA, Ngo Dinh Diem became the leader of South Vietnam over French opposition to him. With a rigged election in which he won 98 percent of the vote, Diem began to consolidate power and canceled the unifying elections called for in the Geneva Accords.

26. "As long as you win"

Diem was autocratic in nature and his regime proved corrupt and inefficient, angering the rural population in the countryside and drawing sharp protest from Buddhists in the major cities. For most of the next decade America would vacillate between propping up the Diem administration and looking for better alternatives. In 1963, with the implicit backing of the Kennedy administration and the CIA, a clandestine group of Vietnamese unhappy with the Diem government seized power. Diem was shot with a revolver and buried in an unmarked grave.[1]

Three weeks after the coup in Vietnam, Kennedy was shot and killed in Dallas. Lyndon Johnson became president and inherited responsibility for the 17,000 American troops stationed in Indochina. At this crossroads stands one of the great tragedies in American history. Johnson was much more interested in domestic policy. He believed in the power of government to lift people out of poverty and had grand plans toward that end. He wanted out of Vietnam. But Johnson had come of age in the time of Munich and appeasement, and he had absorbed the lesson. Never again would America stand by and watch the dominoes fall. If the communists overtook South Vietnam, the rest of Asia would surely follow. And it would all be America's fault, or so the theory went. And so, slowly over the next few years, more and more American boys made their way to Southeast Asia.

In 1966, Gen. Ed Lansdale came out of retirement and took a position as a counterinsurgency specialist working for the U.S. ambassador to South Vietnam, Henry Cabot Lodge. With his years of experience in the CIA, it was thought he could help with the pacification of the South Vietnamese countryside and quell the slow-motion disaster that was unfolding for America in Indochina. He began working with a Vietnamese general who convinced him the best thing America could do was provide security and ensure that honest elections were held. "Give villagers a way to get rid of a corrupt or abusive district chief other than having him killed by VC, and they'll take it very quickly," the general said.

Lansdale explained to Lodge that the U.S. needed to ensure a completely transparent and honest election process for the South Vietnamese people. He said it was the only way to achieve the pacification plan that Johnson and the generals hoped would bring "peace with honor." Lodge responded "with a good deal of reserve, launching into a long commentary that put him on distinctly different ground." The ambassador explained that if anti–American Buddhist political groups gained power they would negotiate a settlement with the North that would not be in America's interest. No, Lodge said, the U.S. would control ballot access for the South Vietnamese in the coming elections, ensuring a victory America wanted.

Lansdale left the meeting dejected, though he had an ace up his sleeve. Richard Nixon was an old friend from Lansdale's time with the CIA in the Eisenhower administration, and he was coming to town. He thought the former vice president could talk some sense into the ambassador. Nixon was on one of his world trips ostensibly in service of his law firm's corporate clients. In the summer of 1966, he was making a stop in Saigon to check out the American situation in Vietnam for himself. Lansdale invited Nixon to dine at his villa with several aides.

Nixon arrived "jet-lagged and rumpled, with the jowls and heavy five o'clock shadow of the Herblock cartoons." He went around and shook hands with everyone present. Daniel Ellsberg, a man Nixon would come to know all too well in the coming years but never met in person again, recorded the scene:

"Well, Ed, what are you up to?" Nixon asked.

"Mr. Vice-President, we want to help General Thang make this the most honest election that's ever been held in Vietnam," Lansdale responded.

"Oh, sure, honest, yes, honest, that's right," Nixon responded.

As he took his seat he winked, nudged Lansdale's arm and slapped his own knee with a chuckle.

"As long as you win!" he said. No one in the room laughed.[2]

In the fall Nixon returned to the United States for what had become a bi-yearly tradition: midterm election campaigning. Every two years since he was first elected to Congress in 1946, Richard Nixon had been one of the leading voices for Republican candidates. Johnson had a mini-meltdown responding to Nixon's criticisms that fall. He complained that Nixon found "fault with his country and his government during a period of October every two years." Johnson derisively called him "a chronic campaigner." Nixon shot back with the self-deprecating humor innate in all good politicians. "I think I can understand how a man can be very, very tired and how his temper can then be short," he said, referencing his famous "last press conference." Republicans gained forty seats in the House and three in the Senate in the 1966 midterm elections.[3]

Nixon was once again becoming the de facto leader of the Republican Party in voters' minds. As a private citizen working at a high-profile law firm, he was able to engage selectively and control his press coverage in a way that was impossible when working inside government. Yet on the issues, Nixon was remarkably silent. On civil rights and the Vietnam War, the two most defining issues of the day, Nixon managed to stay mostly ambivalent and equivocal. He spent most of 1966 criticizing Johnson's approach to inflation.

Come 1967 he was gone again, traveling the world on behalf of soft-drink makers and oil companies. He found time for photo ops with world leaders and the occasional opinion piece in *Reader's Digest* (one of his law firm's clients). Back home, his country was falling apart.

It would be called "the Summer of Love" by many observers, but the sanguine-sounding name belied a much darker truth. On June 18, Jimi Hendrix lit his guitar on fire at the Monterey Pop Festival, creating one of the iconic images of the era. The same day, the *New York Times* reported that thirty-one American GIs were killed and another hundred injured in a Viet Cong ambush. On July 6 the Grateful Dead gave a free concert in Golden Gate Park. A week later, a race riot erupted in Newark, New Jersey, killing twenty-six. Then another one in Detroit killed forty-three a week after Newark. There were smaller riots in Buffalo, Cincinnati and Milwaukee that summer. African Americans found that passing laws was the easy part. Implementing the new racial standards in the face of a resistant public was much harder. Martin Luther King came out against the war and began connecting the immorality of segregation at home with the colonial overtones of the American adventure in Indochina.

The Selective Service Act had long allowed the government to conscript its citizens for a national cause, but was being increasingly relied upon to make up for the lack of recruits willingly enlisting for Uncle Sam's Vietnam crusade. Yet the draft was applied unevenly. The sons of the nation's executives received college deferments while the sons of coal miners and farmers got six months of instruction on how to kill. While the rich debated the strategy and tactics of the war, the poor were loaded on military cargo planes and sent halfway around the world with M16s. As the number of U.S. soldiers in Vietnam swelled, the conflict began hitting Middle America in a way it had not before. Young people began burning their draft cards as anti-war protests spread all across the country.

South Dakota senator George McGovern took to the Senate floor and said, "It would be ironic, indeed, if we devoted so heavy a proportion of our resources on the pacification of Vietnam that we are unable to pacify Los Angeles, Chicago, and Harlem."[4]

A Harvard professor named Timothy Leary encouraged the "flower children" to expand their minds to new heights with LSD. Civil rights leader Stokely Carmichael was shedding his belief in nonviolence and began to speak of "building a movement that will smash everything Western civilization has created."[5]

It was the summer of 1967 that changed "the 1960s" from a numerical delineation of time and place into "the Sixties," a synonym for hope or chaos, depending on one's perspective.

That fall Richard Nixon returned briefly to Whittier. His mother, Hannah, had died after a few months in a nursing home. "I expected it but was not prepared," he would write in a letter to a friend. Hannah was the guiding moral light of Nixon's life. Knowing what she would think kept some of his more duplicitous instincts in check. Once Hannah died, the mendacious side of her second son would blossom for the world to see.[6]

The next year, 1968, was Nixon's twenty-second year on the national political stage. "Politics was not just an alternative occupation for me. It was my life," he said.[7] He had spent the last few years reliving the mistakes of 1960 and '62. He now felt he knew how to avoid the numerous pitfalls inherent in a presidential campaign. He accepted that there is no such thing in politics as a one-man show. He brought in John Mitchell, a partner with his law firm, and H.R. Haldeman to run the day-to-day operations of the campaign, and he did not question his team's every move as he had in 1962. Newspaper editor Pat Buchanan was brought in as speechwriter and a liaison to the conservative wing of the party. And a little-known television producer named Roger Ailes joined the team as a media advisor.

Nixon dispensed with his primary challengers at the Republican National Convention that summer rather easily. Michigan governor George Romney had been stained by the Detroit riot and his response. Nixon's New York neighbor Nelson Rockefeller waffled back and forth before finally jumping in the race too late. Nixon's biggest challenge came from the man who held the job for which he had last run. Two years into his first term as governor of California, Ronald Reagan had captured the hearts of the John Birch wing of the Republican Party. Nixon was ready, though. All that campaigning for Goldwater in 1964 had endeared him to just enough conservatives. With the help of Strom Thurmond's strong-arming of Southern delegates on his behalf, Nixon captured the nomination on the first ballot.

As Nixon surveyed his prospects later that year, he was cautiously optimistic. The man he originally assumed he would be facing, Lyndon Johnson, had shocked the nation when at the end of an Oval Office address in March he announced he would not seek re-election. LBJ's chief rival, Robert Kennedy, had been assassinated in June. The Democrats were in disarray as they convened in Chicago. They nominated Vice President Hubert Humphrey in the proverbial smoke-filled room, at the International Amphitheatre. Across the street in Grant Park protesters clashed with police as news cameras rolled.

Third-party challengers rarely do well in American presidential history, but there are some notable exceptions. One of those was George Corley Wallace. Born in a small Alabama town in 1919, by the 1950s Wallace was a circuit judge. He held moderate views on race, according to those who knew him. At least moderate by 1950s Alabama standards. He lost his 1958 run for governor to an arch-segregationist, after which he vowed to never "get outniggered again."[8] Norman Mailer wrote of him, "If every politician is an actor, only a few are consummately talented. Wallace is talented."⁹

He made a conscious decision to use race division as a means of getting ahead, and in mid-twentieth-century Alabama the strategy worked. He was elected governor in 1962. By 1968 he had made a national name for himself by opposing civil rights laws. Feeling the Democrats had abandoned their principles, he left the party and helped form the American Independent Party. He launched a bid for president on a platform of segregation and was immediately polling at 20 percent nationally.

Wallace told voters he would deal with agitators the old-fashioned way. "We don't have riots in Alabama … first one of 'em to pick up a brick gets a bullet in the brain, that's all," he said.¹⁰ Humphrey meanwhile tried to walk a rhetorical tightrope. He couldn't criticize the administration. He was a part of it. But he had to offer something different. The result was a lethargic campaign that failed to inspire even the most ardent party loyalists. Richard Nixon just said as little as possible.

Roger Ailes had studied Nixon's TV past and he knew what was missing from his boss's appearances. All the nonstop campaigning and rallies had left Nixon looking haggard and unable to think as quickly as he might have otherwise. Ailes convinced the campaign to focus on one big event a day. The idea became known as "in the arena," a phrase Nixon would use to title one of his memoirs. In darkened television studios in different cities, Nixon would stand surrounded by voters and field questions. Viewers saw a man with no notes, standing as others were sitting, answering tough questions. "The look has guts," Ailes would remark.¹¹ The events were held near airports at midday. Just enough time for reporters to send off video to the network studios in New York for the nightly news, but not quite enough time for highly scrutinized editing.

Nixon was answering real voters' questions; they were not screened by the campaign ahead of time. But by focusing on one event a day, Nixon was always sharp and agile. The campaign wasn't directing which clips the news should air, but there was less room for gaffes and missteps for the press to focus on. By contrast, Humphrey ran around the country, doing up to a dozen events a day. Ample time to utter some contradictory statements or criticism of the administration that would become the lead story.

The theme of Nixon's campaign was "Law and Order." Nixon used the phrase in almost every public remark he made in 1968. It was the fourth summer in a row that riots had overtaken major metropolises and medium-sized urban conclaves alike. Violent crime in the United States tripled from 1960 to 1969, according to Justice Department statistics. Nixon's television ads showed rioters setting fire to businesses, mobs roaming inner-city neighborhoods and brandishing weapons. There was no narration, just ominous music. In the end, one word: "Nixon."

When Nixon said that "the first civil right of every American is to be free of domestic violence,"[12] the implication was clear even if all the ne'er-do-wells in his ads were white. "Riots, street crime, anti–Vietnam marches, poor people's marches, drugs, pornography, welfarism, rising taxes, all had a common thread," wrote a prominent historian looking back on the election fifteen years later. "In the public perception, all these things merged."[13]

Wallace's campaign began steadily hemorrhaging support after he picked retired Air Force commander Curtis LeMay as his running mate. LeMay seemed to have no compunction about using nuclear weapons anytime the U.S. needed to achieve a foreign policy objective. He had been the inspiration for Stanley Kubrick's *Dr. Strangelove*. It was too tough an approach for a war-weary public.

Many of Wallace's supporters were traditional Democrats and Humphrey saw a bump in the polls from Wallace defectors. As the weather turned cooler, Nixon and Humphrey appeared to be running neck and neck, with neither man receiving a majority, as Wallace hung on to his support in the Deep South. Nixon was worried and proposed a gentleman's agreement to Humphrey: They would support whoever won the popular vote should the Electoral College tie and the election be decided in the House of Representatives. Humphrey politely declined the offer, saying they should follow the constitutional process to its natural end.

Nixon had seen this movie before. Democrats and their Franklin allies were going to steal this thing from him again if he wasn't careful. But this time he had an insurance policy. They called her the Dragon Lady.

Alexander Sachs was a credible source. The Harvard-educated economist and banker had predicted the Great Depression and the rise of Hitler. In 1939 he was tasked with delivering a letter to FDR from Albert Einstein. The letter warned of Nazi Germany's pursuit of an atomic bomb. FDR started the Manhattan Project days later. By 1968 Sachs was working on Wall Street and one day in early October he had lunch with Eugene Rostow, Johnson's under secretary of state for political affairs. They were discussing the gossip bouncing around Wall Street when Sachs dropped a bomb: Richard Nixon was interfering with the peace talks underway in Paris to end the Vietnam War. "He is trying to frustrate the President by inciting Saigon to step up its demands," he said. Sachs knew Rostow would tell his brother, Walt, the national security advisor, who would surely tell his boss, Lyndon Johnson.[14]

"This is treason!" Johnson screamed when he heard the news. He

26. "As long as you win"

ordered FBI surveillance on the Nixon campaign and South Vietnamese Embassy.[15]

Shortly after Johnson's election in 1964, he had begun escalating the Vietnam War. He authorized Operation Rolling Thunder to demonstrate American air-power superiority. It was thought America could bomb the North Vietnamese into submission. It didn't work. Aided by Russian- and Chinese–produced air defense systems, the North had shot down over nine hundred U.S. planes by 1968. The campaign failed to result in even modest decreases in the number of enemy combatants. After three years and almost one million tonnages of bombs, the futility of the operation became crystal clear.

The Tet Offensive beginning in January of 1968 further damaged troop morale and the American public's appetite for continuing the war. Two months later Johnson announced he would not seek re-election; he said he was doing so to focus on peace. He wanted to bring the war to an honorable end before he left office. Vietnam had frustrated his whole term. He felt his presidency had been consumed by the war and he wanted his legacy to be a peace accord.

Moscow did not want to see Nixon become president. As polls showed him consistently leading that summer, they reached out to the Johnson administration. If he would halt the bombing, they could bring the North to the negotiating table. Both sides hoped an ancillary benefit to the conclusion of the conflict would be a Humphrey presidency. In October, Johnson called off the bombings and announced new peace talks in Paris.

Richard Nixon's stance on Vietnam throughout his term as vice president had been one of escalation. Nixon was the nation's foremost communist fighter and he genuinely believed in dominoes, slippery slopes, and the dangers of communist aggression. But, as usual, as public opinion began to change, so did Nixon's public stance. Over the course of the 1960s Nixon would hold almost every position about the war conceivable outside of total withdrawal or nuclear bombardment. From 1966 to 1968 his public stance was essentially just to disagree with Johnson's policy, all the while insisting on victory. When Johnson told the country in March that he was focusing on peace for the rest of his term, Nixon was thrilled to announce his own moratorium on discussing Vietnam. "Let's not destroy the chances for peace with a mouthful of words," he said. "Put yourself in the position of the enemy. He is negotiating with Lyndon Johnson ... and then he reads in the paper that, not a senator, not a congressman, not an editor, but a potential president of the United States will give him a better deal than President Johnson is offering him.... [I]t will destroy any chance for the negotiations... The enemy will wait for the next man." And yet destroying the chances for peace is exactly what Richard Nixon did.[16]

Anna Chennault was the widow of an American hero. Her husband, Claire, led the "Flying Tigers" in aerial dogfights over China during World War II. His squadron would be romanticized in films starring John Wayne and Fred Astaire in the years that followed. When Claire died in 1958, Anna was left with a sizable fortune and became a prominent member of Washington society, particularly in Republican fundraising circles.

The Chinese-born Chennault had regular access to South Vietnamese President Nguyen Van Thieu as well as other pro-Western leaders in Asia. She believed the communist North must be defeated and wrote to Nixon that an increase in bombing would make the North "bow down for peace." Nixon first met the woman called the Dragon Lady in the early fifties in Taiwan. They became social acquaintances and she raised money for Nixon's various campaigns over the next two decades. In July of 1968 they met at Nixon's New York apartment along with John Mitchell and South Vietnam ambassador Bui Diem. Nixon told the ambassador that if he was elected, South Vietnam could "rest assured" that he would find a way "to winning this war." He concluded the meeting by telling Diem, "If you have a message for me, please give it to Anna, and she will relay it to me, and I will do the same."[17]

The Johnson administration was pressuring Thieu and South Vietnam to come to the negotiating table. Moscow was cajoling Ho Chi Minh and the North. The peace deal proposed was not perfectly aligned to American or South Vietnamese goals but, as Walt Rostow wrote that October, "we have the best deal we now can get—vastly better than any we thought we could get since 1961." In Johnson's mind, peace had never been so close at hand.

Nixon sent for the Dragon Lady. H.R. Haldeman noted an instruction from Nixon to "keep Anna Chennault working on SVN." An FBI wiretap on Anna's phone caught her telling Ambassador Diem that she had a "message from her boss" to tell the South to "hold on, we are going to win." The pressure worked. Thieu never signed on to the deal and the talks fell apart.

Johnson was furious, but he was in a jam. To reveal he knew that Nixon was involved would be to reveal that he had been spying on a foreign ally and a domestic opponent. Johnson called Republican senator Everett Dirksen and vented his anger.

"I'm reading their hand, Everett. This is treason," Johnson said.

"I know," Dirksen admits on the tapes, sounding apologetic.[18]

Dirksen sent word to the Nixon campaign that the jig was up. Haldeman's copious notes provide history with the story: "LBJ called Dirksen—says he knows Repubs through D. Lady are keeping SVN in present position[. I]f this proves true—and persists—he will go to nation & blast Reps & RN."[19]

26. "As long as you win"

Once Nixon had talked to Haldeman, he called Johnson. He feigned ignorance and denied everything. There was "no credibility to that" stuff about "the China lobby," he told the president. "We've got to get this goddamn war off the plate," he said. "And I really feel this, that—and I feel this very deeply—that I think you've gotten a bad rap on this thing ... the war apparently now is about where it could be brought to an end, and if we can get it done now, fine, that's what [we] ought to do. Just the quicker the better, and the hell with the political credit. Believe me, that's the way I feel about it."[20]

Johnson knew Nixon was lying. He had loads of circumstantial evidence but no smoking gun. He never went to the press.

After the election the story trickled out via journalists, but Nixon would always deny everything. He told David Frost in their famous 1977 interviews that he "had no knowledge" and "did nothing to undercut the South Vietnamese," adding that he "couldn't have done that in conscience." The name Anna Chennault is never mentioned in his memoirs.

LBJ left his records on the incident in an envelope with instructions that it not be opened for fifty years. Johnson died in 1973 and his presidential library opened the file in 1995. What came to be known as the X Envelope held all of Johnson's correspondence on the affair. But it was not until 2015 that historian John Farrell uncovered Haldeman's notes tucked away in a White House Special Files box at the Nixon Library, conclusively linking Nixon to the plot.

Nixon spent the night of the election at the Waldorf in New York. Around midnight Humphrey was leading in the popular vote and it looked like the whole race could come down to Illinois again. Pat Nixon went in the bathroom and threw up.

But the West and Upper South broke decisively for Nixon and by 11 a.m. the next day the press was calling him president-elect. Nixon won the election with 43.2 percent of the popular vote. Humphrey was a half percentage point behind, with Wallace getting 13.5 percent nationally. The family went back to their Fifth Avenue apartment and found an empty pantry after months of campaigning. They celebrated with tomato soup and scrambled eggs. Afterwards, Nixon went into his study overlooking Fifth Avenue and blasted *Victory at Sea* on his stereo loud enough that Nelson Rockefeller could hear.[21]

27

"Weirdest day so far"

Richard Nixon was inaugurated on a cold and rainy January day because of course he was. Nixon was an Orthogonian. It was Franklins like Kennedy who got crisp days with bright sunshine reflected off new fallen snow. The bean boys didn't receive such favor from divine providence. As his limousine made its way from the Capitol to the White House, the route was lined with long haired, blue-jean-clad protesters.

"One. Two. Three. Four. We Don't Want Your Fucking War."

Vietnam "was the overriding factor in Nixon's first term. It overshadowed everything, all the time, in every discussion, in every opportunity and every problem," Bob Haldeman would recall years later.

Nixon campaigned in 1968 by saying as little about the conflict in Vietnam as possible. When pressed by reporters he implied he had a secret plan to end the war, though he never actually said that. Nixon's plan was threatening to bomb the North back to the Stone Age and using tactical nuclear weapons, if necessary, in hopes that Ho Chi Minh would negotiate. He believed overwhelming American force would compel Hanoi to negotiate on American terms.

"I call it the Madman Theory, Bob. I want the North Vietnamese to believe I'll do anything to stop the war," he told his aide as they walked along a Key Biscayne beach before the inauguration. As Nixon took office, nearly three hundred U.S. soldiers were dying every week in Vietnam.[1]

The North Vietnamese guerrilla war against the South and its American allies relied heavily on supply lines that ran through neighboring Laos and Cambodia. The two adjacent countries were officially neutral in the conflict. If Nixon attacked inside their sovereign territory, it would be seen as an unconscionable escalation in the eyes of an American public that had elected Nixon to end the conflict. Therefore, secrecy was paramount.

Operation Menu was the code name. The Breakfast attack began on March 18, 1969. B-52 bombers annihilated the jungle canopy and everything below it. U.S. soldiers sent in to scour the area afterwards reported a landscape of moonlike craters and uprooted trees as enemy soldiers and peasant farmers stumbled around bloodied and confused. After Breakfast came Lunch. And then Snack and Dinner and so on. Operation Menu would continue bombing the Cambodian jungle for months on end. The State Department was not told about the escalation until after it was underway. No one in Congress had been notified.

Ho Chi Minh was taken aback by the escalation, but also recognized something key: Nixon was doing it in secret. He knew that would not last, and he was right. On May 9 the *New York Times* broke the story with a front-page headline, "Raids in Cambodia by US Unprotested."

In a Florida hotel room, national security advisor Henry Kissinger threw down his paper in disgust, incensed at the leak. "Outrageous! ... We must crush these people! We must destroy them!"

A game of whodunit cascaded through the White House. Kissinger suspected Secretary of Defense Melvin Laird. Kissinger phoned him that morning, pulling Laird off the golf course to take his call.

"You son of a bitch," Kissinger bellowed at the head of the Defense Department as he came on the line. Laird hung up on him.

Nixon and Kissinger decided leaks of this kind endangered national security and they could not stand. They contacted J. Edgar Hoover at the FBI and asked for wiretaps to be installed on Laird as well as twelve other administration officials and four newspaper reporters. Without a court order. Without any evidence of wrongdoing whatsoever. The eavesdropping produced little other than Washington gossip. One wiretap even caught Laird refusing a reporter's request to leak sensitive material.[2]

Richard Nixon was an idiosyncratic fellow and he spent his first weeks in the White House obsessing over small details. The shower jets Johnson had installed were too strong. "It nearly flung me out of the stall," he claimed.[3] They were replaced. The fireplace was upgraded because he could not get it to crackle right. He dug down into the minutia of White House tipping policy; head waiters should get ten dollars, wine stewards five, and the waiter serving the president should get 25 percent of the bill, he instructed. He ordered all the art in the various embassies replaced: "This administration is going to turn away from ... offbeat art, music and literature."[4] He would eventually build a bowling alley in the White House basement.

From FDR to LBJ the White House taping system had expanded. Roosevelt installed the first microphones and taped his press conferences. Truman added a microphone under a lampshade to capture conversations in the Executive Mansion. Eisenhower recorded phone calls to and from the Oval Office and Kennedy and Johnson each left behind hundreds of hours of recorded conversations. Nixon was not a big fan of electronics, though, and he found the system cumbersome and unnecessary. One of the many changes Nixon made to the White House upon moving in was dismantling the taping system (though he later reinstalled it).

But for all his curious quirks, he was very much a man of his generation. And men of his generation drank alcohol. When one sat down to discuss weighty topics in wood-paneled rooms with leatherbound books, one did it with a drink in hand.

"He could never handle liquor," former press secretary Jim Bassett remembered.

On the White House tapes, ice can be heard clinking in glasses as Nixon's voice slurs, his rants becoming more paranoid and delusional. By the time Nixon entered the White House he had begun taking Dilantin, a sleeping pill intended to help with his insomnia. The combination of alcohol and pills could have deleterious effects. Once, on a late-night call with special counsel Charles Colson, Nixon went silent in mid-conversation. Colson panicked, thinking the president had suffered a heart attack or stroke. The next day Nixon apologized profusely; jet lag had just caught up with him, he said.[5]

The first year of Nixon's presidency did not go well. Barely over one hundred days in, he had escalated the war he had promised to end. The antiwar movement, already a potent force, was growing even larger on college campuses across the country. In April three hundred students took over the Harvard University administration building. Forty-nine were injured, 184 arrested. In November a quarter million people marched against the war in Washington.

It wasn't just the students. An economist from MIT wrote in *Newsweek*, "If Mr. Nixon were to announce defeat in Vietnam and cutting of our losses, the market would jump 50 points."[6] Radio announcer Paul Harvey, a man dubbed by *Esquire* magazine as "the voice of the Silent Majority," told his listeners, "America's six percent section of the planet's mothers cannot bear enough boy babies to police Asia—and the nation can't bleed to death trying."[7]

In May, the Battle of Hamburger Hill encapsulated the insanity of the war. Seventy-two Americans died taking a defensive fortification of little strategic value, only to have the U.S. abandon the hill weeks later. In September Ho Chi Minh died, but his revolution continued strong as ever. The Madman Theory wasn't working. Nixon had claimed to Haldeman before the inauguration that his approach would have Ho "in Paris in two days begging for peace."[8] Ho never came to the Paris talks, and the increased U.S. bombing risked drawing the Russians or Chinese into the conflict on the side of the North. Moreover, the leaks about the bombings had emboldened and expanded the ranks of the antiwar movement.

Frustrated, Nixon introduced a new strategy, Vietnamization. This was the idea that the U.S. could train the South Vietnamese to do what they could not: defend their government from communist takeover. American GIs just needed to win the hearts and minds of the people, Nixon told the public. The strategy allowed Nixon to begin bringing some soldiers home.

Privately, Nixon had known since 1966 that victory with a World War II–style battleship surrender was a fantasy in Indochina. As had Johnson before him. And Kennedy before him. But Nixon, like the others, did not believe the U.S. should be seen as retreating. By the spring of 1970 Vietnamization was not working as hoped, and on average over a hundred American soldiers were still dying every week. Nixon announced more troop withdrawals and then, ten days later, on April 30, turned around and announced an escalation. It was a move only Tricky Dick could pull off.

In a prime-time address to the nation Nixon announced that American boys needed to undertake a ground invasion into Cambodia. To hear Nixon explain it, putting U.S. troops on the ground in a neutral country was not really an expansion of the war. It was a continuation of strategy. The speech was singularly focused on convincing the silent majority. Nixon knew the college campuses would erupt, and he was right.

According to the White House, telegrams and letters poured in supporting the president's expansion of the war while the campuses and streets of the larger American cities exploded in rage. Nixon was caught on tape the next day at the Pentagon calling the antiwar protesters "bums."[9] A protest was planned for May 9 on the National Mall.

On May 4, Nixon woke up from a nap and H.R. Haldeman, now chief of staff, informed him that there had been a shooting at Kent State University. The details were still murky, but it appeared the National Guard had fired on student protesters and four of them were dead. Nixon was "very disturbed. Afraid his decision set it off," according to Haldeman's notes. He seemed agitated and deflated. He "talked about how we can get through to the students, turn this stuff off." Nixon wrote in his memoir that the days following Kent State were "among the darkest of my Presidency." Yet, two days later Haldeman wrote in his diary that the president was "[v]ery aware that the goal of the Left is to panic us, so we must not fall into that trap."

A press conference was planned for the 8th. Nixon explained that this escalation was necessary and that despite it, he still planned to bring an additional 150,000 troops home. Haldeman wrote that the press conference was "masterful." He said that Nixon "really zinged the bad guys," referring to the reporters and news organizations Nixon and his team believed were in a coordinated effort to bring him down.[10]

As often was the case, Nixon spent the hours after his nationally televised appearance with a drink in hand, calling supporters and friends for their take on his performance. In the early-morning hours of May 9, the president made forty-six phone calls. He called aides and reporters. He called his wife and daughters. He called clergymen Billy Graham and Norman Vincent Peale. Nixon then retired to the Lincoln Sitting Room, where he played Rachmaninoff's Second Piano Concerto on the stereo. When the album ended, he looked out over the National Mall. He could see protesters beginning to gather. He summoned his valet, Manolo Sanchez, and his astonished Secret Service agents. He told them to get the limousine; he wanted to go talk to the protesters.

As a pink sky lit the dawn of what would be a perfect spring day, Nixon and Sanchez left the agents behind and climbed the marble steps of the Lincoln Memorial. Protesters stared in disbelief.[11]

"I know that probably most of you think I'm an S.O.B., but I want you to know that I understand just how you feel," Nixon said.[12]

He tried to make small talk and find common ground. A protester told him he was from California, and Nixon tried to talk about surfing. When one mentioned he had come from Syracuse University, Nixon asked about the school's football team. Nixon was still wearing makeup from his press conference, now considerably smudged. "He looked like he had a mask on," one protester remembered.

In his memoir Nixon explained that he tried to "lift them a bit out of the miserable intellectual wasteland in which they now wander aimlessly around." He talked about Churchill and Chamberlain, trying to tie his generation's fight against totalitarianism to the current one. He said that his goal in Vietnam was the same as theirs, to end the war.

A young protester from Detroit, Bob Moustakas, recalled that the atmosphere was akin to a high school party in a friend's basement when the parents came down to see if everything was all right.

As the sun rose higher in the sky and the crowd at the Lincoln Memorial began to grow, Nixon said he had to go. He shook hands with the protesters and walked back toward the limo.

But Nixon was not done. He decided he needed to show Sanchez the Capitol as well. He walked onto the House floor and sat at his old desk. He told Sanchez to get on the rotunda and make a speech, which a delirious and possibly still drunk Nixon applauded. By now it was almost eight in the morning. Haldeman and domestic affairs advisor John Ehrlichman had been called and they were rushing into town from their suburban homes. They found their boss in the Capitol building and implored him to get back to the White House. There were 100,000 people who hated his guts descending on the city as they spoke, and this wasn't safe, they said. Nixon insisted on first having breakfast at the Mayflower Hotel. He sat at the table reminiscing about eating corned beef hash and eggs at the restaurant as a congressman, his voice wistful for simpler times.[13]

Finally, after breakfast, Haldeman convinced him it was not safe to walk back to the White House. They took the limo and returned shortly after 9 a.m.

"Weirdest day so far," Haldeman recorded in his diary.

Eighteen months in, the stress of the job was getting to the president. The alcohol and pills were consumed more frequently and in larger amounts, exacerbating the exhaustion. "I am concerned about his condition," Haldeman wrote in his diary. "He has had very little sleep for a long time and his judgment, temper and mood suffer badly as a result."[14]

He spent the next weekend in Florida relaxing as much as a man like Richard Nixon ever relaxed. He spent the summer and fall reassuring Americans that his policy of Vietnamization was the right one. The boys would be coming home soon after winning an honorable peace. Nixon campaigned that fall ahead of the midterms, hoping his silent majority would buoy his policies with resounding victories for Republicans. The result was a mixed bag, with Democrats gaining twelve seats in the House while Republicans picked up one seat in the Senate. Democrats still maintained control of both chambers.

In early 1971, Nixon changed his mind about one of the micromanaging changes he had made upon his inauguration. He had big plans for the next few years, and he wanted his decision-making process preserved for history. He had an aide, Alexander Butterfield, install a new taping system. One that did not need to be turned off and on but was sound-activated. The new system did not just include the Oval Office, it extended to the Cabinet Room, his office in the Executive Office Building and eventually Camp David. In the beginning there were fewer than ten people aware of its existence. Over the next two years the vast majority of people involved in conversations with Nixon had no idea they were being recorded. He never intended the tapes to become public; they would help him write his memoirs and be selectively edited, if need be, to score political points. It was the most consequential decision Richard Nixon ever made.

The June 13 edition of the *New York Times* that year ran a photo of a smiling bride and her father on the front page. The story was about the main social event in Washington, the marriage of President Nixon's daughter Tricia to Edward Cox at the White House. The ceremony had gone off without a hitch. It was the sixteenth wedding held at the Executive Mansion and the first to take place in the Rose Garden. That was the story in the lefthand column. The right side of the page held more ominous news: "Vietnam Archive: Pentagon Study Traces 3 Decades of US Involvement."[15]

Alexander Haig, the deputy national security advisor, called Nixon at a quarter past noon and found the president in high spirits. They discussed the casualty counts in Vietnam and Haig let him know he would have a report to him by Monday.

"Okay. Nothing else important in the world?" Nixon asked.

"Yes, sir. Very significant. This goddamn *New York Times* exposé of the most highly classified documents of the war," Haig responded.

"Oh, that! I see. I didn't read that story. Do you mean that was leaked out of the Pentagon?"

"Sir, it [is] the whole study that was done for McNamara and then carried on after McNamara left by Clifford and the peaceniks over there. This is a devastating security breach of the greatest magnitude of anything I've seen."[16] (Robert McNamara and Clark Clifford were secretaries of defense in the Kennedy and Johnson presidencies.)

Haig was not being hyperbolic. Never before had classified material been leaked to the American press on such a scale. The documents revealed for the first time that the U.S. had been directly involved in Indochina since the Truman years, directly contradicting the public statements of every president and Pentagon official for the last twenty-five years. They showed particular duplicitousness on the part of Nixon's immediate predecessors, Kennedy and Johnson, as the war gradually escalated.

Daniel Ellsberg was one of the authors of the study. He had graduated summa cum laude from Harvard, a student of Henry Kissinger's. He had served two years as a counterinsurgency expert in Vietnam. He now worked for the Rand Corporation but maintained contacts within the government. He knew the war was unwinnable. He knew that Nixon knew the war was unwinnable. He saw how Vietnamization was simply prolonging the inevitable. It made it possible to draw down American troops and end the draft, but the bombings continued, and American boys and Asian civilians were continuing to die at an alarming rate. He wondered what it all was for.

He leaked the Pentagon Papers, as they would come to be known, in the hopes that it would provide Nixon a way out. Some cover to blame the war on Democrats and their deceit. Withdraw the troops and end the madness once and for all. But that's not how Richard Nixon saw it.

"If this thing flies, … they're going to do the same to you,"[17] Kissinger warned his boss.

Nixon began to imagine the possible scenarios playing out. His contacts with Anna Chennault, the falsified documents of the Menu campaign, the wiretapping of government officials without a court order. Who knew what else the press and their Franklin allies might try to dredge up? Nixon came to see the Pentagon Papers as a conspiracy to bring him down even though, ironically, the documents were much more critical of his predecessors. The study had ended in early 1968 before he even took office.

Nixon's Justice Department filed suit to stop publication. They won a preliminary injunction against the *Times* and so the *Washington Post* picked up the story. When an injunction shut them down, the *Boston Globe* hopped on board. And then sixteen other newspapers. The Supreme Court took the case on an expedited basis and, seventeen days after the initial publication, ruled 6–3 in favor of the newspapers' right to publish the documents.

Nixon took an issue that he easily could have parlayed to his political advantage and turned it around on himself. It was one of the clumsiest acts in a life full of so much political acumen. Nixon was becoming more and more paranoid. "They are using any means," he told aides. "We are going to use any means."[18] One week after the publication of the Pentagon Papers, the Special Investigations Unit inside the White House was born. Nixon needed "a small group of tough guys," he said. They called themselves the Plumbers because they plugged leaks. In time, their mandate would expand.

Nixon saw Ted Kennedy as his greatest threat to being reelected to the presidency in 1972. As the battle over the Pentagon Papers played out in court, he asked his aides to find a way to amplify the scurrilous chapters of the Kennedy years. Instructing them to leak the incriminating documents, he said, with no hint of irony in his voice, that "the public is entitled to know."[19]

28

My Own Worst Nightmare

On March 30, 1969, the NAACP gave the Spingarn Medal to Sammy Davis, Jr. The award was presented annually by the organization for the "highest or noblest achievement by an American Negro during the preceding year or years." It remains their top honor. Sammy stepped on stage to receive the medal in a Nehru jacket and a new hairstyle. He was no longer putting pomade in his hair. Natural hair was in, and Sammy showed up to the ceremony with an afro.

"I have gone through some powerful changes during the past three years. I know my heritage now and I thank young black people for making me aware that I am an American of African descent," the forty-four-year-old entertainer told what *Jet* magazine called a "well-integrated, overwhelmingly middle-class audience."

In his speech he expressed gratitude and humility at the honor, saying he was "a little ashamed of the fact that I haven't done more."

In reality Sammy had done quite a bit. He had been writing checks, organizing benefit concerts, and signing his name to fundraising letters since the 1950s. He had marched in Selma and stood with Martin Luther King on the steps of the Lincoln Memorial. Sammy was the civil rights movement's bridge to middle-class white America. He warned the audience about "playing the game of 'I'll out-black you.' Everyone should be allowed to be as black as he or she can be."[1]

By the late sixties elements of the civil rights movement were turning increasingly militant. The Black Panther Party for Self-Defense was born in Oakland in 1966. It was a reaction to what one historian called "the most racist police force outside of Mississippi."[2] Bobby Seale and Huey Newton wore army fatigues and discussed philosophy. They encouraged African Americans to exercise their 2nd Amendment right and arm themselves. Nonviolence was not working, they believed, and a new approach, more militaristic, was needed for Blacks to achieve parity with whites. Their movement went nationwide by the end of the sixties. Sammy was never really comfortable with the Black Panthers but would seek their acceptance for years.

In his memoir, Sammy relates the story of a clandestine meeting with Ron Karenga, whom he called "the most feared as well as the most respected civil rights activist in LA." Karenga was the co-founder of the Black nationalist group US Organization. He walked into the back of a dimly lit restaurant on Central Avenue in LA and found Karenga with a group of armed men wearing sunglasses.

"Hi, Ron. Guys," Sammy said by way of introduction.

They stared back at him with no response.

"Hey, brothers, you think I'm scared of you?" Sammy asked. Then, with a classic comedic pause, "Well ... you right there."

He smiled that showbiz smile but the self-deprecating humor that had played so well in nightclubs over the years found no reception with the stone-faced militants.

"Mr. Davis, what is it you want?" Karenga asked.

Another man chimed in, "And you're not our brother."

Sammy said he only wanted to help. He had been involved in the civil rights movement for years and wanted to do his part. Eventually the acrimonious tone subsided, and Sammy began to dig down into what they hoped to accomplish. Their ends were very much the same as those of SNCC or SCLC, but their means were different. The Black nationalist of the late sixties wanted better jobs, housing and educational equality for African Americans just as Sammy did.

"Fear is a necessary commodity, Mr. Davis. Far too little has happened and far too little is going to happen until white people are afraid of black people for a while," one of Karenga's lieutenants explained.

"Labor didn't make its gains on goodwill. Only the threat of a strike, or violence, or a riot brought management to the table to talk. So we intimidate," Karenga added.

Sammy recognized their point even if he was more partial to other means. "But why intimidate me?" he asked as he rubbed his hand on his face. "This don't exactly come off, ya know, I'm not Al Jolson."

"But you ain't black either," the lieutenant shot back.

"I've met some people who disagree with you," Sammy said.[3]

Sammy left the meeting hurt and confused. He would continue to attempt to make inroads to the Panthers. His FBI file describes how Sammy spent thousands of dollars financing a feature film for the Panthers titled *The Murder of Fred Hampton* in 1970.

Despite mountains of historical evidence showing his financial and personal commitment to the cause, many members of the African American community viewed Sammy as an Uncle Tom figure. He felt as if he was never fully accepted.

"I didn't deserve to be an outsider. But I was. I was a member of the black race but not the black community," Sammy wrote in his autobiography.

On April 4, 1968, Sammy was rehearsing in New York for a limited engagement of *Golden Boy* scheduled to run in London that summer. Murphy Bennett, Sammy's longtime assistant, came running to the stage. "Dr. King ... they shot him. He's dead."

Sammy had feared this day would come and worried what people might do. King's vision was nonviolence and Sammy wanted the public's reaction to reflect that.

He called Johnny Carson, drove over to NBC Studios and taped a message for the *Tonight Show*. He was interviewed on ABC and CBS. When Americans tuned in to the six o'clock news that night, they saw Sammy Davis pleading for calm. "The next seventy-two hours could mark the destiny of the next hundred years," he said.

His plea fell on deaf ears. Riots broke out in sixty-eight American cities over the next week.

Sammy was shaken by the loss of Dr. King. He had known him well and participated in the movement with him since the mid-fifties. But Sammy still had hope. He believed in Robert Kennedy. Over the course of the 1960s Sammy had gotten to know Bobby much better than he ever knew JFK. Jack was an acquaintance, but Bobby was Sammy's friend. They had vacationed together in Maryland and Hyannis Port, where Kennedy took Davis sailing. Robert Kennedy was certainly more committed to the cause of civil rights than his brother, and Davis became enamored with him.

"I believed—as I had never believed before in any political person—that marvelous things were coming, that Robert Kennedy was going to lead America into a new age in which all Americans would be free and rich and love each other," Davis wrote in 1989.

When Bobby announced he would run for president, Sammy was eager to help. He attended fundraisers in New York and LA and campaigned on college campuses in Indiana and Illinois. He talked to the senator and wished him luck in the California primary before he left for London. He expressed his regret he could not be on his home turf to help more.

"If we're lucky enough to win, it won't seem right you not being there," Kennedy told him.

Golden Boy opened on June 4 at the London Palladium to rave reviews from the often hard to please British press. The next day, Bobby Kennedy was shot and killed after giving his victory speech in California. Sammy spent the next twelve weeks in London drinking heavily. "Since Bobby had been killed, more often than not I was waking up on the couch still dressed," he wrote.

28. My Own Worst Nightmare

The London scene of the late sixties was perfectly suited for escaping grief and depression. Shows every evening to glowing audiences moved into all-night parties. Sammy would sleep through the morning and spend the afternoon getting ready to do it all again. He wrote that London allowed him to escape the "guilt from a failed marriage, three children with a sometimes father, being broke, the wearisome fact of being black in a white world—push all that shit behind you, to be handled at some other time."

While in England Sammy was scheduled to do a few numbers on a TV special hosted by Tom Jones.

"I'd like you to sing 'Bojangles,'" Jones told Davis in rehearsals.

"I can't do that song. I hate it," Davis replied.

Finally, after some back-and-forth, Sammy said, "Tom, you sing it and I'll act it."

The producers colored Sammy's hair gray, and he acted the part of a drunken minstrel whose best days were behind him, tap-dancing in jail. Afterwards the producers pleaded with Sammy to take the lead and sing it as well. They said he was a natural. He refused, later explaining:

> I wanted nothing to do with it, with the character. It was the story of a dancer who became a drunk, a bum, and he died in jail.... The song spooked me. I had seen too many performers who'd slid from headlining to playing joints, then toilets, then finally beer halls and passing the hat ... the song was my own nightmare. I was afraid that was how I was going to end.

After seeing the video the producers and Jones were raving about, Sammy was more convinced than ever. He left the television studio telling Jones emphatically, "I'm not singing that song."[4]

Sammy arrived back in the United States in the fall of 1968 to what felt like a changed world. The counterculture movement had exploded into the mainstream. Sammy always wanted to be on the cutting edge, and he embraced the stylistic changes. He began wearing headbands and big gaudy rings, an open-collar paisley shirt with a gold medallion flung around his neck and draped over his chest. He looked a far cry from the tuxedo-clad crooner of the early Rat Pack days.

Sammy finished 1968 by recording "I've Gotta Be Me." The song was written by Walter Marks and the record produced by Jimmy Bowen. It proved a surprise minor hit as it stayed on the *Billboard* Top 40 chart for eleven weeks. The song became a staple of Davis's live show and a fitting anthem for a man growing more eccentric with the times.

Altovise Gore grew up in Queens. She was brown-skinned and tall, with long legs and dark, suggestive eyes. She was born in 1943, the only daughter of a career navy man and a homemaker. She was described as a loner by her peers at the High School for Performing Arts but excelled in dance class, leading to a job in the prestigious Alvin Ailey troupe. She danced on Broadway in the 1960s, working with stars such as Harry Belafonte and Noel Coward. She was hired to dance in *Golden Boy* for the show's London run. She became a frequent post-show guest of Sammy's in his hotel suite.

"I fell for him because of his mind," she told an interviewer once.

She began touring with Sammy full-time after the European run. He lavished gifts on her: earrings and bracelets and her favorite accessories, high-heeled boots. They made her almost a foot taller than Sammy. Eighteen years apart, the two made a memorable sight as the paparazzi trailed them through airports. Sammy began introducing Altovise to everyone. First Murphy, then his father and Will. He took her around to Hollywood parties and introduced her to Lucille Ball and Frank Sinatra. While May had shunned the spotlight, Altovise embraced it. Not overly concerned with fame, she enjoyed the things fame brought her.

"Altovise didn't want to be famous. She wanted to be moneyed," her fellow dancer Lolly Fountain said.

One night after a show at the Latin Casino in Philadelphia, the new couple were having dinner with Jerry "the Geator" Blavat, a local radio personality, and Sammy's mother. She had come back into Sammy's life in an on-again, off-again kind of way.

"I want to get married," Sammy said, and turned to face Altovise. "Let's get married tomorrow," he proposed. Altovise shrieked with joy. It was no secret by this point that she wanted to be the third Mrs. Sammy Davis, Jr.

Under the table, Elvira Davis kicked the DJ and whispered in his ear. "This stupid-ass son of a bitch doesn't know what he's doing."[5]

Sammy and Altovise were married at the courthouse in Philadelphia the next day. Elvira Davis did not attend.

Sammy's wedding gift to Altovise was a black mink coat. It was the same thing he had given to his first wife, Loray White, whom the Mob had forced him to marry. There was a noticeable, if possibly subconscious difference, though. Loray's coat had been white.

Sammy felt he needed a new home for his new bride. He purchased 1151 Summit Drive in the heart of Beverly Hills. The home had once belonged to his friends Tony Curtis and Janet Leigh, and Sammy had spent considerable time there. When he found out it was for sale, he jumped at the opportunity to own a piece of old Hollywood.

In the 1960s, Sammy had recorded twenty-two albums for Reprise Records, Frank Sinatra's label. His current manager, Sy Marsh, believed the label was not giving him his due. He thought Sammy should be making more money than he was off record sales.

"He got the leftover shit. All these guys wrote for Frank," Marsh explained. Sammy and Marsh had ended the decade with a hit in "I've Gotta Be Me" and they wanted more. Marsh was not sure for whom Sammy should be recording, but he put out some feelers in the industry and received a surprising phone call.

Berry Gordy started Motown Records in Detroit in 1959. By the end of the sixties, he had grown it into one of the most successful music enterprises in the world. He had single-handily launched the careers of Smokey Robinson, The Jackson 5, and Diana Ross, among many others. Gordy called Motown "The Sound of Young America." He offered Sammy a two-album deal. The world's hottest producer and the world's greatest entertainer together. They called a press conference and announced the deal.

Motown Records released the album *Something for Everyone* in the spring of 1970. It contained nothing for anyone. Sammy had fallen in love with the band Blood, Sweat & Tears and included three of their songs. He recorded "In the Ghetto," which had been a hit for Elvis. The album cover was beyond absurd: Sammy dressed in a white robe holding a bust of Beethoven and surrounded by a gaggle of scantily clad women. The singles all failed to gain any traction and the album was panned by critics. The label executives complained that Sammy just didn't have the Motown sound.

Sammy agreed. "You know, I'm not a Motown singer. I can do it, but I'm not comfortable," he explained to Sy Marsh.

There was still a contract for another album and Sammy went back to the Motown studios. Gordy had tasked Marvin Gaye with writing material for Sammy, but Gaye's burgeoning cocaine problem got in the way. The second attempt at making a Motown album went worse than the first. By the end of the second recording session, everyone knew this experiment wasn't working. Motown delayed the release of the first single. Then they pushed it back again.

"Berry, when the fuck you going to put out our records?" Marsh asked, barging into Gordy's office.

"I got a problem. Our salespeople say Sammy doesn't have the Motown sound," Gordy responded.

"Fuck the Motown sound. What about the Sammy sound?" Marsh shot back, growing increasingly angry. "I want the masters back," he said as he stormed out.

It was the kind of music-business power play that rarely works, and Marsh was as surprised as anybody when Gordy sent the tapes to his Hollywood office. "You must have caught that nigger in bed fucking somebody," Sammy joked to Marsh the day the recordings arrived.[6]

Marsh still believed Sammy could have another hit record. He just needed to find the right label and producer.

Mike Curb was born in Savannah, Georgia, but grew up in Compton, California. His father was an FBI agent. Curb, who is white, became profoundly influenced by the African American artists of the time. He dropped out of college at nineteen after having some success in writing advertising jingles. He took the royalties and started Curb Records. A few years later at age twenty-five, he merged his label with MGM Records. He called his house band the Mike Curb Congregation and they began recording their own material as well as producing other artists.

The Congregation cut an Anthony Newley–Leslie Bricusse song titled "The Candy Man." The song had been written for the film *Willie Wonka & the Chocolate Factory*. Curb thought the song was dynamite, but the Congregation's version went nowhere on the radio.

The Mike Curb Congregation was booked at Caesars Palace in Las Vegas, opening for Sammy. Curb cajoled Sammy to cut the tune. Sammy had done plenty of the legendary songwriting team's songs before, but he felt this one was too much fluff. It was almost a children's song, he thought. He was a swinging cat on the scene, not a babysitter. By his own admission he was an absent father who barely saw his own children. How could he ever do this song? "I'm going to sing to kids? Like Julie Andrews? Who's gonna buy this? It's stupid."[7]

Curb was convincing, though. He brought up Sammy's Achilles heel, Frank Sinatra. "You remember 'High Hopes' with Sinatra? That was Sinatra singing with kids. Sinatra did a fun song like that. Why don't you do a fun song?"[8]

Curb's coaxing and Sy Marsh reminding him of the money at stake led Sammy to Curb's studio on the corner of Fairfax and Melrose in LA. He was handed a lyric sheet and he went into the booth. One take and then he was gone.

The album *Sammy Davis Jr. Now* was released and the lead track shot up the charts. "The Candy Man" hit number one, Sammy's first record to do so. Sammy called it "incredible, absurd, ridiculous," saying it was "the one record in my life that I least expected...." He embraced it as only Sammy could, and began performing the song with a pail of candies he would toss to the audience as he sang.[9]

Sammy entered the 1970s at the top of his game in many ways. For three decades he had adapted to the times and maintained a presence in the American consciousness. The dynamic kid in the middle of the Trio in the '40s was succeeded by the eager, talented young star of the '50s. In the early '60s the Rat Pack shtick embodied the postwar economic-boom ethos

28. My Own Worst Nightmare

and made him a household name. By the late '60s he had morphed into a socially conscious soul brother. The 1970s seemed wide open.

Hollywood roles were still few and far between. But he had a hit record now and had long sold out nightclubs across the country. He earned six figures for his engagements in Las Vegas. By the late sixties and into the seventies he regularly guest-starred on TV shows like *Batman*, *I Dream of Jeannie*, and many others. But he had become so well known that most times he played himself. Sammy Davis, Jr., was as famous as anyone could possibly hope to be. He had achieved a level of success unimaginable in the vaudeville days of his youth.

In 1971, Altovise came running into their bedroom on Summit Ridge Drive and woke Sammy up.

"The White House is calling!"[10]

29

"Folkies born in a new age"

As the 1960s faded away, Jerry Jeff Walker was riding high. He had a hit song and a record deal. He had performed all over the country and on national television with appearances on *The Merv Griffin Show* and *The Dick Cavett Show*. Even his hometown newspaper took note: "Ron, or Jerry Jeff Walker as he is known in theatrical circuits, was an outstanding basketball player for the Yellowjackets."[1]

Back in Miami as the new decade dawned, Jerry Jeff traded his motorcycle for a 1947 Packard and fell in with a wild-eyed hippie named Murphy. Despite his newest record's slow sales, Jerry Jeff's booking prospects increased. He and Murphy would crash at her place in Coconut Grove so he could fly to gigs from Miami. When there were no gigs, the two would take off in the Packard for Key West. On one of those trips they brought with them a young songwriter from Nashville named Jimmy Buffett.

Key West in the early '70s was still a sleepy town of writers and smugglers. In addition to its literary history with Hemingway and Tennessee Williams, younger writers like Jim Harrison and Thomas McGuane were calling it home. Hunter Thompson would spend time there in the '70s. Smuggling was an unofficial city business, with marijuana unloaded on public docks along with the day's shrimp and oysters. But "it was not a music town," Jerry Jeff would say. "It was full of people who specialized in screwing off and were tempting me to do the same." He knew he needed a change of pace, but Key West kept luring him back and getting him in trouble. He was arrested for another DUI but paid a lawyer, who happened to be the son of a local judge, five hundred dollars to make the charge disappear. That is how Key West worked back then.

He was getting word from around town that he should probably leave. "They knew I wasn't a smuggler, but they also knew I was trouble," he would write. Tom McGuane told him one night, "Man, don't waste your talents like this ... maybe Key West just doesn't work for you."

Jerry Jeff said he "didn't feel like I was going anywhere unique." He

29. "Folkies born in a new age"

wanted a band. But not like Circus Maximus. And not like the studio guys that the record company sent to him to play on his records. "I wanted a bunch of guys who would let the rough side drag," he said. He was not finding that in Key West.

On his thirtieth birthday he was drinking in a bar with his guitar at his feet. He called it "a real smugglers hangout, full of lowlifes." Trouble was brewing in his mind. He wasn't happy and he needed a change, but he didn't know how. A woman played "Happy Birthday" in German on the bar jukebox to try and cheer him up. It didn't work. In a flare of dramatics Jerry Jeff picked up his guitar and smashed it on the bar. He left the pieces strewn across the bar as he walked out, got in the Packard, and drove to the airport. He bought a ticket to Houston, where he rented a car and drove to Austin. It had rained during the entire flight from Miami to Houston. As he broke past the city limits and headed west, the sun came out, blue skies the whole drive to Austin. It was a good omen, he thought.

He arrived back in Austin and immediately found old friends and made new ones. "Your problem is you are too well-liked," his grandmother used to tell him.

In 1971 the Texas Legislature approved sales of liquor by the drink. This led to more bars and more live music, which in turn led to more musicians coming to Austin. Willie Nelson and Michael Martin Murphey were both back in town and recording. "The Live Music Capital of the World" is how the Chamber of Commerce currently sells the city. In the early '70s that idea was being born.

Jerry Jeff remembered his early days in town this way:

> Long hair and cowboy hats, rockers gobbling acid bumping into freaks bumping into redneck bands. Country fiddlers in backroad honky-tonks, working cowboys playing Bob Wills swing, folkies born in a new age. All living in Austin, smoking plentiful Mexican weed and having a good time.

Jerry Jeff found himself playing with a regular band around Austin. Bob Livingston, aka Cosmic Bob, and Gary P. Nunn led a rotating cast who excelled at "letting the rough side drag." The success of "Mr. Bojangles" landed Jerry Jeff a three-album record deal with MCA. On the weekends he began driving out into the Hill Country to relax. He felt he had found what he needed. "For the first time since I hitchhiked out of Oneonta, I was putting down roots, in my own restless way."[2]

PART 4

30

"Like some song you can't unlearn"

Jerry Jeff Walker was in New York City in mid-1972 mixing his first record for MCA when he passed by Town Hall. Parked on the sidewalk outside the iconic New York venue was a truck, cables running out of it and into a window. "Dale Ashby and Father Sound Recording" a sign on the truck read. Jerry Jeff knocked on the door.

"Are you recording something?" he asked.

"Yes, doing a symphony here tonight," replied Dale Ashby.

"Can you drive this studio to Texas?" Jerry Jeff was about to make another impulsive career move.

"Sure," Ashby said.

"Luckenbach, Texas?" Jerry Jeff asked specifically.

"If it's on a map, we will get there," Ashby assured him.

Jerry Jeff walked into his manager Michael Brovsky's office and tossed him Dale Ashby's business card. His next album was going to be live. Recorded at an abandoned dancehall in an old Texas ghost town known as Luckenbach.

"Oh, and there is no electricity in Luckenbach. Well, there's electricity but when you open the beer cooler all the lights flicker," he told Brovsky as he left him to figure out the details.[1]

The State of Texas no longer erects signs pointing the way to Luckenbach. Tourists steal them as fast as they go up. But it isn't that hard to find once you leave the sprawl of Austin behind. The town was a Comanche trading post when Albert Luckenbach settled there in 1849. A few years later, he moved his family about fifteen miles up the road to a town that became known as Albert. But the post office he helped open in Luckenbach would remain, and by the turn of the century the town was home to about five hundred people. In the 1960s, Lyndon Johnson's ranch, known as the "Texas White House," sat eleven miles away. But Luckenbach sat empty. Various economic factors had made the town's population dwindle. The only buildings left standing were the old post office and a late-nineteenth-century dancehall, not used in years.

Then Hondo Crouch happened upon the place. Hondo was a true Texas original. A sheep rancher and poet, he gave out business cards that read "Hondo Crouch—Imagineer—Authorized Distributor."[2] Hondo went to the University of Texas in the 1930s and was an All-American swimmer. In the early '40s he met Shatzie Stieler and in 1943 they married. She was the daughter of a prominent rancher and Republican politician. Adolf Stieler was a state delegate to the Republican National Convention five times as well as a personal friend of Dwight Eisenhower. He was one of the largest landowners in the Texas Hill Country and was named "Goat King of the World" by *Life* magazine in 1945.[3]

Hondo took to the family trade well enough and in time prospered as a Hill Country sheep farmer himself. He gained a reputation as a gregarious eccentric unconcerned with the goings-on of the outside world. He once ran into an old classmate from college, John Connally, at a UT football game.

"Hondo! I haven't seen you in years! What are you doing now?" Connally asked.

"Oh, I'm still herdin' goats up in the hills, what are you doing now?" Hondo replied.

At the time John Connally was the governor of Texas. It was Hondo's world, other people just lived in it. In 1970, he and Shatzie spent thirty thousand dollars and bought Luckenbach.[4]

Hondo built a makeshift bar at one end of the dancehall and took on a partner to bartend. They sold thirty-five-cent beer and it became a popular place to spend a weekend afternoon. It catered to a mix of locals and young Austinites fleeing the city. And it became a gathering spot for the aspiring songwriters flooding Austin in the early '70s. People strummed guitars and swapped songs under the trees. Local farmers with distinctive Tex–German accents and Mexican laborers drank beer and told stories. All the while, "Hondo whittled and bullcrastinated about deer huntin and the moon," Jerry Jeff said.

Jerry Jeff first met Hondo in the mid-sixties at the 11th Door, a music club in Austin. Hondo's son-in-law was an aspiring folk singer as well and was on the bill. By the end of the night Hondo had stolen the show, singing Mexican love songs and telling stories. "Doin' Hondo," as Jerry Jeff would say. He added, "I've never been able to figure out if Hondo gets on stage or the stage gets under him." He was immediately drawn to Hondo's energy. "Being a lover of dreamers, drunks, and desperados (Hondo embodies the good qualities of all three), I made sure over the following years to ramble through Hondo's existence at least once a year," Jerry Jeff wrote of his friend.[5]

30. "Like some song you can't unlearn"

Back living in Austin, Jerry Jeff started making the trip out to Luckenbach to get away from it all when he wasn't on the road. He would pick Hondo up at his ranch and Hondo would drive Jerry Jeff's new Cadillac along the back-country roads while Jerry Jeff sat in the front seat, feet on the dash, picking guitar. He came to idolize the old man, with his unique perspective on life.

Jerry Jeff showed up in Luckenbach with Dale Ashby and his mobile studio in late summer 1973. They brought haybales into the dancehall to help with the acoustics. Microphones were set up all around the room. Jerry Jeff wanted to record live. He showed the band his songs and the chord changes and then he just wanted to jam. See what came out. What came out was a masterpiece that would shape the coming decade of "outlaw country music" and become a cult classic.

He called the album *Viva Terlingua* after a poster for a chili contest Hondo had judged in the town of Terlingua. It sold 60,000 copies in the state of Texas alone on its way to selling a half million internationally. Jerry Jeff was thirty-two years old. He had written a hit song for others and now he had a hit of his own.

One night in 1974, Jerry Jeff found himself at a party in Austin at the home of a woman named Susan Streit. He was carrying around the rough mixes of his new album, *Walker's Collectibles*. Susan was playing the Rolling Stones on the stereo and Jerry Jeff would sneak up and change the music to his new record when she wasn't looking. Eventually they met at the turntable.

"Are you the asshole who keeps changing my records?" Susan asked indignantly.

Jerry Jeff confessed, saying this was going to be his new record and he wanted to see how it sounded through different stereo systems.

"What do you mean? You actually carry your own music when you come to a party at someone else's house?" she replied.

Jerry Jeff was taken aback and immediately fell in love. He apologized and offered to take her to dinner to make up for it.

Susan Streit was the polar opposite of Jerry Jeff Walker in many ways. She was born to a wealthy, conservative West Texas family. She had graduated from the University of Texas and gone to work in the state legislature for legendary Texas congressman Charlie Wilson, a man who would eventually be played by Tom Hanks in a Hollywood film about an episode in his political career. "She wore dressy clothes, and I wore jeans.... She worked days and I worked nights," Jerry Jeff wrote of the early days of their relationship.

Yet the pair became inseparable. On a late fall evening in 1974, the two were cruising in Jerry Jeff's Cadillac convertible. As they pulled into the gravel driveway of his Austin home, he turned to her and said, "Well, I guess we ought to get married." Susan looked at him. "OK," she replied.

Jerry Jeff exploded. "Hell, I thought you were smarter than that!" he screamed as he got out. He grabbed a tire iron, smashed the headlights of his own car and walked off toward the house. Susan laughed off the incident as just another one of Jerry Jeff's antics. They were married a few weeks later on December 12, 1974, in Luckenbach.

The checks got bigger. The venues got bigger. And so did the parties. Jerry Jeff wrote that he was "raising the pursuit of wildness and weirdness to a fine art." Booze had always flown freely around Jerry Jeff, but now the drugs got harder and more accessible. It was partly the times and partly his own insatiable need for new experiences, his general ardor for life.

Earlier that year he and the band had been booked on a package show in New Orleans with Willie Nelson and Jimmy Buffett. The governor of Louisiana, Edwin Edwards, wanted to meet Willie before the show. Jerry Jeff and Buffett were invited along "to be nice," Jerry Jeff said. He had been up all night drinking and doing cocaine with his old friends in the Quarter and forgot about the meeting until the phone rang in his hotel the next

Jerry Jeff Walker performing in the mid–1970s (Photofest).

morning. There was a patrol car downstairs waiting to take him to the Governor's Mansion, the man on the phone explained.

He and Susan got in with the officer and headed to the airport to pick up Willie first. When they arrived, Billy Cooper, one of Willie's entourage, explained that Willie wasn't going to make it. So, the three of them took off to the mansion. When they arrived, Buffett was waiting for them. When he saw the bedraggled trio coming up the steps, he laughed. "Tuck your shirts in and let me do the talking." Susan smiled and handed Buffett a gram of cocaine.

The governor politely received the two troubadours, Susan, and Billy, concealing his disappointment at Willie's absence. The foursome was so high on cocaine they would not have noticed anyway. They talked through most of the meal and barely ate. As the governor finished eating, he looked at them with a wry smile.

"Could I get you some coffee or dessert? Or Valium?"

Billy Cooper spoke up. "Now you're getting warm, Gov."[6]

Writer Larry L. King gained national attention when he wrote the Broadway hit *The Best Little Whorehouse in Texas* in 1978. He met Jerry Jeff sometime in the early '70s. Once when Jerry Jeff was playing in New York, he decided he would visit his buddy. After his show, Jerry Jeff and writer Bud Shrake took a limo to a "sedate cocktail party ... for delicate academicians and their wives" that King was hosting at Princeton University. Jerry Jeff "appeared very much unannounced, dressed like a buffalo hunter," and began taking the party's volume up a level. He mocked the highfalutin vibe, stepping on gowns and proclaiming his need for Lone Star beer. Eventually he tired of the show he was producing and King, eager to rid the Ivy League party of his outlaw acquaintances, offered his car to Jerry Jeff and his crew. King wrote that they took off "in a snowstorm, at supersonic speeds and in a rental car charged to my American Express. The car was found abandoned in midtown Manhattan, long on traffic tickets and short on operable parts. Jerry Jeff's explanation was that he couldn't remember being in a car that night."[7]

As the royalty checks continued to grow, Jerry Jeff decided he no longer wanted to charter a bus to travel. He chartered planes. He and the band flew to whatever city they were scheduled to perform at, rented a fleet of cars, and raced to the hotel. Jerry Jeff would always speed out onto the interstate first and take the lead, but often he had no idea where he was going. "He'd decide he was going the wrong way and suddenly do some kind of illegal turnaround, and you'd have four or five other cars trying to do the same turnaround. It was kind of funny, but we were just lucky we didn't get killed," band member Gary P. Nunn recalled in 2004.

"You know, out of the three or four years that we played with him, I can't remember ever seeing him in bed. We might catch him napping on the plane, but he never slept," Nunn marveled about their mid-seventies escapades.[8]

The party rolled on. Jerry Jeff's live shows gained a reputation. Would he show up? How drunk or high on coke would he be? A *New York Times* article that portrayed him as more of a drunk than an artist resulted in a tearful phone call from his mother.

Ron Crosby was legally Jerry Jeff Walker, but now he began to acquire new nicknames as well: Scamp Walker, Jacky Jack Double Trouble, and Dr. Snowflake. He allegedly relieved himself in a beer pitcher on stage. He reportedly showed up and played a show in his underwear. Jerry Jeff would always insist they were his swim trunks, that he had simply been at the pool before the show.

A writer turned up at his Austin home and found a TV floating in the swimming pool. Why was it there, he asked? "Sonofabitch never would sink," Jerry Jeff replied. He had tossed it in the pool when he felt it was distracting him from writing.[9]

He played the 1976 Super Bowl pre-party for the Dallas Cowboys in Miami. Bill Murray joined him onstage and they sang classic rock songs from the fifties. A few weeks later, annoyed at the flight time from Atlanta to Chattanooga, he opted instead to purchase a 1954 Lincoln and drive himself the hundred-plus miles. He got lost and missed his slot opening for Willie Nelson. The promoter was furious. He told security to not let Walker in if he showed up. Jerry Jeff did show halfway through Willie's set. He somehow made it through security, got on stage and jammed with Willie and the band. When the show ended, the promoter had him arrested for trespassing. He turned thirty-four the next morning in a Chattanooga jail.

In 1977, Jerry Jeff returned to Luckenbach to record more live material. Hondo read his poem "Luckenbach Moon" on the front porch of the general store over Jerry Jeff's subtle guitar picking while Dale Ashby's truck captured it all. Some songs were recorded in the old dancehall the same way they had done in '73. These would be packaged on a double album with material Ashby had recorded over Jerry Jeff's last few years of touring.

That fall Jerry Jeff got word that Hondo had died of a heart attack. "I was stunned and confused. I got drunk for a week and missed the funeral. Truth is, I didn't want to go anyway. That was to admit that his death was real," he wrote in his autobiography.

Jerry Jeff brought poet Charles John Quarto to a studio in Austin and included some of his work on the new double album, which he titled *A Man Must Carry On*.

30. "Like some song you can't unlearn"

Hondo, he took his time, which took his turn
He was so easy to remember
Like some song you can't unlearn....¹⁰

Jerry Jeff would not return to Luckenbach for a decade.

Jerry Jeff Walker made nine albums in six years. Between 1972 and 1978 he performed over two hundred dates a year. "I didn't just burn the candle at both ends, I was also finding new ends to light. Somebody somewhere may one day cram more living into a few years. But I doubt it," he wrote about the era.

In late 1977 Susan found out she was pregnant. She left the touring party. Jerry Jeff plowed on. A new record deal with Elektra found him flush with money and in Miami to record. It was "an area awash with cocaine. And we were in a crash and burn frame of mind," he said. The resulting album was not his best work.

In April 1978, his daughter was born. Susan kicked him out. "The druggies and hangers-on weren't welcome at the house" anymore, he said. "And I qualified on at least one of those counts." He took to sleeping in his car when not on the road playing shows.

Then the lawsuits came. American Express sued him for $90,000 in unpaid bills. "We had been flying everyone first class, racking up massive hotel bills.... Once we lost a rental car, just flat forgot about it.... I was spinning my wheels. The faster the money came in, the faster it went out." The IRS came calling as well. They said he had

Jerry Jeff Walker promotional photograph, 1978 (Photofest).

massively underpaid his last four years of taxes. He knew things had to change; he wanted to change. The death of Hondo and the birth of his first child had galvanized a sense of mortality in him.

Jerry Jeff recorded his last contractually obligated album for Elektra and gave it the ironic title of *Too Old to Change*. The day after the recording session was over, he went cold turkey. "I quit drugs, whiskey, cigarettes, and red meat. I went home to Susan, and I slept."[11]

31

"They're not colorblind"

On July 1, 1971, Sammy Davis, Jr., and an entourage of six were greeted by President Nixon as they walked into the Oval Office.

"Well, how are you? Good to see you again. All your, ah, your team here, eh?" Nixon began as White House photographers snapped photos for posterity and the wire services.

Nixon smiled and joked, "We want to record this in living color! Not in black and white, you know what I mean?" On the tapes, you hear belly laughs from Davis and his crew. "You know, I saw you before you were born, you know! Remember, Chicago. The Soft Shoe, a speakeasy there.... Do you still got the energy to do all that?" Nixon says, referring to the 1954 performance of the Will Mastin Trio.

"No, no," Davis responds in a rare display of humility. It had actually been at the Copa in New York where the then vice president had first seen him perform. More small talk ensues before Nixon turns to sports.

"Any of you golfers?" he asks.

"I am," Davis responds.

"You play out there with Dean Martin and that whole bunch. I bet you play Bel-Air."

"No, I don't, I'm afraid, sir, they're not colorblind," Davis responded, informing the apparently unaware president that his Southern California golf course of choice was a segregated institution.

"No?" says Nixon.

"I can't get into Bel-Air," Sammy says as members of his entourage nervously laugh. "I'd like to, but I can't play that course. I usually play Hillcrest."

"Hillcrest? It's hard to get into there, too."[1]

Richard Nixon's record on civil rights is the most puzzling of his complicated legacy. A prominent scholarly work on the subject is subtitled "Explaining an Enigma."[2] Much has been made of Nixon's "Southern strategy" in the election of 1968. No doubt, the support of Strom Thurmond was crucial in securing the Republican nomination and keeping

Wallace voters in check in the general election. Nixon's rhetoric has rightly been called "Wallace without the accent." "He was never as blatant as George Wallace or Lester Maddox, but he delivered a clear message that was hard to miss," John Ehrlichman said. "Nods and winks," one legal scholar called it.

When Nixon entered office, only 186,000 out of roughly three million African American children in the South attended integrated schools despite the Supreme Court's 1954 decision ordering desegregation. But by the end of 1970, the number was almost two million. In Nixon's first term the amount of money available for civil rights programs increased from $75 million to $2.6 billion. The money greased the wheels for dealing with intransigent Southerners. For a time, public schools in the South were more integrated than those in the North. "Make it happen, but don't make it seem like Appomattox," was how speechwriter William Safire saw Nixon's position.

Scholars of the subject largely agree it worked. Under Nixon's leadership, lawsuits and the threat of denying federal aid to noncompliant districts "broke white Southern resistance" in relatively short order.[3]

"No man can be fully free while his neighbor is not. To go forward at all is to go forward together. This means black and white together, as one nation, not two. The laws have caught up with our conscience. What remains is to give life to what is in the law," Nixon proclaimed on his cold and rainy inauguration day.[4] Yet, when one studies Nixon and civil rights, one can't help but feel there are three sides to the coin.

Later that year he told a senator from Georgia that on segregation he planned to "do what is legally required, but not to be evangelic."

Nixon endorsed the Philadelphia Plan that made integration of the workforce a central prerequisite to obtaining federal contracts. A cynical observer might say Nixon saw it as an opportunity to drive a wedge between minorities and labor unions, both key Democratic voting blocks. And that may be true. But the end result was decades of federal policy promoting desegregation in some of the most segregated industries in America.

Nixon's first two nominees to fill vacancies on the Supreme Court were Southerners who had promoted segregation. Both were rejected by Congress. Nixon often told aides he loathed the idea of being thought of as racist. "My feelings on race, as you know, are if anything ultra-liberal," he wrote in a memo.

And yet Richard Nixon left behind hours of taped conversations that would say otherwise. Most of his ire was directed at Jews and media elites whom he felt looked down on men like him. He did his fair share of looking down as well, though. In a rambling Oval Office conversation with

Donald Rumsfeld, a future secretary of defense but at the time a young political appointee, Nixon summarized his feelings on African Americans by saying that "most of them basically are just out of the trees."[5]

Black America by and large did not trust Richard Nixon. In 1971 the newly formed Congressional Black Caucus boycotted his State of the Union address. They said he was stifling the racial progress of the previous years. During the 1968 campaign a reporter in Cleveland told Nixon, "Negros are a little afraid of you." While there were few African Americans appointed to key positions in his administration, there was Robert J. Brown.

Brown was born into poverty in North Carolina. In 1960 he founded the public-relations firm B&C Associates and built it into a million-dollar company. He was an early associate of Dr. King and became a major activist and fundraiser for the civil rights movement. He was among the people invited by Coretta Scott King to accompany her to Memphis the day after Dr. King's murder. By 1968 he began to feel that the Democratic Party was taking Black votes for granted. He thought that Johnson and Humphrey's policies leaned too much on welfare. He wanted to see federal investment in Black communities to help them achieve their own economic independence.

He was approached by some mutual acquaintances working for Nixon's campaign. They sold him hard on coming over to their side. "He identifies with the underprivileged and poor," they told him. "The Quakers believe we should help all people in need." They were laying it on thick; like Nixon, Brown had attended a Quaker school as a boy. With some reluctance Brown accepted a position as a paid consultant with the campaign.

He and Nixon grew to know each other during the campaign and when Nixon won, he offered Brown a job in the White House. He told Brown he would be his "point man" on issues relating to the Black community. He was given the title of "Special Assistant to the President."[6]

Barely two months into his administration, Nixon signed an executive order creating the Office of Minority Business Enterprise inside the Commerce Department. Brown served as the head of the organization and reported directly to the president. The aim was to promote lending to Black–owned businesses through government support of free-market mechanisms.

"We didn't need handouts; we needed access to capital," Brown wrote in his memoir.[7]

In 1970 Nixon created the National Advisory Council on Economic Opportunity. Every president has created commissions of the sort. Business leaders, academics, and celebrities all sharing ideas. Little normally comes out of them except photos of participants in the White House and resume lines about working with an administration. Nixon decided he wanted Sammy on the new council. He sent Bob Brown to Beverly Hills to cajole him.

Brown and Davis knew each other. They had worked together as major fundraisers for Martin Luther King, Jr., and SCLC. Brown met Sammy and Altovise at their new Summit Ridge Drive home.

"Sammy, the president has spoken highly of you and he wants your help with some of our programs," Brown opened his pitch.

Sammy later wrote that he was astounded. "Bob, I'm a Democrat and strongly associated with the Kennedys," he said.

"Understood. But don't close the door on Nixon. Use his power to accomplish the things you and I believe in," Brown responded. He went on to explain the administration's push to support Black capitalism and he let it be known that the outspoken football star Jim Brown had agreed to serve.[8]

Sammy Davis, Jr., and Richard Nixon in the Oval Office, July 1, 1971 (courtesy Richard Nixon Presidential Library and Museum).

31. "They're not colorblind"

Sammy later wrote about his skepticism; he called friends like Harry Belafonte for advice. He may have listened to their concerns about Nixon's policies but in the end, the child of vaudeville could not resist the idea of White House meetings and photo ops with the president.

He showed up in July 1971 in a brown suit and tie and Gucci briefcase. He wore a gold chain with a giant peace sign over his tie. Nixon signed a proclamation naming him to the council. The photograph made almost every paper in the country.

Despite their awkward golf-course small talk, Sammy was fascinated with Nixon. Sammy knew celebrity and Sammy knew money. But this was power. The last time Sammy had been at the White House, Kennedy's men had rushed him and his white wife to a side room to avoid the photographers. Now Nixon smiled for the camera, telling the world Sammy was part of his team.

The entourage left the room with presidential trinkets, and Sammy and Nixon sat down for a one-on-one. Nixon pontificated about the problems with American youth and said he thought Sammy could be part of the solution.

"Inspiring young people," he said. "You can go out and make an appearance and you say to them, 'Sammy Davis, Jr., says it,' it will really send them. It will turn them on. Whereas if they hear a preacher say it, maybe not; the teacher, maybe not; the judge, certainly it's too late."

"Ah yes," Davis responded.

Nixon continued with themes from his speeches and campaign, genuinely trying to sell Davis. "The elite in this country are practically the least capable of governing. I mean that. When you find what is happening to the children of the so-called better families."

"Yes," Davis chimed in.

"Believe me, that's where the real problem is. They should be leading; they should be standing up. But the fashionable thing for them is to, you know, go to pot, or worse."

Their conversation would continue for another twenty minutes, with the pair discussing Tolstoy and Willie Mays, among other topics. After Sammy left, Nixon can be heard on tape praising him to an aide.

"He was married to that Swedish girl for a while," Nixon says for no apparent reason as the labor secretary walks in.[9]

Sammy Davis left his Oval Office meeting convinced that all his peers in the civil rights movement were wrong about Nixon. He would tell the *New York Times* the following year, "There's an honesty about the man [that] I love."[10] He started flying in every month for council meetings. He loved carrying his briefcase around Washington, dropping by the Eisenhower Executive Office Building and hamming it up with Bob Brown.

Handshakes and hugs with some of the most prominent African American business leaders, men Davis called "the soul brothers" in a letter to Nixon.

In early 1972 singer Mahalia Jackson died. The White House staff reached out to Sammy to be Nixon's official emissary to the funeral. They sent a private plane to Las Vegas. Sammy flew to Chicago and sat next to Mayor Daley in the front row, representing the president of the United States. The air force flew him back to Vegas in time for his show that evening.

Sammy wrote Nixon on February 3, 1972, "Bob and I have had several meetings concerning the upcoming election. (Needless to say, if you want an old ex–Democrat, you've got him!)"[11]

Nixon did want Sammy's support in 1972. But first he had another mission for the ex–Democrat. He needed him in Vietnam.

32

"How did that happen?"

Sammy and his traveling crew of twenty-five left the Ambassador Hotel in Los Angeles and loaded onto an army transport plane in February 1972. Hawaii, Guam, and then Vietnam. They ate box lunches and TV dinners as they flew over the Pacific Ocean. "It was awful," remembered Shirley Rhodes, the wife of Sammy's bandleader, George Rhodes. Sammy had been all bluster and confidence after first accepting Nixon's request to entertain the troops; "wasn't a black cat ever [so] important that [he] went to Vietnam," he had oddly bragged to Sy Marsh. As they landed, Sammy was fidgety and nervous. "We were both scared," Altovise would recall years later.

There was good reason to be scared. America was in the waning days of the Vietnam War, and losing. Upon his return, Sammy wrote in a piece for *Ebony* magazine about an attack on an airbase that killed six American servicemen the day after his performance there. He wrote in his memoir of hearing gunfire and rocket shells at night as he tried to sleep.

The protest movements back home were starting to attract large numbers of former combat veterans. By and large, the public's appetite for the war had waned and they wanted out. Many active-duty soldiers on the ground in Indochina felt the same. They knew about the Pentagon Papers. They knew the war was a lost cause. As the futility of the war became more and more obvious to the average American GI, drug use skyrocketed. By the time Sammy showed up, the American army was rife with dissent and disillusionment.

Sammy spent ten days in Vietnam doing shows. In Danang the army built a stage and he performed for twenty thousand GIs. Other times he performed for as few as twenty-five soldiers at an airbase. He told jokes, danced and sang. He had brought along folk singer Lynn Kellogg to warm up the crowd. Comedian Timmie Rogers was part of the vaudeville-style traveling show as well.

In the middle of the show Sammy would single out his new wife, dressed in hot pants and an army shirt tied at her belly button to show maximum cleavage. His all-male audiences would whistle and holler as Altovise took her turn as the star she never was back home.

"That ain't my old lady, that's my wife, man. Don't let me come out here and have to cut somebody," Sammy joked, and the GIs laughed.[1]

Part of Sammy's mission in Vietnam was to investigate complaints by civil rights leaders that Black soldiers were being singled out for harsher punishment for drug offenses. Soldiers would score cocaine and weed when they were on leave in South Vietnamese cities. When caught, they were thrown into a makeshift military prison to detox.

Sammy walked into one of these detox centers during his tour of Vietnam and was treated with the same skepticism he had received from the Black Panthers back home.

"Hi, guys," he said as he flashed his show-business smile.

"Motherfucker, what are you doing here?"

Sammy explained he was there on a mission from the president himself. That he wanted to do some good, to try and help the situation.

"Bullshit. You are here to use us for a TV special. To do yourself some good," one GI responded.[2]

Sammy talked them down. He told them he could be in Vegas making a hundred grand a week. Eating steak and caviar. Driving in a brand-new rag-top Rolls-Royce. Instead, he was here, on the other side of the world, trying to help his Black brothers. There was no TV special being made from this trip. He wasn't Bob Hope, he explained. He had been in the army too. He knew how hard it had been, and he wanted to help.

The spiel worked. Soldiers began confiding in Sammy about their troubles. Sammy cautioned the GIs about drug use as Sy Marsh looked away to keep from laughing at the absurdity. Sammy loved cocaine and weed as much as anyone.

They asked him to contact loved ones back home for them. And when Sammy returned to the states, he personally called the mothers and fathers of the GIs he had spoken with. The GIs asked that Sammy get them ice cream. He said he would mention it to the top brass.

Sammy landed back in the U.S. feeling he had played the part superbly. To Sammy, the Vietnam trip had been another role to play. But this time it wasn't Hollywood's old guard he was trying to impress with his performance, it was the president of the United States. He wrote for *Ebony* magazine, "I can't discuss too much about my findings there, but I've already made my report to the President."[3] He thought it sounded right out of a movie. The Nixon White House agreed. An internal memo from Bob Brown predicted, "We can get some good mileage out of this one."[4]

In his meeting with Nixon, Sammy relayed some of the GIs' concerns. He said he did not think the men caught using drugs should be kept in barbed-wire enclosures with armed guards. They were just kids in a hard situation and drugs were their escape. When they came down from their high and found themselves in an American prison on foreign soil, their attitudes hardened. They needed help, not cages, Sammy pleaded. Nixon said he agreed; the barbed wire would come down.

They talked a while longer, Nixon fawning over the great job Sammy had done for the country. Sammy then made a pitch for Nixon to attend a dinner in Washington later that week being held by some top Black Republicans. No president had ever attended such an event. Nixon shied away from all Black events, due to a mixture of personal uncomfortableness and political calculation. He hedged, telling Sammy he would think about it.

"I have some close people delegated to attend. I respect the Negro Republicans. I know they influence the black voters...." Nixon trailed off and paused a moment. "Incidentally, is it OK to say 'black'?" he asked Sammy.

"Yes, Mr. President. We say 'black' now. 'Negro' and 'colored' are not in use."

Nixon wrote in bold letters on his yellow notepad. "Black is preferred, colored is not." He then looked up at Sammy. "How did that happen?"[5]

Later that week, Sammy served as the entertainment for the group of Black Republicans. Nixon had never committed to coming to the dinner and Sammy figured it was a lost cause. He rationalized it, saying the president was a busy man and if he could have made it, he would have. About an hour in, Bob Brown came and whispered in Sammy's ear. "The man is on his way over. You pulled off a coup," he informed Sammy hyperbolically.

Sammy was on stage when Nixon entered the hall. He walked right through the audience, shaking hands with the attendees. He reached the stage and took the podium. "Sammy told me I had to be here," he said to thunderous applause.[6] He gave a five-minute speech praising Sammy's work for the administration and his own policies to help the Black community and then he was gone, shaking hands all the way out. The dinner organizers were shocked. Nixon needed more from Sammy in the coming months; it was an election year, after all. Sammy didn't connect those dots, though. He was on top of the world; he had personally delivered the president.

As the evening wound down Sammy was introduced to Daniel "Chappie" James, the highest-ranking Black member of the military. Sammy asked the general if there was any way to get the troops in Vietnam some ice cream. James, a dour and serious man, stared blankly at the entertainer before walking away.

Nineteen seventy-two was arguably the height of Sammy Davis, Jr.'s, career, and not just from his newfound prominence in Washington, D.C.

Sammy had a gold record for the first time. "The Candy Man" had continued to climb the charts and had become a staple of Sammy's live shows. He also made one his most memorable appearances on TV.

Producer Norman Lear created a show in the early '70s that skewered American life. *All in the Family* centered around the stereotypical archetype of a Nixon voter, Archie Bunker. The veteran actor Carroll O'Connor was tapped to play Lear's creation and Archie Bunker soon became an American phenomenon. Archie took on all the controversial issues in American life with a thick New York accent and a no-nonsense blue-collar attitude. Feminism, abortion, homosexuality, race—nothing was off-limits. Archie became a hero to a certain, mostly white, demographic.

The show took place for the most part in the living room of the home Archie shared with his wife (whom he called a "dingbat"), his hippie daughter, and his son-in-law (whom he called "Meathead"). ABC passed on the show, but Lear eventually landed it as a midseason replacement on CBS. The show first aired in January 1971, and it came with a disclaimer:

> The program you are about to see is *All in The Family*. It seeks to throw a humorous spotlight on our frailties, prejudices, and concerns. By making them a source of laughter, we hope to show—in mature fashion—just how absurd they are.[7]

By summer, it was America's top-rated sitcom. "Archie Bunker for President" stickers began popping up on cars all over the country. In May 1971, Nixon watched an episode and he opined to John Ehrlichman as his secret taping system preserved his thoughts for history: "Archie is sitting here with his hippie son-in-law, married to the screwball daughter.... The son-in-law apparently goes both ways." What led Nixon to believe Meathead was bisexual is not immediately clear on the tape, but he goes into a lengthy dissertation on the ill effects of homosexuality:

> The point that I make is that, goddamn it, I do not think that you glorify on public television homosexuality. You don't glorify it, John, any more than you glorify, uh, whores.
> I don't want to see this country to go that way. You know what happened to the Greeks. Homosexuality destroyed them. Sure, Aristotle was a homo, we all know that, so was Socrates.

Socrates "never had the influence television had," Ehrlichman adds, to his boss's delight.[8]

Nixon was not a fan of the show, but Sammy was. While Nixon hated what he saw as the glorification of sexual liberation, Sammy loved the edgy, sarcastic take on race. He desperately wanted to be on the show. He lobbied Norman Lear for a part, but Lear could not envision a fictional role

32. "How did that happen?"

for Sammy. But Sammy was nothing if not persistent, and he eventually convinced Lear he should guest-star as himself.

The episode aired in February 1972 and begins as Archie informs his family about the famous passenger in his cab that day. They take turns guessing who it could be. They coax out of him that the famous man in question is Black. The son-in-law guesses Harry Belafonte. Archie responds that Belafonte "ain't Black, he's dipped in caramel."

They learn it is Sammy, that he left his briefcase in the back of Archie's cab and that he is going to stop by and pick it up on his way to the airport. Sammy arrives at the Bunker home and sits down for coffee. Archie tells Sammy it is an honor to have him there.

"I was just telling my family before you came in, Sammy Davis, Jr., is maybe the greatest credit to his race."

Sammy, smoking a cigarette, gives a wry smile. "Well, thank you very much, I'm sure you've done good for yours too."

The next ten minutes feature Archie making comments about race and Sammy giving whip-smart sarcastic responses that seem to go over Archie's head.

"Ya being colored, I know you had no choice in that. But what made you want to turn Jew?" Archie asks.

The studio audience howls in laughter as Sammy looks dumbfounded. Before he can answer, a neighbor at the door claims Archie's attention. Then Archie's daughter chimes in, "I'm sorry, Mr. Davis, sometimes my father says the wrong things."

"Yeah, I've noticed that."

"But he's not a bad guy, Mr. Davis. I mean, like, he'd never burn a cross on your lawn."

"No, but if he saw one burning, he's liable to toast a marshmallow on it."

Archie returns and there is talk of Sammy's last appearance on the *Tonight Show*, with Raquel Welch. Some jokes are made about whites and Blacks kissing on television, and Sammy sarcastically responds that there is a "kissing clause" in his contract.

Archie says he likes to consult the Bible on these things. "If God had meant us to be together, he'd have put us together. But look what he done? He put you over in Africa and he put the rest of us in all the white countries."

A bewildered Sammy stares at him as the audience roars with laughter.

"Well, you must have told him where we were, 'cause somebody came and got us."

As Sammy gets up to depart for the airport, he asks for a picture with his new friend Archie Bunker. On the count of three, as the picture snaps, Sammy plants a kiss on Archie's cheek. The studio audience laughs for over a minute; their response had to be cut short for the broadcast. Sammy smiles and walks out the door as Archie shrugs, "What the hell, he said it was in his contract."[9]

"Sammy's Visit" was the highest-rated half-hour episode in television history at that point. The kiss was an undeniable cultural touchstone; it got all of America talking. Blacks and whites did not kiss on network television in 1972. Men kissing men, even on the cheek, was even more taboo. Sammy's most thorough biographer wrote, "It wasn't just a kiss. It was the thunder hooves of history rolled up into a kiss."[10] The reaction was swift and harsh. The hate mail that piled up at CBS and Sammy's Hollywood office was staggering. Sammy's secretary and manager hid a lot of it from him. Norman Lear just shook his head, perplexed that the humorous spotlight he sought to shine on the country's frailties and prejudices was not coming through as absurdity to many Americans.

What Richard Nixon thought about Sammy's appearance on the show was not recorded for history. But Nixon was certainly not done with Sammy Davis, Jr. He called Mike Curb in the early summer of 1972. He asked if the Curb Congregation and Sammy would come perform in Miami that August for the Republican National Convention. Curb explained he was happy to, but that he did not manage Sammy. He added that his label was looking for a suitable venue to present Sammy with his first gold record. Miami during the convention might be perfect. He encouraged the president to call Sammy and invite him down.

Sammy was gleeful in his acceptance. Nixon arranged for him to fly to Miami on an oil executive's private plane. The second night of the convention, he sat in the private box of the first family. Sammy sported a tailor-made plaid suit with wide lapels, rings on each hand, and sat smoking cigarettes and laughing the night away with the Nixons, the embodiment of white America.

On August 22, the night before Nixon was formally renominated, Sammy performed at a youth rally at the Miami Beach Convention Center. The 26th Amendment had been ratified and the 1972 election was the first to include voters between the ages of 18 and 21. In the middle of the show, a phalanx of Secret Service agents began parting the crowd. Chants of "four more years" erupted. Nixon walked through the hall and toward the stage. He took the microphone and thanked the youth delegates for their support and then began to heap effusive praise on Davis. He talked about seeing Davis in the '50s in New York. He called him the greatest entertainer in the world. He then addressed the naysayers. A reporter had asked Sammy the

32. "How did that happen?"

Sammy Davis, Jr., and Richard Nixon on stage together at the Republican National Convention in Miami in 1972 (courtesy Richard Nixon Presidential Library and Museum).

night before about critics who said he had sold out by supporting Nixon. Nixon decided to answer the reporter's question for Davis.

"You aren't going to buy Sammy Davis by inviting him to the White House. You buy him by doing something for America."[11]

Standing behind and to the left of the president, Sammy was moved. All those years of segregated hotels and back-door entrances. Moving step by step up the ladder and still playing second fiddle to Frank and the gang. The Kennedys and their backstabbing two-faced political posturing, a greivance he shared with Nixon. It all came flooding back. Sammy was overcome with emotion as he stepped up and gave Nixon a bear hug from behind. Sammy looked childlike in his appreciation and deepfelt admiration for the president. Nixon's face was a series of pained contortions. It came from behind, and so he was genuinely surprised to feel Sammy's embrace. But it is as if in those five seconds every reaction from every constituency raced through Nixon's mind as he heard the click of a thousand camera shutters.

The hug became a front-page headline and once again Sammy Davis, Jr., was the talk of America. First the kiss and now the hug. The thunder hooves of history were moving faster and faster.

33

What Were They Doing?

W. Mark Felt was hired by the FBI in the 1940s and he rose steadily through the ranks. He worked as a spy for the agency during World War II and was special agent in charge of investigating the Las Vegas Mob in the '50s and '60s. By 1971, Felt had been promoted to deputy assistant director. When J. Edgar Hoover died in May of 1972, his deputy and possible lover, Clyde Tolson, resigned his position as the number two, inherited Hoover's estate, and retired. This made Felt next in line to become director and he thought the job was his. But according to Felt, "twenty-six hours and ten minutes after he announced Hoover's death," Richard Nixon appointed an old friend, L. Patrick Gray, as acting director. Felt was not happy. "I was resentful an outsider was taking over," he wrote later.

Gray was a Nixon man. He had left the navy in 1960 to work on Nixon's campaign and most recently had been assistant attorney general of the Civil Division in the Department of Justice. Acting director of the FBI was a big promotion. But Gray was not quite up for the job, telling Felt, "I'm expecting you to run day-to-day operations.... I will not be able to handle much paperwork." Gray would be the director and embrace the perks of the job, but Felt would do the work.

Six weeks into this arrangement, on Saturday June 17, the FBI night supervisor in Washington called Felt at home. He had something to report he thought was quite serious. A few hours before, five men wearing business suits and rubber gloves had been arrested at the Democratic National Committee headquarters inside the Watergate office complex. They had on them hundreds of dollars in cash as well as photographic and wiretapping equipment.

"What in the world were they doing?" Felt asked incredulously.[1]

For the next two and half years, all of America would be asking much the same question.

Richard Nixon was an ends-justify-the-means kind of guy. From Helen Gahagan Douglas to Alger Hiss to Anna Chennault to Cambodia, it was part of his base understanding of how politics worked. By 1971, Nixon was growing increasingly paranoid and his Plumbers were being tasked with more and more operations of dubious legality. G. Gordon Liddy was a forty-one-year-old ex–army officer with a penchant for Nazi regalia. Howard Hunt, fifty-three, was a former CIA agent with the botched Bay of Pigs invasion on his resume. They ran the Plumbers with money funneled through the Committee to Re-elect the President, an organization that would be remembered in history with the unfortunate acronym CREEP.

The Plumbers stayed busy as the 1972 campaign got underway, but they didn't make much progress. As George McGovern became the Democratic front runner, they attempted to bug his headquarters, to no avail. Liddy cased the building and even shot out a streetlight to create better conditions for a break-in. But four different times they tried and failed to gain access and install listening devices. Liddy and Hunt were under pressure to produce results. They had a quarter-million-dollar budget from CREEP and nothing to show for it. As the summer began, they set their sights on the Watergate offices of the DNC.

Hunt recruited James McCord, an old friend from the CIA who was serving as security chief for CREEP, to lead the operation. They then enlisted four men who would come to be known as "the Cubans." The Castro–hating exiles were eager to help when they were told they would be uncovering evidence that Castro was surreptitiously funding the Democrats. On May 28 McCord and the four Cubans succeeded in gaining access to the office, but the bugs they planted on the telephones failed to work. And so, on June 17 they went back to fix their mistake by installing a microphone in the smoke detector.

The five men carefully picked locks and put duct tape over latches as they made their way through the building. It was supposed to make for a quicker escape, but the taped-over locks made security guard Frank Wills suspicious and he called the D.C. police. Plainclothes detectives showed up and followed the trail of duct-taped doors to the offices of the DNC, where they surprised and arrested the five men. Liddy and Hunt listened to the whole thing from their command post in the Watergate. They fled, leaving mountains of evidence behind. The D.C. cops immediately grasped the seriousness of the situation and called the FBI.[2]

Richard Nixon was on vacation the weekend of the burglary. He did not know about it ahead of time, but he did know what the Plumbers were up to in general. And as the story broke and the press began asking questions, Nixon was captured on tape three days after the break-in scheming how to sweep it under the rug. He called it "containment." Under the American legal code, it is called obstruction of justice.

Hush money was approved. The Cubans were fanatics, scared that McGovern would ally with Castro. They would ask for mercy from the court. Apologize for their passion and patriotism. As first-time offenders they would get off easy. And after a reasonable interval could expect presidential clemency. This was the plan that first Monday when the White House press secretary said he would have no comment "on a third-rate burglary attempt."

The plan soon met logistical roadblocks. Lawrence O'Brien, a Kennedy confidant and chair of the DNC whose personal office had been breached, was lobbing attacks in the press. He thought the break-in was clearly an inside job exposing "the ugliest questions about the integrity of the political process." Quick guilty pleas and requests for mercy would almost guarantee a civil suit from O'Brien and the Democrats. A civil suit could result in embarrassing depositions and the need for top Nixon aides to perjure themselves.

To complicate matters, the FBI's new acting director was on a mission to get to the bottom of the story. Gray was a longtime Nixon confidant, and he was going to see to it that this amateur larceny would not be allowed to embarrass the president. As part of his investigation Gray called the director of the CIA, Richard Helms, and noted how many ex–CIA people seemed to be involved in this troublesome problem. Helms denied any agency involvement, but Gray was suspicious; of course they would deny it. He floated his idea to campaign chair John Mitchell, who took it to White House counsel John Dean. A lightbulb flickered in their minds and they presented a plan to Nixon.

This was a black-bag CIA job, off the books, they said. It was aimed at containing fallout from the Bay of Pigs invasion, which Howard Hunt had been involved in. They would claim to the FBI that O'Brien had secret files that would embarrass the CIA and they were fearful he would release them. Nixon ran through scenarios in their taped brainstorming session: "Just say this is a comedy of errors, without getting into it: 'The president believes this is going to open the whole Bay of Pigs thing again.'" He ended the meeting with an emphatic instruction: "Call the FBI … don't go any further into this case, period!"

Meanwhile at CREEP, Liddy, Hunt, Mitchell, and others began shredding documents as fast as they could. Gray would eventually acquiesce to the president's suggestions and get in on the game too, burning files that implicated the Plumbers with his Christmas trash later that year. Within weeks of the break-in, a half dozen of Nixon's top aides and lieutenants were involved in a massive cover-up.

And yet it was almost certainly unnecessary. The press by and large did not give the Watergate story much oxygen in the early days. The D.C. police released statements early in the investigation insinuating that it was unlikely the burglary was planned from "up high, because it was bungled

33. What Were They Doing?

too badly to have been the case." At a June 29 televised press conference, Nixon's first in thirteen months, no one asked about Watergate. As the fall rolled around and the 1972 election campaign kicked into high gear, there were lingering questions, but the cover-up was working quite well.[3]

What Nixon and his team did not know was that the number two man at the FBI, Mark Felt, had befriended a young *Washington Post* reporter some years earlier. The reporter, Bob Woodward, had stayed in touch with Felt, seeking a mentor of sorts for coping with life in the hectic and competitive world of Washington. Felt, as the number two, saw all the files the bureau gathered on the "third-rate burglary." He realized there was a cover-up afoot and he saw that his boss was involved. He began meeting Woodward late at night in an underground parking garage in Virginia, just across the Potomac River. He would confirm or deny gossip Woodward had heard. Felt pointed Woodward to the right path without ever handing him classified documents. Woodward told his editors about his contact, and some started jokingly referring to the mystery man as Deep Throat, after the currently popular pornographic movie.[4]

34

"As far uptown as I'm ever going to get"

"Why? Why?" Eartha Kitt screamed at Sammy in the airport. She had seen him on the plane and kept her composure, but when she saw him again in the terminal she exploded.

"Did you have to kiss him?" she screamed as passing travelers gawked at the feuding celebrities.

Sammy tried to explain his reasoning. He brought up how Nixon was doing positive things for Blacks. He talked about the Office of Minority Business Enterprise and Black capitalism. Kitt's voice rose in anger as the subject turned from TV to politics. How could he not see what Nixon was really up to? She stormed off and left Sammy embarrassed and confused.[1]

In the fall of 1972, despite a slow drip of press reports about corruption and illegal activity, Richard Nixon won a second term as president of the United States in the largest landslide in American history to that point. The Democratic coalition of the New Deal era was officially dead. The party fissures over civil rights and Vietnam, combined with Nixon's effective use of innuendo to court segregationist Democrats, realigned the geographic center of American politics for the next fifty years. Archie Bunker's America had spoken loud and clear.

Every month and sometimes twice a month, Nixon held an "Evening at the White House." The events brought dignitaries, cabinet officials, members of Congress, and political contributors together. They were held in the East Room and often featured some of America's most popular entertainers. In early 1972, as the Pentagon Papers were revealing the futility of the Vietnam War in precise detail, the Ray Conniff Singers were invited to perform in celebration of *Reader's Digest*'s fiftieth anniversary. DeWitt and Lila Acheson Wallace, the magazine's founders, were longtime Nixon supporters.

Nixon, serving as master of ceremonies, told the assembled guests, "If the music is square, it's because I like it that way!"[2] The Ray Conniff Singers were an incredibly popular group in 1972, but they were not the critics' darling. A twenty-first-century critic would call the group "essentially a cover band for elevator music." Conniff led the twenty-five-member male and female choral group backed by a twelve-piece band. Carole Feraci was a Canadian singer who had been hired by Conniff just two weeks prior to the White House gig. In the moments before the band was to begin, she stepped to the microphone and unfurled a homemade bandanna that read, "Stop the Killing." She stared right at the president in the front row and spoke in a calm, collected voice.

"Mr. President, stop the bombing of human beings, animals and vegetation. You go to church on Sunday and pray to Jesus Christ. If Jesus Christ were in this room tonight, you would not dare drop another bomb...."

When she finished, an uncomfortable silence hung in the air. The bassist hit two awkward notes. Ray Conniff, not knowing what else to do, clapped his hands, counted to four and began playing "Ma! He's Making Eyes at Me." When the song was over Conniff apologized for Feraci's outburst as members of the crowd shouted to throw her out. Which Conniff then did. Feraci was questioned by the Secret Service, escorted to the White House gates and told never to return.[3]

There was no worry about protests on March 3, 1973, with Sammy coming to perform. The evening was billed as a salute to the Apollo 17 astronauts who had just returned to the earthly realm after a twelve-day space flight and a little under twenty-four hours on the surface of the Moon. As of the early twenty-first century, they are the last humans to have walked on the Moon. For the first Evening at the White House of 1973, Sammy and Nixon would honor them in the East Room.

The day dawned cold and gray in Washington and the constant rain held up some of the two hundred and forty congressmen, business executives and Washington socialites who crowded into the East Room. "The yellow acacias and pink azaleas which filled the grand hall soon dispelled the gloomy weather," it was reported.[4] The assembled guests dined on crabmeat mousse and prime tenderloin as Louis Martini cabernet flowed. Nixon introduced Sammy with effusive praise. He told the audience that Sammy had grown up poor but "he overcame the poverty and prejudice and went clear to the top." He compared what he called America's "can-do spirit" that led Apollo 17 to the Moon with Sammy's own "spirit of 'yes I can.'" Nixon called Sammy "a great American."

With that, Nixon took his seat and Sammy stepped to the microphone. He thanked the president and joked, "Where else but in America could one grown man hug another grown man and get invited to his house?" The audience roared with laughter.

All the years of struggling, both in his career and for the causes he believed in, had come to fruition. The vaudeville kid was performing at the White House. "This is about as far uptown as I'm ever going to get," he quipped as he launched into "The Candy Man."[5] He kept the groove uptempo with "I've Gotta Be Me." He did a medley of popular songs and broke out his impressions of Sinatra and Dean Martin, among others. The latter bit had him "guzzling the microphone and singing into a highball glass." The audience ate it up.

He closed with "Mr. Bojangles." "Using just a derby hat as a prop and using tremendous economy of movement, and some dramatic spotlighting, Sammy created the poignant old hoofer in his New Orleans cell right there on the East Room stage," an observer said.[6] He finished to a standing ovation. "It brings tears to your eyes," Nixon told a *Washington Post* reporter about Sammy's version of "Bojangles."[7]

Something had gotten to him. Maybe it was the story of hope embedded in the struggle of the aging dancer. Maybe it was Nixon's own identification with the down and out. Nixon viewed his personal story as one of a common man fighting against the elites. He thought he and Sammy shared that in common, and maybe the song pulled those emotions to the surface. Cynical Nixon observers might say he was just still the student of his old English professor at Whittier College, Albert Upton. The actor who knew how to feign emotion to connect with an audience. And there may be some truth to that. But White House recordings would suggest otherwise. Nixon brought up Sammy's performance and how marvelous it was to almost everyone he talked to for the next few days.

The night went on and a military band continued the entertainment while the guests danced. Nixon asked Altovise to dance and without missing a beat Sammy took Pat Nixon's hand. They whirled across the floor, Pat twirling and dipping to Sammy's lead. Sammy was in awe, dancing with the First Lady, his wife with the president; he couldn't believe it. The foursome stood in a receiving line shaking hands with the astronauts, senators and Supreme Court justices—"the people who ran the country," as Sammy would later write.

Around 2 a.m., Sammy and Altovise retired to the Lincoln Bedroom. They were the first African Americans to sleep in the White House. Booker T. Washington had famously visited and dined with Teddy Roosevelt. FDR and Eisenhower both welcomed the president of Liberia. And of course, enslaved people had built and worked the grounds for decades prior to the Civil War. But no American of African descent had ever been invited to stay overnight. Sammy and his wife were so amazed they hardly slept.[8]

The next morning, Nixon made a series of phone calls before departing for Camp David. He mentioned Sammy, his performance, and the history-making overnight stay to almost everyone. Speaking to his secretary of state that morning, he said, "Incidentally, I didn't know it, because I thought with the Kennedys and the Rat Packers, but this is the first time he had ever performed at the White House and the first time a n—..." He stopped himself but without missing a beat continued, "an American Black has ever stayed overnight in the White House."[9]

"It was the greatest thrill of my life," Sammy told *Jet* magazine that May.[10]

Before Nixon left for Maryland on March 4, he and Sammy ate breakfast in his private dining room. Sammy pressed Nixon to support the United Negro College Fund and beef up support for Black entrepreneurs. Absolutely, Nixon assured him. It was a top priority.

Onstage the night before, Sammy had proposed an idea: a welcome-home dinner for all the POWs who had just been released from North Vietnam. "Sammy Davis Offers to Stage P.O.W. Gala," read the *New York Times* headline the next day,[11] and Nixon soon agreed it was a fantastic idea. Dictating a lengthy memo to Bob Haldeman from Camp David, Nixon said the idea was "very appealing." He had a producer in mind and wanted Bob Hope to be involved. Provided he could "de-emphasize some of the girlie stuff," Nixon said.[12]

Two months later, the show was on. Nixon had recruited Bob Hope as he had wanted. Sammy was "somewhat upset by the efforts of some other entertainers to climb aboard this particular bandwagon." He felt that since it was his idea, he should be the "main attraction." Sammy's original idea was for a closed-circuit television fundraiser that he would headline at a thousand dollars a ticket, raising money for the POWs and their families. Nixon and his team took the idea and made it a more mainstream affair.[13]

An enormous tent was erected on the White House lawn and six hundred ex–POWs were treated to a five-course dinner and an evening of entertainment. Among the ex–POWs in attendance were future senator and presidential candidate John McCain. He and his wife sat at the same table as Vice President Spiro Agnew. Seated at various tables among the former captives were celebrities like John Wayne and Jimmy Stewart.

Bob Hope and Sammy gave the headline performances and Irving Berlin closed out the night, leading the assembled guests in his song "God Bless America." The concert was broadcast live on ABC. The concert Sammy suggested remains the largest event ever held at the Executive Mansion.

Nixon gave a rousing speech, but when the entertainment was over, he retired early. It was to be one of the last happy days in the White House for Nixon. Just four days after Sammy's performance, his lawyer, John Dean, warned him that there was "a cancer within—close to the presidency, that's growing. It's growing daily."

Welcome home dinner for prisoners of war in Vietnam, May 25, 1973. The event was the brainchild of Sammy Davis, Jr., and remains the largest event ever held at the Executive Mansion. From left: Richard Nixon, Vic Damone, Irving Berlin, Sammy Davis, Jr., Pat Nixon, and Bob Hope (courtesy Richard Nixon Presidential Library and Museum).

Nixon won the '72 election by as much as he did because of the weakness of his opponent, George McGovern. The Watergate scandal was always right below the surface. Mark Felt was steering Bob Woodward and his fellow *Post* reporter Carl Bernstein along a trail of criminality that led to the White House. Two weeks before his second inauguration, the burglars went on trial and were all convicted. The judge warned them of long prison sentences if they did not open up about what they knew. Nixon can be heard on tape discussing how to keep them quiet: "You could get a million dollars, and you could get it in cash. I know where it could be gotten."[14]

On March 23, 1973, James McCord sent a letter to Judge John Sirica, who was presiding over the trial, alleging a wider conspiracy of higher-ups. Sirica read the letter aloud in open court and the press went wild.

Attorney General Elliot Richardson appointed a special prosecutor named Archibald Cox—a Harvard man who had worked for Kennedy and Johnson, Nixon would complain—to investigate further. Democratic senator Sam Ervin launched a committee to examine the alleged shenanigans of the 1972 election as well. Longtime aides Haldeman and Ehrlichman were forced to resign, and Nixon went on TV to proclaim his innocence. The cover-up had been going quite well for a year, but now people were going to be called to testify under oath. Nixon's ability to control the narrative was slipping away.

Weeks earlier, as the POWs enjoyed their newfound freedom dancing on the White House lawn, Nixon withdrew to the Lincoln Sitting Room. "My father seemed drained, like the emotion of the night had been too much for him," his daughter Julie remembered. He sat by the window listening to the sound of the party still going strong and made phone calls to confidants, as was his custom. He tried to tell a few jokes, "but it was almost painful for us to see how sad Daddy's face looked despite the laughter," his other daughter, Tricia, wrote in her diary. Nixon hung up the phone and the three sat there in silence for a moment.

"Do you think I should resign?" Nixon queried his daughters out of the blue.

They responded in "a wave of exclamations. 'Don't you dare! Don't think of it!'"[15]

As for Sammy, Eartha Kitt was not the only friend angry with him over his embrace of Nixon. Of course, Sammy was not the only high-profile Black to support Nixon. Floyd McKissick, the former leader of the civil rights group CORE (Congress of Racial Equality), had switched parties with much the same logic as Bob Brown. Blacks needed economic opportunity, not handouts. Soul singer James Brown endorsed Nixon. As did baseball great Jackie Robinson (though Robinson had first supported Nelson Rockefeller). But it was only Sammy who received a backlash that would in many ways define the rest of his career.

Sammy was accustomed to traveling the country in style. He was normally the only Black in first class on the airplane. The only Black staying at the five-star hotel. But it was Blacks who took his ticket as he boarded and Blacks who delivered his room service and carried his bags. For years they were excited to see him. They called him brother and slapped him on the back and asked for autographs. But not anymore. Now he was just "Mr. Davis."

After Dr. King was assassinated, the civil rights movement splintered into many competing factions. The PUSH (People United to Save Humanity) coalition, headed by Jesse Jackson, soon became one of the leading national organizations advocating for the movement. Jackson had been on the balcony of the Lorraine Motel as King was murdered. By the early '70s he wore a leather jacket and gold medallion. He was a preacher like King, but he was younger. One historian said his sermons had "the lilt of poet and rebel." To some in the movement he was too brash and too hungry for media attention, but he gained a large following.

Fresh off his embrace of Nixon, Sammy wanted to be part of the 1972 Black Expo in Chicago being organized by PUSH that fall. He believed in the cause and saw it as a way to get back in the good graces of the community. Ossie Davis, Bill Cosby, and B.B. King, among others, were scheduled to perform. Sy Marsh contacted Jackson and said Sammy wanted to help. Twenty-five thousand dollars is what it would cost, Jackson told him. If Sammy could donate that amount to PUSH, he could perform at the Expo. Of course, Sammy did not have the money. He was always spending the next paycheck before it was in the bank. He told Marsh to figure it out, though. He wanted to be there. "I had to borrow the money from Vegas," Marsh recalled in an interview years later.

Sammy flew from London to Chicago and Marsh gave Jackson the check. On stage, Jackson told the crowd he had a surprise for them and introduced "Brother Sammy Davis." Sammy walked onstage to a chorus of boos. He was "in a state of shock," Marsh recalled.[16] According to the *New York Times*, Sammy told the crowd, "I am a black man and I have the right to my political opinion."[17] The boos got louder. "It struck me with a physical force, knocking the wind out of me," Sammy would later write.[18]

"The worst moment in my life was being booed by my people in Chicago. I cannot begin to tell you what that did to me. Nothing has ever hurt me that much," he would tell *Ebony* magazine almost a decade later.[19]

Jackson told the crowd how important Sammy had been to the movement over the years. "If it wasn't for people like Sammy Davis, you wouldn't be here," he said, trying to quiet the crowd. Nothing worked. Sammy and the band struggled through "I've Gotta Be Me" and Sammy departed the stage.[20]

"Once I got into performing, the entertainer in me came out. But in doing that … in pushing the human being down and letting the entertainer take over, I felt a terrible sense of shame," Sammy explained in an interview. "They weren't booing 'the entertainer'—they were booing the human being."[21]

Sy Marsh described the scene in more literal terms: "Sammy sang a song, came off and said, 'Fuck 'em. They don't want me, I don't want them.' He got blind drunk that night, and cried."[22]

35

"All kinds of prisons"

It was late winter 1974 and Samuel Byck was muttering into a tape recorder as he drove through downtown Baltimore. He was on his way to the airport, but he made a pit stop at the post office to mail his recording to a reporter first. When Byck arrived at the airport, he entered the terminal and shot a police officer in the back. He then ran to the gate of Delta flight 593 and, waving his gun, boarded the plane.

"Fly this plane out of here!" he screamed.

The pilot explained that the wheel blocks were still in place. It was impossible for the aircraft to take off. Byck shot the co-pilot.

"The next one will be in the head," he told the captain.

The pilot tried one more round of reasoning with the would-be hijacker and Byck shot him as well. He then ordered a passenger caught up in the melee to fly the plane.

"Emergency! Emergency! We are all shot!" the pilot radioed the tower.

Just then a police officer aimed his gun at the cockpit window and fired. Byck was hit in the shoulder and fell to the ground. He put a bullet in his brain as the cops rushed in.

The recording Byck mailed to syndicated columnist Jack Anderson outlined his plan to hijack the aircraft and fly it into the White House, killing Richard Nixon. The attack was widely reported in the press and inspired a 2004 movie. In February of 1974, there was no shortage of people looking to get rid of Richard Nixon.[1]

The Senate Watergate hearings had gripped America in the summer of 1973. "What did the president know and when did he know it?" Sen. Howard Baker famously asked. The four Democrats and three Republicans of the Senate Watergate Committee presided over almost daily hearings, determined to find answers. The hearings were broadcast by all three networks live, interrupting profitable daytime programming. Some Americans were fascinated with the daily civics lesson while others lamented the loss of their favorite soap operas and game shows, but everyone had an opinion.

John Dean testified under oath, alleging the conspiracy went straight to Nixon. But for a time, it was simply his word against the president's. By July 4 it looked like Nixon might survive this political crisis as well. But a week later, the game changed again. Alexander Butterfield, Haldeman's chief assistant, was one of only seven people who knew about the existence of the White House taping system. When Sen. Fred Thompson asked him if he knew of the clandestine recordings, he looked uncomfortable, as if he realized the firestorm he was about to set off.

"I was aware of such a system, yes sir," Butterfield told the committee.[2]

Nixon was in the hospital being treated for pneumonia when he got the news. Two White House lawyers hovered over his bed arguing about his next move. Fred Buzhardt urged him to immediately destroy the tapes. They had not yet been subpoenaed and his allies in Congress would not punish him for doing what he pleased with his private records. Leonard Garment argued the other side. He told him destroying the tapes would look like an admission of guilt and could potentially still be seen as obstruction. He did not *need* to destroy them, Garment claimed; executive privilege meant he would not legally be required to turn them over.

Nixon thought it over. He had seen Truman and Eisenhower before him deftly navigate the executive privilege argument and he thought he could do the same. Besides, he had appointed three members of the current Supreme Court. Their ideology on this subject fit his, he thought. So he did not burn the tapes, and Archibald Cox filed suit to gain access to them.

Nixon appealed, and all through the late summer and early fall of 1973 he worked the court of public opinion as he tried to broker a compromise. On Friday, October 19, he offered to have conservative Mississippi senator John Stennis listen to the tapes and summarize them for Cox. Cox refused the odd offer, demanding unfettered access. The next day Nixon ordered Attorney General Richardson to fire Cox. Richardson refused and resigned, as did his deputy, William Ruckelshaus. Solicitor General Robert Bork took over and did the president's bidding. The press called it "the Saturday Night Massacre" and said the country had entered a period of constitutional crisis.

Nixon remained upbeat and defiant in public. But in the evening he sat alone drinking, his mood becoming sullen. "Rustle of Spring," his mother's favorite song, echoed through the Executive Mansion as he pounded on the piano late into the night.

A new special prosecutor, Leon Jaworski, was appointed. He likewise demanded to hear the tapes. A month later, Nixon gave his famous "I am not a crook" press conference in Florida. A mere four days later, the White House admitted that an eighteen-and-a-half-minute gap existed on a tape

35. "All kinds of prisons"

from June 20, 1972, three days after the break-in. The White House said that the erasure was purely accidental and blamed it on Nixon's secretary. The public was fast coming to believe their president was indeed a crook.

The appeals about the tapes dragged on and in March 1974, Haldeman, Ehrlichman and five others were indicted. Nixon was named as an "unindicted co-conspirator." Still clinging to threadbare support in the Congress against his impeachment, Nixon released his own transcripts of the tapes in April. The highly edited versions satisfied no one and in May, the Congress began impeachment proceedings. In July the Supreme Court ruled unanimously in Jaworski's favor, saying Nixon must release the tapes.

On August 5 he released a transcript of a June 23 conversation with Haldeman. It became known as "the smoking gun." The conversation revealed there was no doubt that Nixon was aware of and participated in the cover-up of the Watergate burglary. The next day a group of Republican senators were dispatched to the White House to let Nixon know it was over. What was left of his firewall to stave off impeachment had collapsed. If he did not resign, he would be removed by the Senate.

On August 8 he told the nation in a televised address that he would resign at noon the next day. In a tear-filled farewell from the East Room of the White House, he talked of his long career and his childhood. He called his mother a saint and gave an ironic piece of advice: "Always remember, others may hate you, but those who hate you don't win unless you hate them, and then you destroy yourself."

He and Pat walked a red carpet to the presidential helicopter as his staff and supporters cheered him. He turned and gave a final smile and wave to the crowd before boarding. On the helicopter, the couple sat quiet for a time. Pat, staring out the window as the National Mall faded from view, broke the silence. "It's so sad," she said.

The chopper took them to Air Force One, which flew them one last time to California. They took separate cabins for the flight. Nixon made a drink. As they flew somewhere over the heartland, the clock struck noon, and the uniquely American exile of Richard Nixon began.[3]

It was on a rocky hillside overlooking the ocean that Nixon learned he would not be going to prison. Vice President Gerald Ford became president when Nixon resigned, and on September 8, he pardoned him for all offenses against the United States. He told the country via a television address that the "long national nightmare" was over. A mostly horrified country thought the pardon was another crooked deal.

The Nixons returned to La Casa Pacifica, as they called it. They had purchased the beachfront mansion shortly after Nixon's inauguration in 1969. It was a grand estate by any measure. "The Western White House," as the press dubbed it, had nine thousand square feet of living space overlooking the Pacific, with curated gardens, a three-hole golf course and a swimming pool.

Nixon woke every morning, dressed, and went to his office with a view of the water. He read the papers and worked on his memoir. But few people called or wrote. Like an old dancer waiting for someone to ask "please," Nixon would sit and stare at the ocean for long periods. "There are all kinds of prisons," Bob Haldeman's wife told an interviewer.

Nixon once loved the place, having sparred with Russian leader Leonid Brezhnev and plotted with Kissinger inside its walls. But now he hated it. And he could barely afford it. He left office with a generous six-month transition budget, but when it ran out, he at one point had only five hundred dollars in his bank account.

He would not be broke for long, though. The public did not want Nixon as president, but they were still plenty interested in what he had to say. He signed a book deal for his story and auctioned off the rights to a televised interview to the highest bidder. British journalist David Frost paid him $600,000 plus a share of the profits for twelve interviews to be aired in four 90-minute segments.

In his memoirs and interviews after leaving the White House, Nixon never really took full responsibility for the fiasco that led to his undoing. His defense became a version of "everyone else did it too." And history would vindicate him on that particular point, regardless of its merits as a defense.

Watergate changed the political landscape in ways both trivial and profound. For decades after, every political scandal, no matter how minor, was saddled with the "-gate" suffix. But it also led to a groundswell of support for reforming the old way of doing business. Many felt the Watergate revelations were just the tip of the iceberg, and they were right.

In 1975, Idaho senator Frank Church held hearings on a variety of abuses committed by a broad swath of government agencies. The CIA ran assassination teams in foreign countries, with varying degrees of success. The FBI kept tabs on American citizens it deemed subversive. The National Security Agency was intercepting telegrams and bugging phones.

It was revealed that the CIA installed two-way mirrors at a brothel in San Francisco and gave unwitting customers LSD to observe the effects. Moreover, the FBI possessed a list of 26,000 names of American citizens to be rounded up should a "national emergency" be declared. The Church Committee brought to light the extent of domestic and international spying the government had been involved in for decades. Many Americans were shocked.

The Church Committee findings were in no way exculpatory of

35. "All kinds of prisons"   213

Richard Nixon. They found plenty of abuses of power to go along with Watergate on Nixon's watch, like the 1973 CIA–backed overthrow of the democratically elected government in Chile. But to Nixon and his supporters, it was the same old double standard. The Kennedys bugged people and the press called it Camelot. When Nixon did it, he was Tricky Dick.[4]

In the 1980s the Nixons sold La Casa Pacifica and moved east. "We are just slowly dying here," Pat confided in her daughter. Tricia and Julie and the Nixons' growing number of grandchildren lived in New York. They purchased a brownstone at 142 E. 65th Street in midtown Manhattan, a few blocks from Central Park. They were surrounded by Franklins. JFK's buddy Theodore White lived across the street. David Rockefeller was a neighbor. The backyard abutted the home of historian Arthur Schlesinger, Jr. One Halloween the Secret Service handed out candy bars to the Schlesingers' son. He was wearing a Nixon mask.

After a few years they traded the brownstone for a sprawling estate twenty miles north of the city in Saddle Brook, New Jersey. Nixon dedicated the last twenty years of his life to what he had always done, campaigning. But no longer for any office, rather for his place in history. His memoir sold over a million copies, and he wrote nine other books before his death. He hosted dinner parties, sometimes twice a month. News anchors, authors, and political pundits marveled as they were greeted at the door by America's thirty-seventh president. He sat at the end of the table and opined on world affairs while expensive French wine flowed.

In 1986 he gave an off-the-cuff speech to the American Newspaper Publishers Association. He was asked what he had learned from Watergate. "Just destroy the tapes," he told the assembled journalists as they laughed and applauded. Katharine Graham, publisher of his old nemesis the *Washington Post*, was in the audience. They were photographed laughing together, and she gave what one biographer described as "an order disguised as a suggestion to the editors" of *Newsweek* (which she also owned) to put Nixon on the cover. In May, Nixon smiled at the country from supermarket checkout and big-city newsstands. "He's Back," the headline read. Inside, the weekly called him "the sage of Saddle Brook."

Ford and Jimmy Carter both kept Nixon at arm's length but Reagan embraced his advice, in secret. The two exchanged numerous letters and Nixon offered copious guidance on strategic relations with Russia, though Reagan did not always act on his suggestions. Nixon and George H.W. Bush had had a frosty relationship since Nixon's days in office, and that continued through the Bush presidency. But Bill Clinton took Nixon's call early in his administration and the two found common ground as policy wonks.

"He was very respectful, with no sickening bullshit. It was the best conversation with a president I've had since I was president," Nixon told an aide, adding, "He really let his hair down. This guy does a lot of thinking."[5]

After Mark Felt left the FBI, he found himself in legal trouble over actions he had taken as deputy director against a leftist group, the Weather Underground. Nixon testified on his behalf. Felt was convicted nonetheless but was pardoned by Ronald Reagan in 1981. Upon hearing of the pardon, Nixon sent Felt a bottle of champagne with an ironic note, "Justice always prevails."

Richard Nixon never learned that Mark Felt was Deep Throat and the man most responsible for keeping the Watergate story alive and thus forcing his resignation. Felt admitted his role near the end of his life and it was confirmed by Bob Woodward in 2006.[6]

In 1993, Pat finally succumbed to lung cancer after years of battling emphysema. Nixon was devastated. Much has been written about his relationship with Pat, especially in the worst years of Nixon's presidency. Many called it loveless and a marriage for show. Personal artifacts and letters between the two that they left behind certainly throw that view into question. And anyone who has seen the photographs of the distraught man at her funeral would come to the opposite conclusion.

Nixon made it about another year. Shortly after putting the finishing touches on his ninth book, he was found by a housekeeper on the porch of his New Jersey home, clutching the doorframe, the right side of his face drooping. "I knew right away," she said. He had suffered a stroke and, four days later, on April 22, 1994, Richard Nixon died.

Nixon's life was one of the great American tragedies of the twentieth century. Brilliant and capable, he found himself consumed by self-doubt, anger, and paranoia. Former aides and family members talked of a light and dark side to the man. They claimed that while there was an undeniable duplicity to his thinking, he was at heart a good person and family man. They often argued that Watergate got out of hand precisely because he was so bad at "dirty tricks." In a thorough 2015 study of his life, biographer Evan Thomas concluded:

> Nixon's strengths were his weaknesses and vice versa. The drive that propelled him also crippled him. The underdog's sensitivity that made him farsighted also blinded him. He wanted to show that he was hard because he felt soft. He learned how to be popular because he felt rejected. He was the lonely everyman to the end.[7]

In October 1974, shortly after his departure from the White House, Nixon developed phlebitis in his leg. The doctors told him the blood clot could go to his heart and kill him. His former deputy communications director, Ken Clawson, came to La Casa Pacifica to visit his old boss. They

35. "All kinds of prisons"

talked of their years together at the top of American politics and the trials and tribulations they had seen. They stared at the ocean and Clawson asked Nixon about his leg, which was propped up on an ottoman.

"They say it's very bad, but I've already told them to go to hell. I've told them I wasn't setting foot outside the wall around my property no matter what. They can cut off the damn leg, let it rot, or just wait for the clot to reach the end zone. I don't care."

Clawson stared at him in silence, not sure how to respond.

"You see, don't you? You've got to be tough," Nixon continued. "You can't break, my boy, even when there is nothing left. You can't admit, even to yourself, that it is gone. Now, some people we both know think that you go stand in the middle of the bullring and cry, '*mea culpa, mea culpa*,' while the crowd is hissing and booing and spitting on you. But a man doesn't cry."

Clawson looked at the former president and tears began rolling down Nixon's cheeks.[8]

36

The Party of the Century

The cops weren't sure how long the old man had been dead. They figured a few days. In mid–March 1979, a neighbor knocked on his door and got no answer. He became worried and called the police. Inside the East Hollywood apartment, amid top hats and tap shoes, they found the ghost of vaudeville. At one hundred years old, Will Mastin was dead.

The obituaries were short. The one most widely circulated around the country came from the Associated Press. It was seventy-nine words. Mastin outlived everyone who truly understood what he had accomplished. Saving his pennies in late-nineteenth-century Alabama, he somehow escaped and lived a life few Black men of his time could even dream of. He was a successful businessman and entertainer for nearly sixty years. He took what Sam Lucas and Bert Williams had accomplished and raised the bar for what was possible. Will Mastin died with very little money but no debt. In his final years, he simply began giving away his money to various churches around Los Angeles.

Sammy got the phone call backstage in Reno and was on the next plane to LA. A few days later they laid his uncle in the ground at Forest Lawn Memorial Park. His tombstone read merely, "Will Mastin, Sr.—He Was a Vaudevillian."[1]

In the years before Will passed, Sammy's life was fast-paced and turbulent. In 1972, Donald Rumsfeld and his wife, Joyce, were what the *New York Times* called "Nixon's unofficial Ambassadors to Beverly Hills." Though the paper noted that they didn't really look the part. The Rumsfelds became fast friends with Sammy during the campaign and went to visit him in Vegas shortly after the convention. Sammy took them to the Hilton to meet Elvis. As they left, Sammy began imitating Elvis's accent and swiveling his hips, leaving Joyce Rumsfeld howling with laughter.

"What are we going to do with you, Sammy?" she asked.

"Well, you're stuck with me for the next four years!"[2]

It was not to be, though. When Nixon resigned, people would heckle Sammy on the street about it. In his memoir he wrote about the

36. The Party of the Century

experience, saying he was still "bewildered over the whole Nixon episode." He added, "[P]eople started throwing the crap at me in a nasty way. They wagged their fingers and enjoyed pointing out how wrong I had been.... I was pretty close to a nervous breakdown."[3]

"I lost a lot of friends because of my support for the president—and that's forever, man," he told *Jet* magazine.[4]

In the summer of 1973 he told *Variety*, "My support for the man continues unchanged.... I admire the man very much." But as 1974 dawned and it became clear Nixon was done, Sammy changed his tune: "Nixon is not to be explained, he is not to be rationalized at all."[5]

Still, he felt burned by the criticism and was defensive. People "assumed that I was having some tax problems ... ain't none of that true," he said. "I supported him because of some things that he promised to do for my people. Because of what he said he would do for the soul brothers."

"Now, I make 100,000 dollars a week, and the President makes [$]250,000 a year. What was the President going to do for me?" Sammy asked an *Ebony* magazine interviewer rhetorically. "I was promised that certain things would be done for rural blacks and that there would be urban programs. 'Just let us win, Sam,' I was told. 'I promise you we'll do this, and we'll do that.'"[6]

But he would maintain an admiration for the man. "I had long talks with the guy face to face, and I must say, even now, he impressed me," he wrote in 1980.[7]

Richard Nixon famously said at the 1972 Republican convention that you could not buy Sammy Davis, Jr. No president "has ever said that about a performer," Sammy would brag.[8] The comment made Sammy so swept away with emotion that he spontaneously hugged the president. The controversy it ignited was just one of many Sammy had started and sometimes courted over the years. But the image became indelible to the cultural understanding of Sammy Davis, Jr. "They took that picture, and that's the one they used. I became the lackey and the ass-kisser."[9]

Sammy loved money but money was simply a tool, a means to achieve fame and power. He spent it faster than he made it his whole life, but it rarely mattered, there was always a Skinny D'Amato or Sam Giancana to plug the holes.

Nixon bought Sammy with the access to power that he longed for. The president gave him a title and a reason to fly to Washington and carry a Gucci briefcase. He had achieved stardom and while he was notoriously bad with money, he managed to live a very monied lifestyle with relative ease. In Sammy's mind, the next step up was power. Kennedy had denied it to him. He had embarrassed him. And here was Nixon, offering the thing he desperately wanted. Nixon fed Sammy's ego in a way no one else could.

When it all came crashing down, Sammy was one of the collateral victims. The years after the Nixon resignation were some of Sammy's strangest and least productive. He did not appear in any feature films from 1974 to 1981. His drinking and cocaine use skyrocketed. He became fascinated with the new world of commercial pornography. He would call the studios that produced porn and purchase their latest reel-to-reel films. He would hold screenings on Summit Ridge Drive and often some of the stars of the film would attend. The parties would rage all night as the number of younger guests increased. The kids Sammy had derided as "youth freaks" in the late sixties were now members of his entourage. He and Altovise decided to have an open marriage.

Frank Sinatra was nowhere to be found amid Sammy's new scene. A bitterness had grown between the men. Frank did not like the parties and drugs, while Sammy complained to mutual friends that Frank was acting like a bully. And just like that, they were done. Seeing each other at social events in the coming years, the men would not speak.

"At one time in my life, I was his little mascot, but I'm not his little mascot anymore," Sammy told the press.[10]

In 1975 ABC greenlighted a talk show featuring Sammy as the host. On *Sammy and Company*, Davis would guffaw with Bob Hope or singer Billy Eckstine in between pre-planned sketches. The show was syndicated and aired mostly late at night. It was canceled midseason 1977. No worries to Sammy, that was just the business. Besides, the party was still going strong on Summit Ridge Drive.

Back in his shag-carpeted lounge amid the bowls of cocaine sitting on the bar for anyone to partake of, a new type of visitor began arriving. Longtime friends Jack and Roxanne Carter dropped by one day and left immediately. "He had heavy-metal-music people over," they told one of his biographers. Satanism and the occult fascinated Sammy and he began to dabble in the art of dark magic. His Beverly Hills home became the site of séance rituals and Sammy painted his nails red. Friends grew fearful and nervous; had Sammy finally crossed a line? Was the Summit Ridge Drive house going to become the Manson family redux? There was talk of some sort of an intervention, but Shirley Rhodes told everyone it was "better just to wait it out." She was right. Sammy emerged from his devil-worship phase, shedding it the same way he traded a Nehru jacket for a polyester shirt. The Hollywood Hills, the land of make-believe, was the perfect place for a child of vaudeville to grow old.[11]

Sammy continued to play nightclubs across the country, which were his main source of income. He was paid handsomely, but he spent lavishly.

"He had no concept of money," said Sy Marsh, who by the late

36. The Party of the Century

seventies had been Sammy's manager for about ten years. "He had no idea that with 100,000 dollars you would be taxed 40,000."[12]

As the 1980s dawned, Sammy and Altovise decided to throw the biggest party they had ever thrown. Tents were erected and flowers and catering brought in. *People* magazine, *Variety*, and other trade magazines ran stories on the soiree. They called it the party of the century. By all accounts it was a lovely affair. The next morning Sy Marsh found Sammy in the kitchen on Summit Ridge Drive.

"It was a wild party," he told him. "Except the hangover is going to last all year. Thank god you're playing Vegas next week."

Sammy stared at him grimly. He knew Sy was about to deliver the unfortunate news of the party's total cost.

"Seventy-five grand," he said. "Sammy, what was the motivation for that?"

"I didn't want people to think I'm broke."[13]

In the 1970s, Sammy lent his name to a golf tournament. Sammy had long loved the game; learning it years before had seemed like an entry into a forbidden part of white society. Now he was the first Black with his own tournament, the Sammy Davis Jr.–Greater Hartford Open. Later in the decade Sammy bought an 8 percent stake (or more accurately, lent his name for an 8 percent stake) in a Las Vegas hotel and casino, the Tropicana. He was the first Black to have an ownership interest on the Las Vegas Strip. Vegas, where he once could not sleep in the same hotel where he performed! It was a stunning achievement in many ways. But after Nixon, few took notice of Sammy's history-making.

Among the multitude of changes Sammy underwent in the seventies, one stands out as prophetic. He began closing his shows with "Mr. Bojangles." By all accounts Sammy truly did not care for the song. It scared him.

"I'll never do it again," he told his manager as he walked offstage after closing his show with the number for the first time.

"What are you talking about? They gave you a standing ovation," Marsh replied.

"I don't want to be the guy standing around at the end and the parade passes him by," Sammy explained.[14]

But he would do the song again. And again, and again. The song became synonymous with Sammy. It was already a hit before Sammy ever heard it. The Nitty Gritty Dirt Band rode it up the charts first. Harry Belafonte, Bob Dylan, and John Denver all recorded it. Whitney Houston, Neil Diamond, and Queen, among many others, would eventually sing the tune. But they all just sang it. They told the listener the story. Sammy *was* the story. He had lived it. Whether he wanted to admit it or not, the American public loved his rendition. They loved it because it fit the narrative of who Sammy was in their collective imagination. The derby hat and cane, Sammy twirling around the stage singing quietly about county fairs and minstrel shows. About dead dogs. About being left behind in a changing world. And the public's perception was fast becoming reality.

Sammy was still playing the same rooms in Vegas and Palm Springs he always had. But as the eighties arrived, the early show might not be full in the back. Sammy began joking onstage about his drinking. Just like Bojangles, he admitted he drank a bit. It began to catch up with him. He complained of stomachaches. He lost his appetite and began losing weight. He awoke one night in a Reno hotel room and "it felt as if I had a flame against my ribs," he wrote. Marsh took him to the hospital for X-rays.

"You have a touch of jaundice with overt signs of liver damage," the doctor told him.[15]

He was told he would need to quit drinking. Sammy was never more than 150 pounds soaking wet. The doctors explained to him that alcohol damages the liver in people with smaller body mass at an exponentially greater rate. For a little while he quit, but after he regained his strength he was back at it, though the pains of age moderated some of the excess.

But the combination of time off from performing and smaller checks when he was exasperated his money woes. Sy Marsh convinced him to invest in a company they formed called SYNI (for Sy & I) to take advantage of the government's loopholes. Sy called it a tax shelter, but in time the IRS would call it tax evasion. The need for money led Sammy to start the SDJ Food Corporation. The company hawked bar-b-q sauces and spices with Sammy's face on the packaging. It went belly-up after a few years.

In 1981 Sammy had what would be considered his last hit. *Cannonball Run* featured Burt Reynolds as the leading man with supporting roles for Sammy and Dean Martin as crooks masquerading as priests. It was a reunion of sorts. Sammy and Dean back on the set together. Reminiscing about old times, gossiping and complaining about Frank. The critics yawned but the film grossed an impressive profit and spawned a sequel. A little more bread to keep the IRS wolf at bay.

He sold his Rolls-Royce as part of a plan to get solvent. Then turned around and spent $12,000 on an Andy Warhol silkscreen painting of a soup can. He would guest-star on a television show and then throw a wrap party for the cast that cost more than he made for his appearance. Sammy had less regard for money than any star before or since. When he was a child, Will Mastin doled out cash to his cast members from a paper bag. It seemed like a game to Sammy; how much would he get today? As an adult, nothing had changed.

36. The Party of the Century

As the eighties wore on, Altovise and Sammy drifted farther apart and argued about the definition of "open" in their marriage. She would take off traveling for weeks at a time and then ring their Beverly Hills home with a message for the staff, saying, "Tell Sammy I'm coming in and to get rid of whoever he's got with him there."[16]

Sammy soldiered on, playing Vegas mostly but still touring sporadically. The audiences were smaller than they used to be. His body was slowly giving out, his hip in constant pain now. But people still wanted to see the ghost. The vision of days gone by on the stage in front of them. What he long said he feared had come to pass. He became Bojangles and Bojangles became him with every twirl of the cane.

A young comedian named Billy Crystal began making a name for himself on the comedy-club circuit. In 1984 he joined the cast of *Saturday Night Live*. One of his most popular bits was an impression of Sammy. Hunched over and squinting, Crystal, wearing blackface, held a half-burnt cigarette with massive rings on each finger. He would use the lingo of the Rat Pack days that now seemed passe. Jokes about being a Black Jew. Jokes about Republican politics. The mimic being mimicked. Sammy took it all in stride. After all, hadn't he made a name for himself with jokes about Edward G. Robinson? But sometimes after a few drinks, his fragile ego would poke through. He would ask Murphy or Sy or George, did he really look and sound like that?

Ringo Starr and Billy Crystal (as Sammy Davis, Jr.) on *Saturday Night Live*, **December 8, 1984 (Photofest).**

Sammy's longtime bandleader George Rhodes died suddenly of a heart attack in 1985. A few years later his father, Sam Sr., passed away in his sleep. His tap shoes found their way to the historical society in Wilmington, where they are still on display. He had become an honored citizen of a town where he was once almost lynched.

The march of time and the inevitable understanding of one's own mortality tend to make a man forget the small stuff. And such was the case with the Rat Pack. In 1987, Frank and Sammy and Dean met in Palm Springs, just for laughs, as they used to say. It was almost inevitable that someone would suggest a reunion tour, so Sammy just did it himself.

"Smokey, let's do it," Frank agreed. Dean demurred but came around. Plans were made for twenty-plus dates all over the country in the spring and then again in the fall. The tour was announced and shows began selling out immediately.

As usual, Frank and his team were in charge. As the tickets began selling, Sammy was desperate to know what he could expect to make. How much was Frank going to give him out of the paper bag? Too many unknowns, Frank's office told Sammy's office. Finally, after months of Sammy's people badgering Frank's people, an answer came. Sammy could expect to clear six to eight million dollars. He was able to find a bank to refinance the Summit Ridge Drive home. The IRS would hold off on seizing his assets again.

The tour went well at first, selling out theaters and auditoriums. A week into the tour, Frank blew up in Chicago. The hotel had booked the men on different floors.

"Don't unpack. We are going to get out of this dump," Frank told them. Sammy was more than happy to change hotels, but something about the scene set off Dean. He was sick of Frank's shit. He went to the airport and took a private plane home. He was done. Liza Minnelli took Martin's place for the rest of the tour. On with the show.[17]

Midway through the tour Sammy felt a scratch in his throat. Murphy would make him hot tea to soothe the ache, but it was only a temporary reprieve. Once back in LA, Sammy went to the doctor. It was throat cancer. Years of cigarettes had finally caught up with him. The doctors told Sammy they could operate and save his life, but he would never sing the same again. He refused. If he could not perform, he did not want to live.

Sammy returned to the Summit Ridge Drive home he loved, and slowly deteriorated. Visitors streamed in to say their goodbyes as Altovise stayed drunk. Looking to hide objects of value from the IRS, she shipped jewelry, clothing, and cash around the world to various friends. Sammy's impending demise was the worst-kept secret in Hollywood. Reporters and camera crews camped outside the house on death watch.

On May 16, 1990, just as the sun was coming up over Hollywood Hills, Sammy closed his eyes and took his last breath. Altovise spent the days following his death frantically salvaging what she could from the house. Before Sammy was buried, she removed all his jewelry and his glass eye.[18]

37

"Foolish in her eyes"

In early 1980, Jerry Jeff Walker called his accountant. "Transfer all my money and property" to Susan, he told him.

"You mean your pickup truck and car?" the accountant asked incredulously.

"Naw, man! Everything!" Jerry Jeff shot back.

"That is everything, Jerry Jeff. You don't have any money or property. And you're $26,000 in debt."[1]

The 1970s had flown by in a haze of two hundred shows a year, chartered planes, and more cocaine daily than most people do in a lifetime.

Even four decades later, remembrances of his life were filled with stories of how Jerry Jeff never slept. He once told a journalist, "You're older than I am, but I've been up more hours." But the hard living caught up with him as it does to most who try to push the limits with drugs and alcohol. While his peers like Nelson and Buffett saw their album sales and venue sizes grow, Walker remained on the outside looking in, with concert promoters and fans growing increasingly skeptical of his onstage antics, wondering in what mental state he might arrive to perform.

"The folk rock-country-desperado image has proven too elusive to gain him superstardom," one critic opined.[2]

"You start to live the way you figure stars should live. Room service, limos, groupies and parties. You pay for every cent of this whether you realize it or not. Occasionally your management team comes to see how you're doing; they fly first class, stay first class, and charge it all to you," Jerry Jeff wrote in his memoir.[3]

There were a multitude of reasons Jerry Jeff needed to change his life. The IRS was after him, as was American Express for unpaid bills. He had a three-year-old daughter at home. But most of all he had a deep love for his wife, and she told him it was time.

"Susan, who's so pretty and smart, who's only done one thing wrong and that was when she married me, wants to know what I'm going to do! And I can't look foolish in her eyes," he told his manager.[4]

And so, he went cold turkey. People asked him how he did it and he told them he started by walking to his mailbox, which sat down the end of a long driveway. Then he would run back. Never one to halfheartedly undertake an endeavor, by 1982 Jerry Jeff was running marathons and espousing the benefits of juice cleansing to anyone who would listen. *Running* magazine featured a profile on the unlikely convert to the sport. An Austin journalist said he had "become the model Whole Foods cowboy."[5]

"Running is the balance to all the bad things I do to my body. 'The blowout' is what I call the run. It blows the pipes out," Jerry Jeff said.[6]

MCA released a greatest-hits package in 1981 that sold well, but for the most part Jerry Jeff spent the early '80s raising a family and getting his life together. He was seriously in debt as the new decade dawned, but he had an ace up his sleeve still. The royalty checks for "Mr. Bojangles" that came to the mailbox helped jump-start his health kick.

By the mid–'80s Jerry Jeff was in firm control of himself again. He and Susan had added a son to their brood, and as the children started school, Susan began to talk about going back to work. So, Jerry Jeff offered her a job. He wanted her to be his manager. She was the only person he trusted and if she wanted to work, she should work for him, he said.

"If I do run your business, we're not dealing with any assholes, OK?" she said. Jerry Jeff agreed. The pair started their own record label, Tried & True Music. It was an almost unheard-of proposition in 1986. Without major-label support he would never be able to maintain a presence on radio or get press for his new music, business insiders scoffed. But Jerry Jeff and Susan plowed ahead. Jerry Jeff recorded a new album on a four-track tape recorder in his Austin living room. He began selling the homemade tape at shows. The album, *Gypsy Songman*, had twenty songs, some new, some old, that spanned his career to that point.

They started a mailing list and a newsletter, reaching out to the fans in a more personal way. Jerry Jeff began touring with just his acoustic guitar, coming back full circle to how things had started. He was sober and making all his scheduled performances. The mailing list and fan base grew.

Years later he would marvel at his wife's accomplishment in resurrecting his career from his burnout days. "I guess I'm the only asshole she continues to do business with."[7]

While Jerry Jeff had profoundly changed his life, he still loved to drink beer and watch football and basketball. And there were some nights with old friends that conjured up the blurry '70s. But the hard stuff was gone for the most part. An interviewer queried Susan in the 1990s if she was concerned that her husband might fall off the wagon. "Jerry Jeff can still do a pretty good impression of the old Jerry Jeff from time to time. But, nah, I'm not worried," she said.[8]

And there was not much reason to worry. By the mid-'90s Jerry Jeff was arguably at the height of his performing career. He wasn't necessarily playing the biggest venues he had ever played or racking up his highest album sales, but he had developed a group of hardcore devotees who would in turn spread his musical ethos to a new generation. In the early twenty-first century, Texas Music is its own subgenre, with a DIY infrastructure patterned off Jerry Jeff Walker and Tried & True Music.

He bought a plane and hired a pilot to fly him to gigs. His road manager was his golfing buddy, and on days off or before shows they snuck in eighteen holes. He bought a house in New Orleans just blocks from where he had met Bojangles. He bought a beachfront mansion in Belize and began holding retreats there. Part concert festival, part tropical vacation, they attracted fans who bought travel packages and arrived with the family for a week of music and relaxation. As the twentieth century faded away, Jerry Jeff Walker was living a life most could only dream of.

In 1994 at a gig in Virginia, President Clinton and Vice President Al Gore showed up to sing along. Clinton had initially seen Walker in 1972 and had remained a fan. The *Wall Street Journal* reported that the Secret Service was supremely annoyed, as the president and the VP were not supposed to both attend the same event, for security reasons. Walker enthusiastically supported Clinton for both elections in the '90s but overall did not venture into politics much.

He had been invited to the White House by Jimmy Carter in 1977 but the president was late to their lunch. After waiting around for a bit, Walker said, as quoted by the *Chicago Tribune*, "I just don't think the President and I are going to get it on because I can't spend one more minute in this damn White House and he don't go to bars."[9]

When it came to the "story widely guffawed around Austin"[10] about "Mr. Bojangles" having reduced Nixon to tears, Walker said, "Dammit, ol' Nixon just liked that song because his little buddy Sammy Davis Jr. sang it."[11]

Jerry Jeff's song has been covered hundreds of times. It was his wife's hard work and his own renewed focus on sharper performances and engaging with his fans that made him a Texas legend. It was "Mr. Bojangles" that bought him a plane and beachfront homes. In 1987, Jerry Jeff received an award for the song's being played over two million times on the radio. Then in 1998 he got another for its three-millionth spin. Jerry Jeff claimed Nina Simone rendered his favorite version and that he did not particularly care for Sammy's take on the tune. He said:

> It serves a purpose, I guess. It's that show business/theatrical thing. I take a more direct approach. The one thing I always thought was different was Sammy starts fairly well dressed, always undoes his tie and disintegrates. I always thought the guy

comes out behind a rumple of beat-up clothes and then he starts to shine by the end of the song. That's how I always thought of him. A disheveled heap who in the cell kind of explodes about.[12]

But it is undoubtably Sammy's performance that is most associated with the song. For a period in the early '80s, Jerry Jeff was in conversations with a Hollywood producer to turn the Bojangles story into a movie.

"You'll have to change the script. Your character of Bojangles is white," the producer told Jerry Jeff.

"Bojangles is white too," Jerry Jeff explained to the movie man. In 1965, when he had been thrown into the New Orleans drunk tank, jails were still segregated.

"You'll have a hard time convincing this town he is white," the man responded, showing how thoroughly Sammy had taken over the image of Bojangles.[13]

"The movie business is really weird," Jerry Jeff concluded, and the project never happened.[14]

Jerry Jeff Walker died on October 23, 2020, after a three-year battle with lung cancer. Condolences poured in from around the world. Dan Rather, Lyle Lovett and Bill Clinton, among others, remembered Scamp Walker as an outsized personality and first-rate artist. His legacy looms large in the State of Texas; a life-sized bronze statue was erected in Luckenbach in his honor.

Of Jerry Jeff's many legacies, possibly his most lasting is the influence he had on a younger generation of songwriters who carry his torch and keep his music alive. One of those acolytes is Todd Daniel Snider. Snider first saw Jerry Jeff in his mid-'80s revival as a folk singer, and it sparked a lifelong love of his music.

Snider staked out a career path not all that different from Jerry Jeff's. He signed a major-label record deal in the '90s and toured with a rock-'n'-roll band, pushing the boundaries, then reinvented himself as a traveling folkie. By the mid–2000s he was playing many of the same venues that Walker played.

The two became friends over time and Walker recorded one of Snider's songs on his record *Gonzo Stew*. In 2010, Jerry Jeff invited Snider to play a gig with him in Santa Fe, New Mexico. It was one of Jerry Jeff's favorite places to play. After the show, the pair went to a bar at a hotel, La Fonda on the Plaza. They talked about life and music and Jerry Jeff's career.

"We spent a lot of time talking about his albums and how he made them. I like to hear how he found the songs. I could interview him for hours and every now and then he will get tipsy enough to let me," Snider wrote.

The bartender called last call at 2 a.m. and the pair began walking back to their hotel through the empty streets of downtown Santa Fe. Snider heard some music coming from a side street and they walked toward it. They saw "a bedraggled guy … kind of crazy looking" with a banjo and a harmonica around his neck, his hat on the ground for tips. The man began playing descending notes in 6/8 time. He looked at the two drunk strangers and took them for tourists. They stopped and listened, and he began to sing, "I knew a man Bojangles and he danced for you…"

Snider was in awe as he watched his hero watch a street performer sing his own song about street performers back to him. He wasn't sure what to do. He wanted to tell the guy that this was the writer of that song. But he didn't. They just sat and listened. When the man finished singing, Jerry Jeff took all the cash in his pocket, a "fuckload of cash," according to Snider, and put it in the man's hat. Jerry Jeff told the man with the banjo he sounded great and began walking toward his hotel.[15]

Chapter Notes

Chapter 1

1. Jerry Jeff Walker, *Gypsy Songman* (Emeryville, CA: Woodford Press, 1999), pp. 58–62.
2. The details in this opening chapter come from Walker's memoir.

Chapter 2

1. Robert C. Toll, *On with the Show! The First Century of Show Business in America* (New York: Oxford University Press, 1976), pp. 81–120.
2. Eileen Southern, *The Music of Black Americans: A History*, 3rd ed. (New York: W.W. Norton, 1997), p. 242.
3. Robert C. Toll, *On with the Show!*, pp. 121–131.
4. 1860 U.S. Census Records, Madison County, Alabama, Post Office: Huntsville, sheet no. 230, reel no. M653-15, division: the city of Huntsville, page no. 48. Accessed at ancestry.com.
5. 1880 U.S. Census Records, Madison, Alabama, roll 22, page 155C, Enumeration District 209. Accessed at ancestry.com.
6. Wil Haygood, *In Black and White: The Life of Sammy Davis, Jr.* (New York: Billboard, 2005), pp. 60–61.

Chapter 3

1. Wil Haygood, *In Black and White: The Life of Sammy Davis, Jr.* (New York: Billboard, 2005), p. 47.
2. Gary Fishgall, *Gonna Do Great Things: The Life of Sammy Davis, Jr.* (New York: Scribner's, 2003), pp. 5–6.
3. Alex Haley, "Alex Haley Interviews Sammy Davis, Jr.," *Playboy*, December 1966.
4. Haygood, *In Black and White*, pp. 34–39.
5. *Ibid.*, pp. 44–51.
6. Sammy Davis, Jr., Jane Boyar, and Burt Boyar, *Yes I Can: The Story of Sammy Davis, Jr.* (New York: Farrar, Straus & Giroux, 1965), p. 11.
7. Haygood, *In Black and White*, p. 51.
8. Davis, Jr., Boyar, and Boyar, *Yes I Can*, p. 12.

Chapter 4

1. Tom Willman, "Teapot Dome Scandal Drew Nixon into Law, Cousin Says," *Independent* (Long Beach, CA), May 11, 1973.
2. Roger Morris, *Richard Milhous Nixon: The Rise of an American Politician* (New York: Holt, 1990), p. 61.
3. Stephen E. Ambrose, *Nixon, Volume 1: The Education of a Politician, 1913–1962* (New York: Simon & Schuster, 1988), pp. 9–20.
4. John A. Farrell, *Richard Nixon: The Life* (New York: Vintage, 2018), p. 45.
5. *Ibid.*, p. 52.
6. *Ibid.*, p. 47.
7. *Ibid.*, p. 48.
8. Evan Thomas, *Being Nixon: A Man Divided* (New York: Random House, 2016), p. 9.
9. Farrell, *Richard Nixon*, p. 48.
10. Ambrose, *Nixon*, pp. 28–29.
11. *Ibid.*, p. 41.
12. Richard Nixon and Frank Gannon, "Frank Gannon's Interview with Richard Nixon, February 9, 1983, part 3," University of Georgia Libraries, Special Collections.

Chapter 5

1. Stephen E. Ambrose, *Nixon, Volume 1: The Education of a Politician, 1913–1962* (New York: Simon & Schuster, 1988), p. 57.
2. Roger Morris, *Richard Milhous Nixon: The Rise of an American Politician* (New York: Holt, 1990), pp. 116–133.
3. Ambrose, *Nixon*, pp. 65–70.
4. Morris, *Richard Milhous Nixon*, pp. 136–139.
5. Ambrose, *Nixon*, p. 72.
6. Richard Nixon, *The Memoirs of Richard Nixon* (New York: Grosset & Dunlap, 1978), pp. 20–21.
7. Morris, *Richard Milhous Nixon*, p. 177.
8. *Ibid.*, p. 171.
9. Ambrose, *Nixon*, p. 84.

Chapter 6

1. Wil Haygood, *In Black and White: The Life of Sammy Davis, Jr.* (New York: Billboard, 2005), p. 68.
2. Gary Fishgall, *Gonna Do Great Things: The Life of Sammy Davis, Jr.* (New York: Scribner's, 2003), p. 8.
3. Sammy Davis, Jr., Jane Boyar, and Burt Boyar, *Yes I Can: The Story of Sammy Davis, Jr.* (New York: Farrar, Straus & Giroux, 1965), p. 13.
4. *Ibid.*, 14.
5. Haygood, *In Black and White*, p. 67.
6. Davis, Jr., Boyar, and Boyar, *Yes I Can*, p. 15.
7. Haygood, *In Black and White*, p. 31.
8. Haygood, *In Black and White*, pp. 65–66.
9. Davis, Jr., Boyar, and Boyar, *Yes I Can*, p. 15.
10. Robert C. Toll, *On with the Show! The First Century of Show Business in America* (New York: Oxford University Press, 1976), p. 265.
11. Fishgall, *Gonna Do Great Things*, pp. 11–12.
12. *Ibid.*, pp. 14–15.
13. Haygood, *In Black and White*, p. 70.
14. *Rufus Jones for President* (Warner Brothers, 1933).
15. Haygood, *In Black and White*, pp. 74–75.
16. Davis, Jr., Boyar, and Boyar, *Yes I Can*, p. 41.
17. Fishgall, *Gonna Do Great Things*, p. 19.
18. Davis, Jr., Boyar, and Boyar, *Yes I Can*, pp. 42–46.
19. Alex Haley, "Alex Haley Interviews Sammy Davis, Jr.," *Playboy*, December 1966.

Chapter 7

1. Wil Haygood, *In Black and White: The Life of Sammy Davis, Jr.* (New York: Billboard, 2005), p. 96.
2. Sammy Davis, Jr., Jane Boyar, and Burt Boyar. *Why Me? The Sammy Davis, Jr. Story* (New York: Farrar, Straus & Giroux, 1989), pp. 10–13.
3. Haygood, *In Black and White*, p. 103.
4. Davis, Jr., Boyar, and Boyar. *Why Me?*, p. 26.
5. Official Military Personnel File for Sammy Davis, Jr., National Archives Online Database.

Chapter 8

1. Richard Nixon and Frank Gannon, "Frank Gannon's Interview with Richard Nixon, February 9, 1983, part 3," University of Georgia Libraries, Special Collections.
2. Richard Nixon FBI application, National Archives, p. 47.
3. Stephen E. Ambrose, *Nixon, Volume 1: The Education of a Politician, 1913–1962* (New York: Simon & Schuster, 1988), pp. 88–92.
4. David Halberstam, *The Fifties* (New York: Random House, 1994), pp. 324–325.
5. Richard Nixon, *The Memoirs of Richard Nixon* (New York: Grosset & Dunlap, 1978), p. 23.
6. Will Swift, *Pat and Dick: The Nixons, an Intimate Portrait of a Marriage* (New York: Threshold Editions, 2014), pp. 17–23.
7. Roger Morris, *Richard Milhous Nixon: The Rise of an American Politician* (New York: Holt, 1990), p. 237.
8. Ambrose, *Nixon*, pp. 102–103.
9. Morris, *Richard Milhous Nixon*, pp. 244–226.
10. Nixon, *The Memoirs of Richard Nixon*, p. 28.
11. Ambrose, *Nixon*, p. 110.

12. Harrison E. Salisbury, "My Nixon File," *Esquire*, August 1980.
13. Ambrose, *Nixon*, pp. 111–112.
14. Morris, *Richard Milhous Nixon*, p. 252.
15. Ambrose, *Nixon*, p. 112.
16. Donald Jackson, "The Young Nixon," *Life*, 6 November 1970.

Chapter 9

1. Roger Morris, *Richard Milhous Nixon: The Rise of an American Politician* (New York: Holt, 1990), pp. 262–263.
2. George Brown Tindall and David Emory Shi, *America: A Narrative History*, vol. 2, 4th ed. (New York: W.W. Norton, 1996), p. 1293.
3. Morris, *Richard Milhous Nixon*, pp. 270–280.
4. Richard Nixon, *The Memoirs of Richard Nixon* (New York: Grosset & Dunlap, 1978), pp. 34–35.
5. John A. Farrell, *Richard Nixon: The Life* (New York: Vintage, 2018), pp. 15–17.
6. Stephen E. Ambrose, *Nixon, Volume 1: The Education of a Politician, 1913–1962* (New York: Simon & Schuster, 1988), pp. 129–140.
7. Nixon, *The Memoirs of Richard Nixon*, p. 44.
8. Morris, *Richard Milhous Nixon*, p. 343.
9. Susan Jacoby, *Alger Hiss and the Battle for History* (New Haven: Yale University Press, 2010), pp, 11–12.
10. Rick Perlstein, *Nixonland: The Rise of a President and the Fracturing of America*. (New York: Scribner's, 2009), p. 23.
11. Alger Hiss Congressional Testimony, 80th Congress, House Un-American Activities Committee, 5 August 1948.
12. Whittaker Chambers Congressional Testimony, 80th Congress, House Un-American Activities Committee, 17 August 1948.
13. Farrell, *Richard Nixon*, p. 114.

Chapter 10

1. Jerry Jeff Walker, *Gypsy Songman* (Emeryville, CA: Woodford Press, 1999), pp. 5–17.

2. Richard Skanse, "Jerry Jeff Walker: A Man Must Carry On," *Texas Music*, Spring 2004.
3. Walker, *Gypsy Songman*, pp. 19–37.

Chapter 11

1. Jerry Jeff Walker, *Gypsy Songman* (Emeryville, CA: Woodford Press, 1999), pp. 47–60.
2. Arrest Books—First Precinct Jail, New Orleans, Louisiana, 5 July 1965, New Orleans Public Library.

Chapter 12

1. Sammy Davis, Jr., Jane Boyar, and Burt Boyar, *Yes I Can: The Story of Sammy Davis, Jr.* (New York: Farrar, Straus & Giroux, 1965), pp. 76–77.
2. Wil Haygood, *In Black and White: The Life of Sammy Davis, Jr.* (New York: Billboard, 2005), pp. 96–98.
3. *Ibid.*, 104.
4. Davis, Jr., Boyar, and Boyar, *Yes I Can*, pp. 82–88.
5. Gary Fishgall, *Gonna Do Great Things: The Life of Sammy Davis, Jr.* (New York: Scribner's, 2003), p. 41.
6. Haygood, *In Black and White*, p. 107.
7. Davis, Jr., Boyar, and Boyar, *Yes I Can*, p. 82.
8. Haygood, *In Black and White*, pp. 112–114.
9. Davis, Jr., Boyar, and Boyar, *Yes I Can*, p. 88.
10. Haygood, *In Black and White*, pp. 120–121.
11. Davis, Jr., Boyar, and Boyar, *Yes I Can*, p. 131.
12. Fishgall, *Gonna Do Great Things*, p. 57.
13. Haygood, *In Black and White*, p. 121.
14. Fishgall, *Gonna Do Great Things*, pp. 67–68.

Chapter 13

1. Stephen E. Ambrose. *Nixon, Volume 1: The Education of a Politician, 1913–1962* (New York: Simon & Schuster, 1988), p. 211.
2. Greg Mitchell, *Tricky Dick and the*

Pink Lady: Richard Nixon vs. Helen Gahagan Douglas—Sexual Politics and the Red Scare, 1950 (New York: Random House, 1998), pp. 99–106.
   3. Evan Thomas, *Being Nixon: A Man Divided* (New York: Random House, 2016), pp. 56–61.
   4. John A. Farrell, *Richard Nixon: The Life* (New York: Vintage, 2018), pp. 163–176.
   5. Ambrose, *Nixon*, pp. 287–290.

Chapter 14

   1. Wil Haygood, *In Black and White: The Life of Sammy Davis, Jr.* (New York: Billboard, 2005), p. 155.
   2. Gary Fishgall, *Gonna Do Great Things: The Life of Sammy Davis, Jr.* (New York: Scribner's, 2003), pp. 69–73.
   3. Haygood, *In Black and White*, p. 151.
   4. *Ibid.*, pp. 156–173.

Chapter 15

   1. David Halberstam, *The Fifties* (New York: Random House, 1994), p. 49.
   2. Roger Morris, *Richard Milhous Nixon: The Rise of an American Politician* (New York: Holt, 1990), p. 626.
   3. John A. Farrell, *Richard Nixon: The Life* (New York: Vintage, 2018), pp. 212–226.
   4. *Ibid.*, pp. 233–236.
   5. *Ibid.*, pp. 239–244.
   6. George Brown Tindall and David Emory Shi, *America: A Narrative History*, vol. 2, 4th ed. (New York: W.W. Norton, 1996), p. 1377.
   7. Farrell, *Richard Nixon*, pp. 248–259.

Chapter 16

   1. Wil Haygood, *In Black and White: The Life of Sammy Davis, Jr.* (New York: Billboard, 2005), 193.
   2. *Ibid.*, pp. 188–193.
   3. Alex Haley, "Alex Haley Interviews Sammy Davis, Jr.," *Playboy*, December 1966.
   4. Haygood, *In Black and White*, pp. 183–186.
   5. *Ibid.*, pp. 218–221.
   6. Gary Fishgall, *Gonna Do Great Things: The Life of Sammy Davis, Jr..* (New York: Scribner's, 2003), p. 99.
   7. Haygood, *In Black and White*, p. 233.
   8. Fishgall, *Gonna Do Great Things*, p. 100.
   9. Haygood, *In Black and White*, p. 239.

Chapter 17

   1. Wil Haygood, *In Black and White: The Life of Sammy Davis, Jr.* (New York: Billboard, 2005), pp. 254–256.
   2. Sam Kashner, "The Color of Love," *Vanity Fair*, April 1999.
   3. Gary Fishgall, *Gonna Do Great Things: The Life of Sammy Davis, Jr.* (New York: Scribner's, 2003), pp. 110–111.
   4. Haygood, *In Black and White*, p. 263.
   5. Kashner, "The Color of Love."
   6. Alex Haley, "Alex Haley Interviews Sammy Davis, Jr.," *Playboy*, December 1966.
   7. Fishgall, *Gonna Do Great Things*, p. 117.
   8. *Ibid.*, p. 135.
   9. Haygood, *In Black and White*, pp. 285–86.
   10. Fishgall, *Gonna Do Great Things*, p. 131.
   11. "The New Pictures," *Time*, 6 July 1959.
   12. Kim Masters, "David Geffen, Samuel Goldwyn and the Search for the 'Holy Grail' of Missing Movies," *Hollywood Reporter*, 23 February 2017.
   13. Haygood, *In Black and White*, pp. 295–296.

Chapter 18

   1. John A. Farrell, *Richard Nixon: The Life* (New York: Vintage, 2018), p. 266.
   2. Rick Perlstein, *Nixonland: The Rise of a President and the Fracturing of America* (New York: Scribner's, 2008), pp. 47–49.
   3. Farrell, *Richard Nixon*, pp. 280–281.
   4. Perlstein, *Nixonland*, pp. 52–58.
   5. Farrell, *Richard Nixon*, pp. 287–292.

Chapter 19

   1. Sammy Davis, Jr., Jane Boyar, and Burt Boyar. *Why Me? The Sammy Davis, Jr. Story* (New York: Farrar, Straus & Giroux, 1989), p. 103.
   2. Gary Fishgall, *Gonna Do Great*

Things: The Life of Sammy Davis, Jr. (New York: Scribner's, 2003), pp. 140–143.
  3. Wil Haygood, *In Black and White: The Life of Sammy Davis, Jr.* (New York: Billboard, 2005), pp. 304–305.
  4. Fishgall, *Gonna Do Great Things*, pp. 148–153.
  5. *Ocean's 11* (Warner Brothers, 1960).
  6. May Britt, "Why I Married Sammy Davis, Jr.," *Ebony*, January 1961.
  7. Fishgall, *Gonna Do Great Things*, p. 155.
  8. Haygood, *In Black and White*, p. 304.
  9. Davis, Jr., Boyar, and Boyar, *Why Me?*, p. 116.
  10. *Ibid.*, p. 118.

Chapter 20

  1. Jerry Jeff Walker, *Gypsy Songman* (Emeryville, CA: Woodford Press, 1999), pp. 66–83.
  2. Jerry Jeff Walker, *Five Years Gone* (Vanguard Records, 1969).

Chapter 21

  1. Jerry Jeff Walker, *Gypsy Songman* (Emeryville, CA: Woodford Press, 1999), pp. 92–101.
  2. Dave Paulson, "'Mr. Bojangles' Couldn't Have Happened Without the Radio," *Tennessean*, 8 December 2017.

Chapter 22

  1. John A. Farrell, *Richard Nixon: The Life* (New York: Vintage, 2018), pp. 296–304.
  2. Rick Perlstein, *Nixonland: The Rise of a President and the Fracturing of America* (New York: Scribner's, 2008), pp. 59–60.
  3. Matt Lait, "Looking Back at the 1962 Gubernatorial Race," *Los Angeles Times*, 22 March 1992.
  4. Farrell, *Richard Nixon*, pp. 305–306.
  5. Perlstein, *Nixonland*, p. 60.
  6. Farrell, *Richard Nixon*, pp. 305–308.
  7. Lait, "Looking Back at the 1962 Gubernatorial Race."
  8. Farrell, *Richard Nixon*, pp. 310–11.

Chapter 23

  1. Sammy Davis, Jr., Jane Boyar, and Burt Boyar, *Why Me? The Sammy Davis, Jr. Story* (New York: Farrar, Straus & Giroux, 1989), p. 128.
  2. Todd S. Purdum, "From That Day Forth," *Vanity Fair*, February 2011.
  3. Davis, Jr., Boyar, and Boyar, *Why Me?*, pp. 129–130.
  4. Purdum, "From That Day Forth."
  5. Gary Fishgall, *Gonna Do Great Things: The Life of Sammy Davis, Jr.* (New York: Scribner's, 2003), p. 180.
  6. Sammy Davis, Jr., Jane Boyar, and Burt Boyar, *Yes I Can: The Story of Sammy Davis, Jr.* (New York: Farrar, Straus & Giroux, 1965), p. 265.
  7. Emilie Raymond, *Stars for Freedom: Hollywood, Black Celebrities, and the Civil Rights Movement* (Seattle: University of Washington Press, 2015), pp. 54–68.
  8. Fishgall, *Gonna Do Great Things*, pp. 174–176.
  9. Alex Haley, "Alex Haley Interviews Sammy Davis, Jr.," *Playboy*, December 1966.
  10. Wil Haygood, *In Black and White: The Life of Sammy Davis, Jr.* (New York: Billboard, 2005), pp. 313–314.
  11. Fishgall, *Gonna Do Great Things*, p. 180.
  12. Davis, Jr., Boyar, and Boyar, *Why Me?*, p 148.

Chapter 24

  1. Jules Witcover, *The Resurrection of Richard Nixon* (New York: G.P. Putnam's Sons, 1970), pp. 40–42.
  2. "Better to See Once," *Time*, 3 August 1959.
  3. *Ibid.*
  4. Witcover, *The Resurrection of Richard Nixon*, p. 43.
  5. *Ibid.*, p. 42.
  6. *The Jack Paar Program*, NBC, 8 March 1963.
  7. Witcover, *The Resurrection of Richard Nixon*, p. 49.
  8. *Ibid.*, p. 60.
  9. Johnson to Congress, 88th U.S. Congress, 27 November 1963.
  10. Goldwater to Republican National Convention, 16 July 1964.
  11. Rick Perlstein, *Nixonland: The Rise of a President and the Fracturing of America* (New York: Scribner's, 2009), pp. 62–65.

12. Witcover, *The Resurrection of Richard Nixon*, pp. 111–112.

Chapter 25

1. Wil Haygood, *In Black and White: The Life of Sammy Davis, Jr.* (New York: Billboard, 2005), pp. 363–364.
2. Gary Fishgall, *Gonna Do Great Things: The Life of Sammy Davis, Jr.* (New York: Scribner's, 2003), p. 202.
3. Shannon Heupel, "Beyond the Stars: Coleman Woodson, Jr., Returns to Scene of 1965 March at the City of St. Jude," *Montgomery Advertiser*, 26 February 2020.
4. Emilie Raymond, *Stars for Freedom: Hollywood, Black Celebrities, and the Civil Rights Movement* (Seattle: University of Washington Press, 2015), p. 192.
5. *Ibid.*, p. 175.
6. Sammy Davis, Jr., Jane Boyar, and Burt Boyar, *Why Me? The Sammy Davis, Jr. Story* (New York: Farrar, Straus & Giroux, 1989), p. 103.
7. Haygood, *In Black and White*, p. 366.
8. Raymond, *Stars for Freedom*, p. 180.
9. Thomas Thompson, "A Five-Month Ordeal, with a Whole Career at Stake," *Life*, 13 November 1964.
10. Fishgall, *Gonna Do Great Things*, p. 198.
11. Howard Taubman, "Sammy Davis in a Musical 'Golden Boy,'" *New York Times*, 21 October 1964.
12. Thompson, "A Five-Month Ordeal."
13. Fishgall, *Gonna Do Great Things*, p. 203.
14. Haygood, *In Black and White*, p. 384.
15. Fishgall, *Gonna Do Great Things*, pp. 230–231.

Chapter 26

1. George C. Herring, *America's Longest War: The United States and Vietnam, 1950–1975*, 4th ed. (New York: Knopf, 1986), pp. 125–126.
2. Daniel Ellsberg, *Secrets: A Memoir of Vietnam and the Pentagon Papers* (New York: Penguin, 2003), pp. 155–160.
3. John A. Farrell, *Richard Nixon: The Life* (New York: Vintage, 2018), p. 319.
4. Rick Perlstein, *Nixonland: The Rise of a President and the Fracturing of America* (New York: Scribner's, 2008) p. 189.
5. *Ibid.*, p. 124.
6. Farrell, *Richard Nixon*, p. 317.
7. *Ibid.*
8. Leonard Pitts, Jr., "Did Wallace Truly Change His Racist Views?" *Chicago Tribune*, 22 September 1998.
9. Perlstein, *Nixonland*, p. 78.
10. *Ibid.*, p. 341.
11. Farrell, *Richard Nixon*, p. 339.
12. Perlstein, *Nixonland*, p. 334.
13. Farrell, *Richard Nixon*, pp. 330–331.
14. Anthony Summers, *The Arrogance of Power: The Secret World of Richard Nixon* (New York: Viking, 2000), p. 301.
15. Jules Witcover, *The Year The Dream Died: Revisiting 1968 in America* (New York: Grand Central, 1998), p. 410.
16. Perlstein, *Nixonland*, p. 350.
17. Summers, *The Arrogance of Power*, p. 299.
18. Farrell, *Richard Nixon*, pp. 341–343.
19. *Ibid.*, p. 638.
20. Transcript, Nixon to Johnson call, 3 November 1968, Miller Center of Public Affairs, University of Virginia.
21. Farrell, *Richard Nixon*, pp. 343–346.

Chapter 27

1. John A. Farrell, *Richard Nixon: The Life* (New York: Vintage, 2018), pp. 350–362.
2. Rick Perlstein, *Nixonland: The Rise of a President and the Fracturing of America* (New York: Scribner's, 2009), pp. 373–374.
3. Farrell, *Richard Nixon*, p. 349.
4. *Ibid.*, p. 357.
5. *Ibid.*, pp. 411–412.
6. Perlstein, *Nixonland*, p. 472.
7. *Ibid.*, p. 497.
8. *Ibid.*, p. 419.
9. Farrell, *Richard Nixon*, p. 403.
10. H.R. Haldeman, *The Haldeman Diaries: Inside the Nixon White House* (New York: Berkley, 1995), pp. 159–161.
11. Anthony Summers, *The Arrogance of Power: The Secret World of Richard Nixon* (New York: Viking, 2000), pp. 364–365.
12. Richard Nixon, *The Memoirs of Richard Nixon* (New York: Grosset & Dunlap, 1978), p. 462.
13. Anthony Summers, *The Arrogance of Power*, p. 366.

14. Haldeman, *The Haldeman Diaries*, p. 163.
15. Neil Sheehan, "Vietnam Archive: Pentagon Study Traces 3 Decades of U.S. Involvement," *New York Times*, 13 June 1971.
16. Douglas Brinkley and Luke Nichter, *The Nixon Tapes* (Boston: Houghton Mifflin Harcourt, 2014), p. 171.
17. John Farrell, *Richard Nixon*, p. 423.
18. *Ibid.*, p. 427.
19. *Ibid.*, p. 426.

Chapter 28

1. Peter Bailey, "Humble Davis Thanks Blacks," *Jet*, 24 April 1969.
2. Rick Perlstein, *Nixonland: The Rise of a President and the Fracturing of America* (New York: Scribner's, 2009), p. 187.
3. Sammy Davis, Jr., Jane Boyar, and Burt Boyar, *Why Me? The Sammy Davis, Jr. Story* (New York: Farrar, Straus & Giroux, 1989), pp. 192-193.
4. *Ibid.*, pp. 202-221.
5. Wil Haygood, *In Black and White: The Life of Sammy Davis, Jr.* (New York: Billboard, 2005), pp. 405-406.
6. *Ibid.*, pp. 410-416.
7. Davis, Jr., Boyar, and Boyar, *Why Me?*, p. 246.
8. Haygood, *In Black and White*, p. 417.
9. Davis, Jr., Boyar, and Boyar, *Why Me?*, p. 260.
10. *Ibid.*, p. 249.

Chapter 29

1. "Star Athlete Tackles Guitar," *Oneonta Star*, 6 January 1968.
2. Jerry Jeff Walker, *Gypsy Songman* (Emeryville, CA: Woodford Press, 1999), pp. 108-112.

Chapter 30

1. Jerry Jeff Walker, *Gypsy Songman* (Emeryville, CA: Woodford Press, 1999), pp. 119-120.
2. Jerry Jeff Walker, liner notes, *A Man Must Carry On* (MCA Records, 1977).
3. Josh Davidson, "The Man Who Dreamed Up Luckenbach," *Texas Monthly*, July 1984.
4. Becky Crouch Patterson, *Hondo: My Father* (Austin, TX: Shoal Creek, 1979), p. 4.
5. Jerry Jeff Walker, liner notes, *Viva Terlingua* (MCA Records, 1973).
6. Walker, *Gypsy Songman*, pp. 130-142.
7. Larry L. King, *Of Outlaws, Con Men, Whores, Politicians, and Other Artists* (New York: Penguin, 1981), p. 142.
8. Richard Skanse, "Jerry Jeff Walker: A Man Must Carry On," *Texas Music*, Spring 2004.
9. Douglas Kent Hall, "'Mr. Bojangles' Dance: The Odyssey and Oddities of Jerry Jeff Walker," *Rolling Stone*, 19 December 1974.
10. Jerry Jeff Walker and Charles John Quarto, "Like Some Song You Can't Unlearn" (*A Man Must Carry On*, MCA Records, 1977).
11. Walker, *Gypsy Songman*, pp. 161-162.

Chapter 31

1. Nixon White House Recordings, Conversation 534-011, Richard Nixon Presidential Library and Museum (RNL).
2. Hugh Davis Graham, "Richard Nixon and Civil Rights: Explaining an Enigma," *Presidential Studies Quarterly*, vol. 26, no. 1 (1996): 93-106.
3. John A. Farrell, *Richard Nixon: The Life* (New York: Vintage, 2018), pp. 383-393.
4. Richard Nixon, First Inaugural Address, 20 January 1969.
5. Farrell, *Richard Nixon*, pp. 385-390.
6. Robert J. Brown, *You Can't Go Wrong Doing Right: How a Child of Poverty Rose to the White House and Helped Change the World* (New York: Convergent, 2019), pp. 136-138.
7. *Ibid.*, p. 164.
8. Sammy Davis, Jr., Jane Boyar, and Burt Boyar, *Why Me? The Sammy Davis, Jr. Story* (New York: Farrar, Straus & Giroux, 1989), p. 249.
9. Nixon White House Recordings, Conversation 534-011, RNL.
10. James Conaway, "Sammy Davis, Jr. Has Bought the Bus," *New York Times Magazine*, 15 October 1972.
11. Davis to Nixon, 3 February 1972, Jeb Magruder CREEP Box 14, RNL.

Chapter 32

1. Wil Haygood, *In Black and White: The Life of Sammy Davis, Jr.* (New York: Billboard, 2005), pp. 425–426.
2. Sammy Davis, Jr., Jane Boyar, and Burt Boyar, *Why Me? The Sammy Davis, Jr. Story* (New York: Farrar, Straus & Giroux, 1989), p. 253.
3. Sammy Davis, Jr., "Why I Went to the Troops," *Ebony*, June 1972.
4. Brown to Ehrlichman, 15 March 1972, Egil Krogh Box 6, Richard Nixon Presidential Library and Museum (RNL).
5. Davis, Jr., Boyar, and Boyar, *Why Me?*, p. 257.
6. "President Nixon Honors Bob Brown at Washington Hilton Hotel," WHCA SR P-720116, 30 January 1972, RNL.
7. *All in the Family*, pilot episode, CBS, 12 January 1971.
8. Gene Weingarten, "Just What Was He Smoking?," *Washington Post*, 21 March 2002.
9. *All in the Family*, "Sammy's Visit," CBS, 19 February 1972.
10. Haygood, *In Black and White*, p. 421.
11. Richard Nixon, Republican youth rally, Miami Beach Convention Center, 22 August 1972.

Chapter 33

1. Bob Woodward and Carl Bernstein, *The Secret Man: The Story of Watergate's Deep Throat* (New York: Simon & Schuster, 2006), pp. 46–52.
2. John A. Farrell, *Richard Nixon: The Life* (New York: Vintage, 2018), pp. 465–472.
3. Rick Perlstein, *Nixonland: The Rise of a President and the Fracturing of America* (New York: Scribner's, 2008), pp. 678–684.
4. Woodward and Bernstein, *The Secret Man*, p. 4.

Chapter 34

1. Wil Haygood. *In Black and White: The Life of Sammy Davis, Jr.* (New York: Billboard, 2005), p. 434.
2. Bob Thompson, "Richard Nixon and the Oobie-Doobie Girl," *Washington Post*, 27 July 1997.
3. Richard E. Farley, "A Brief History of Artists Giving the President Their Unvarnished Opinion," *Town and Country*, 21 November 2016.
4. Gannon to Nixon, President's Office Files, Box 87, White House Special Files (WHSF), Richard Nixon Presidential Library and Museum (RNL).
5. Evening at the White House, NPC-1211-194-73, 3 March 1973, RNL.
6. Gannon to Nixon, President's Office Files, Box 87, WHSF, RNL.
7. Donnie Radcliffe, "An Evening with 'The Man' and 'Golden Boy,'" *Washington Post*, 5 March 1973.
8. Sammy Davis, Jr., Jane Boyar, and Burt Boyar, *Why Me? The Sammy Davis, Jr. Story* (New York: Farrar, Straus & Giroux, 1989), p. 271.
9. Nixon White House Recordings, Conversation 037–045, RNL.
10. Gary Fishgall, *Gonna Do Great Things: The Life of Sammy Davis, Jr.* (New York: Scribner's, 2003), p. 286.
11. "Sammy Davis Offers to Stage P.O.W. Gala," *New York Times*, 4 March 1973.
12. Nixon to Haldeman, President's Personal File, Box 134, WHSF, RNL.
13. Scott to Haldeman, Social Affairs File, Box, 26, White House Central Files, RNL.
14. John A. Farrell, *Richard Nixon: The Life* (New York: Vintage, 2018), p. 506.
15. Evan Thomas, *Being Nixon: A Man Divided* (New York: Random House, 2016), pp. 455–56.
16. Haygood, *In Black and White*, pp. 434–436.
17. Paul Delaney, "Black Supporters of President Under Fire," *New York Times*, 17 October 1972.
18. Davis, Jr., Boyar, and Boyar, *Why Me?*, p. 267.
19. "Sammy Davis Jr. on Sammy Davis Jr., Sex, Suicide, Success, Richard Nixon, Frank Sinatra, Black and White Women, Blacks and Jews," *Ebony*, March 1980.
20. Davis, Jr., Boyar, and Boyar, *Why Me?*, p. 267.
21. "Sammy Davis Jr. on Sammy Davis Jr., ..."
22. Haygood, *In Black and White*, p. 436.

Chapter 35

1. John A. Farrell. *Richard Nixon: The Life* (New York: Vintage, 2018), pp. 525–526.

2. Alexander Butterfield, Senate Watergate hearing, 13 July 1973, 93rd U.S. Congress.
3. Farrell, *Richard Nixon*, pp. 519–533.
4. *Ibid.*, 534–543.
5. Evan Thomas, *Being Nixon* (New York: Random House, 2016), pp. 513–522.
6. Bob Woodward and Carl Bernstein, *The Secret Man: The Story of Watergate's Deep Throat* (New York: Simon & Schuster, 2006), p. 147.
7. Thomas, *Being Nixon*, p. 528.
8. Robert Sam Anson, *Exile: The Unquiet Oblivion of Richard M. Nixon* (New York: Simon & Schuster, 1984), p. 68.

Chapter 36

1. Wil Haygood, *In Black and White: The Life of Sammy Davis, Jr.* (New York: Billboard, 2005), p. 452.
2. James Conaway, "Sammy Davis, Jr. Has Bought the Bus," *New York Times Magazine*, 15 October 1972.
3. Sammy Davis, Jr., *Hollywood in a Suitcase* (New York: Berkley, 1981), p. 247.
4. Robert A. DeLeon, "Sammy Davis Jr. Talks about Himself, His Wife and His Career," *Jet*, 23 November 1973.
5. Gary Fishgall, *Gonna Do Great Things: The Life of Sammy Davis, Jr.* (New York: Scribner's, 2003), p. 287.
6. "Sammy Davis Jr. on Sammy Davis Jr., Sex, Suicide, Success, Richard Nixon, Frank Sinatra, Black and White Women, Blacks and Jews," *Ebony*, March 1980.
7. Davis, Jr., *Hollywood in a Suitcase*, p. 247.
8. Conaway, "Sammy Davis, Jr. Has Bought the Bus."
9. "Sammy Davis Jr. on Sammy Davis Jr., …"
10. *Ibid.*
11. Haygood, *In Black and White*, p. 443.
12. *Ibid.*, 455.
13. Sammy Davis, Jr., Jane Boyar, and Burt Boyar, *Why Me? The Sammy Davis, Jr. Story* (New York: Farrar, Straus & Giroux, 1989), p. 301.
14. Haygood, *In Black and White*, p. 446.

15. Davis, Jr., Boyar, and Boyar, *Why Me?*, p. 316.
16. Haygood, *In Black and White*, p. 456.
17. *Ibid.*, pp. 465–467.
18. Matt Birkbeck, *Deconstructing Sammy: Music, Money, and Madness* (New York: Amistad, 2009), p. 2.

Chapter 37

1. Larry L. King, "Jacky Jack Is Back," *Washington Post*, 15 May 1980.
2. Roy Blount, Jr., "Running Wild with Jerry Jeff," *Texas Monthly*, May 1979.
3. Jerry Jeff Walker, *Gypsy Songman* (Emeryville, CA: Woodford Press, 1999), p. 164.
4. Blount, Jr., "Running Wild with Jerry Jeff."
5. Dennis Wall, "Beat the Devil," *Third Coast: The Magazine of Contemporary Austin*, June 1985.
6. Don Kardong, "Feet on Solid Ground—Country singer Jerry Jeff Walker takes to the road to clean up his act," *Running*, April 1982.
7. Walker, *Gypsy Songman*, p. 166.
8. Russ DeVault, "Walker's Tried and True Sound Is Attracting a New Generation," *Atlanta Journal-Constitution*, 5 February 1998.
9. Liz Smith, "If Sinatra Jr. Could, He'd Kiss Kiss Goodbye," *Chicago Tribune*, 2 October 1977.
10. Jan Reid, *The Improbable Rise of Redneck Rock* (New York: Da Capo, 1977), p. 108.
11. King, "Jacky Jack Is Back."
12. Mike Greenblatt, "Jerry Jeff Walker: The Magic Is Being Alive," *Aquarian*, 14–21 October 1981.
13. John Moulder, "Jerry Jeff Walker, 'Mr. Bojangles,' Battles Hollywood," *Country Style*, March 1980.
14. Greenblatt, "Jerry Jeff Walker."
15. Todd Snider, *I Never Met a Story I Didn't Like: Mostly True Tall Tales* (Boston: Da Capo, 2014), p. 35.

Bibliography

Books

Ambrose, Stephen. *Nixon, Volume 1: The Education of a Politician, 1913-1962.* 1987. New York: Simon & Schuster, 1988.

Anson, Robert Sam. *Exile: The Unquiet Oblivion of Richard M. Nixon.* New York: Simon & Schuster, 1984.

Birkbeck, Matt. *Deconstructing Sammy: Music, Money, and Madness.* New York: Amistad, 2009.

Brinkley, Douglas, and Luke Nichter. *The Nixon Tapes.* Boston: Houghton Mifflin Harcourt, 2014.

Brown, Robert J. *You Can't Go Wrong Doing Right: How a Child of Poverty Rose to the White House and Helped Change the World.* New York: Convergent, 2019.

Davis, Sammy, Jr. *Hollywood in a Suitcase.* 1980. New York: Berkley, 1981.

Davis, Sammy, Jr., Jane Boyar, and Burt Boyar. *Why Me? The Sammy Davis, Jr. Story.* New York: Farrar, Straus & Giroux, 1989.

_____. *Yes I Can: The Story of Sammy Davis, Jr.* New York: Farrar, Straus & Giroux, 1965.

Early, Gerald. *The Sammy Davis, Jr., Reader.* New York: Farrar, Straus & Giroux, 2001.

Ellsberg, Daniel. *Secrets: A Memoir of Vietnam and the Pentagon Papers.* 2002. New York: Penguin, 2003.

Farrell, John A. *Richard Nixon: The Life.* 2017. New York: Vintage, 2018.

Fishgall, Gary. *Gonna Do Great Things: The Life of Sammy Davis, Jr.* New York: Scribner's, 2003.

Halberstam, David. *The Fifties.* 1993. New York: Fawcett, 1994.

Haldeman, H.R. *The Haldeman Diaries: Inside the Nixon White House.* 1994. New York: Berkley, 1995.

Haygood, Wil. *In Black and White: The Life of Sammy Davis, Jr.* 2003. New York: Billboard, 2005.

Herring, George C. *America's Longest War: The United States and Vietnam, 1950-1975.* 2nd ed. New York: Knopf, 1986.

Jacoby, Susan. *Alger Hiss and the Battle for History.* 2009. New Haven: Yale University Press, 2010.

King, Larry L. *Of Outlaws, Con Men, Whores, Politicians, and Other Artists.* 1980. New York: Penguin, 1981.

Mitchell, Greg. *Tricky Dick and the Pink Lady: Richard Nixon vs. Helen Gahagan Douglas—Sexual Politics and the Red Scare, 1950.* New York: Random House, 1998.

Morris, Roger. *Richard Milhous Nixon: The Rise of an American Politician.* New York: Holt, 1990.

Nixon, Richard. *The Memoirs of Richard Nixon.* New York: Grosset & Dunlap, 1978.

Patterson, Becky Crouch. *Hondo: My Father.* Austin, TX: Shoal Creek, 1979.

Perlstein, Rick. *Nixonland: The Rise of a President and the Fracturing of America.* New York: Scribner's, 2008.

Raymond, Emilie. *Stars for Freedom: Hollywood, Black Celebrities, and the Civil Rights Movement.* Seattle: University of Washington Press, 2015.

Reeves, Richard. *President Kennedy: Profile of Power.* Nowralk, CT: Easton Press, 2000.

Reid, Jan. *The Improbable Rise of Redneck Rock.* New York: Da Capo, 1977.

Snider, Todd. *I Never Met a Story I Didn't Like: Mostly True Tall Tales*. Boston: Da Capo, 2014.
Southern, Eileen. *The Music of Black Americans: A History*. 3rd ed. New York: W.W. Norton, 1997.
Summers, Anthony. *The Arrogance of Power: The Secret World of Richard Nixon*. New York: Viking, 2000.
Swift, Will. *Pat and Dick: The Nixons, an Intimate Portrait of a Marriage*. New York: Threshold, 2014.
Thomas, Evan. *Being Nixon: A Man Divided*. 2015. New York: Random House, 2016.
Tindall, George Brown, and David Emory Shi. *America: A Narrative History*, vol. 2. 4th ed. New York, London: W.W. Norton, 1996.
Toll, Robert C. *On with the Show! The First Century of Show Business in America*. New York: Oxford University Press, 1976.
Walker, Jerry Jeff. *Gypsy Songman*. Emeryville, CA: Woodford Press, 1999.
Witcover, Jules. *The Resurrection of Richard Nixon*. New York: Putnam, 1970.
———. *The Year the Dream Died: Revisiting 1968 in America*. 1997. New York: Grand Central, 1998.
Woodward, Bob, and Carl Bernstein. *The Secret Man: The Story of Watergate's Deep Throat*. 2005. New York: Simon & Schuster, 2006.

Newspapers and Magazines

Bailey, Peter. "Humble Davis Thanks Blacks." *Jet*, 24 April 1969.
"Better to See Once." *Time*, 3 August 1959.
Blount, Roy, Jr. "Running Wild with Jerry Jeff." *Texas Monthly*. May 1979.
Britt, May. "Why I Married Sammy Davis, Jr." *Ebony*, January 1961.
Conaway, James. "Sammy Davis, Jr. Has Bought the Bus." *New York Times Magazine*, 15 October 1972.
Davidson. Josh. "The Man Who Dreamed Up Luckenbach." *Texas Monthly*, July 1984.
Davis, Sammy, Jr. "Why I Went to the Troops." *Ebony*, June 1972.
Delaney, Paul. "Black Supporters of President Under Fire." *New York Times*, 17 October 1972.
DeLeon, Robert A. "Sammy Davis Jr. Talks About Himself, His Wife and His Career." *Jet*, 23 November 1973.
DeVault, Russ. "Walker's Tried and True Sound Is Attracting a New Generation." *Atlanta Journal-Constitution*, 5 February 1998.
Farley, Richard E. "A Brief History of Artists Giving the President Their Unvarnished Opinion." *Town and Country*, 21 November 2016.
Graham, Hugh Davis. "Richard Nixon and Civil Rights: Explaining an Enigma." *Presidential Studies Quarterly* vol. 26, no. 1 (1996): 93–106.
Greenblatt, Mike. "Jerry Jeff Walker: The Magic Is Being Alive." *Aquarian*, 14–21 October 1981.
Haley, Alex. "Alex Haley Interviews Sammy Davis, Jr." *Playboy*, December 1966.
Hall, Douglas Kent. "Mr. Bojangles' Dance: The Odyssey and Oddities of Jerry Jeff Walker." *Rolling Stone*, 19 December 1974.
Heupel, Shannon. "Beyond the Stars: Coleman Woodson, Jr., Returns to Scene of 1965 March at the City of St. Jude." *Montgomery Advertiser*, 26 February 2020.
Jackson, Donald. "The Young Nixon." *Life*, 6 November 1970.
Kardong, Don. "Feet on Solid Ground—Country Singer Jerry Jeff Walker Takes to the Road to Clean Up His Act." *Running*, April 1982.
Kashner, Sam. "The Color of Love." *Vanity Fair*, April 1999.
King, Larry L. "Jacky Jack Is Back." *Washington Post*, 15 May 1980.
Lait, Matt. "Looking Back at the 1962 Gubernatorial Race." *Los Angeles Times*, 22 March 1992.
Masters, Kim. "David Geffen, Samuel Goldwyn and the Search for the 'Holy Grail' of Missing Movies." *Hollywood Reporter*, 23 February 2017.
Moulder, John. "Jerry Jeff Walker, 'Mr. Bojangles,' Battles Hollywood." *Country Style*, March 1980.
"The New Pictures." *Time*, 6 July 1959.
Paulson, Dave. "'Mr. Bojangles' Couldn't Have Happened Without the Radio." *Tennessean*, 8 December 2017.
Pitts, Leonard, Jr. "Did Wallace Truly Change His Racist Views?" *Chicago Tribune*, 22 September 1998.

Purdum, Todd S. "From That Day Forth." *Vanity Fair*, February 2011.
Radcliffe, Donnie. "An Evening with 'The Man' and 'Golden Boy.'" *Washington Post*, 5 March 1973.
Salisbury, Harrison E. "My Nixon File." *Esquire*, August 1980.
"Sammy Davis Jr. on Sammy Davis Jr., Sex, Suicide, Success, Richard Nixon, Frank Sinatra, Black and White Women, Blacks and Jews." *Ebony*, March 1980.
"Sammy Davis Offers to Stage P.O.W. Gala." *New York Times*, 4 March 1973.
Sheehan, Neil. "Vietnam Archive: Pentagon Study Traces 3 Decades of Growing U.S. Involvement." *New York Times*, 13 June 1971.
Skanse, Richard. "Jerry Jeff Walker: A Man Must Carry On." *Texas Music*, Spring 2004.
Smith, Liz. "True Grits." *Chicago Tribune*, 2 October 1977.
"Star Athlete Tackles Guitar." *Oneonta Star*, 6 January 1968.
Taubman, Howard. "Sammy Davis in a Musical 'Golden Boy.'" *New York Times*, 21 October 1964.
Thompson, Bob. "Richard Nixon and the Oobie-Doobie Girl." *Washington Post*, 27 July 1997.
Thompson, Thomas. "A Five-Month Ordeal, with a Whole Career at Stake." *Life*, 13 November 1964.
Wall, Dennis. "Beat the Devil." *Third Coast: The Magazine of Contemporary Austin*, June 1985.
Weingarten, Gene. "Just What Was He Smoking?" *Washington Post*, 21 March 2002.
Willman, Tom. "Teapot Dome Scandal Drew Nixon into Law, Cousin Says." *Independent* (Long Beach, CA), 11 May 1973.

Records, Films and Television

Jerry Jeff Walker LPs:

- *Mr. Bojangles*—ATCO, 1968
- *Five Years Gone*—Vanguard, 1969
- *Viva Terlingua*—MCA, 1973
- *A Man Must Carry On*—MCA, 1977

Sammy Davis, Jr., LPs:

- *Something for Everyone*—Motown, 1970
- *Portrait of Sammy Davis, Jr.*—MGM, 1972
- *Sammy Davis, Jr. Now*—MGM, 1972

Films and Television

The Jack Paar Program. NBC, 8 March 1963.
Ocean's 11, dir. Lewis Milestone, Warner Brothers, 1960.
Rufus Jones for President, dir. Roy Mack, Warner Brothers, 1933. https://www.youtube.com/watch?v=DICgr6m7HOA
All In the Family, "Sammy's Visit." CBS, 19 February 1972.
American Masters, "Sammy Davis, Jr.: I've Gotta Be Me," dir. Sam Pollard. PBS, 2019.

Archival

Files from Richard Nixon Presidential Library and Museum (RNL)

Committee to Re-elect the President (CREEP):

Jeb Magruder, Box 14

White House Special Files (WHSF):

President's Office Files, Box 87
President's Personal File, Box 134
Egil Krogh, Box 6

White House Central Files (WHCF):

Social Affairs File, Box 26

White House Communications Agency Sound Recording:

WHCA SR P-720116

Naval Photographic Center Film Collection:

NPC-1211-194-73

Nixon White House Recordings:

Conversation-534-011
Conversation-037-045

Bibliography

Online Resources

FBI Online Vault:
FBI Application of Richard Nixon, https://vault.fbi.gov/Pres.%20Richard%20Nixons%20FBI%20Application

Sammy Davis, Jr. FBI file, https://vault.fbi.gov/Sammy%20Davis%2C%20Jr

National Archives Online Database:
Military Personnel File, Sammy Davis, Jr., https://catalog.archives.gov/id/57283794

University of Georgia:
Frank Gannon interviews Richard Nixon, https://georgiaoralhistory.libs.uga.edu/gannix

University of Missouri–Kansas City School of Law:
Alger Hiss Congressional Testimony, 5 August 1948, https://www.famous-trials.com/algerhiss/655-8-5testimony

Whitaker Chambers Congressional Testimony, 17 August 1948, https://www.famous-trials.com/algerhiss/654-8-3testimony

University of Virginia Miller Center:
Nixon to Johnson call. 3 November 1968. Transcript: https://prde.upress.virginia.edu/conversations/4006126

Index

Acheson Dean 49, 74
Agnew, Spiro 205
Ailes, Roger 152–153
All About Eve (film) 71
All in the Family (TV show) 194–196
Allen, Steve 70
Anderson, Jack 209
Anna Lucasta (film) 101
Armstrong, Louis 71, 128
Astaire, Fred 71, 156

Bacall, Lauren 110
Baez, Joan 144
Baker, Howard 209
Baldwin, James 130, 132, 144
Ball, Lucille 110, 170
The Band 118
Batman (TV show) 173
Bee Gees 117
Belafonte, Harry 100–101, 116, 126–129, 142–145, 170, 189, 195, 219
Bennett, Tony 144
Benny, Jack 68, 110
Berlin, Irving 205–206
Bernstein, Carl 206
Best Little Whorehouse in Texas (Broadway play) 181
The Birth of the Blues (song) 90
Bishop, Joey 83, 110
Blood, Sweat and Tears 171
Boddy, Manchester 74
Bogart, Humphrey 71, 90, 110
Bork, Robert 210
Brando, Marlon 109
Brezhnev, Leonid 212
Britt, May 109–110, 112–113, 126, 131–133, 143, 145–147, 170
Bromberg, Davis 116
Brown, James 207
Brown, Jim 188
Brown, Pat 123–125
Brown, Robert J. 187–190, 192–193, 207
Buchanan, Pat 152
Buckley, Lord 54

Buffett, Jimmy 174, 180–181, 224
Bush, George H. W. 213
Butterfield, Alexander 163, 209

Cagney, James 34, 68
The Candy Man (song) 172, 194, 204
Cantor, Eddie 83, 91
Carmichael, Stokely 151
Carson, Johnny 168
Carter, Jimmy 213, 226
Cass, Mama 115
Chambers, Whittaker 49–50
Chapman, Charlie 31
Chapman, Lita Grey 31
Chennault, Anna 156–157, 164, 198
Church, Frank 212
Churchill, Winston 45
Clark, Guy 115
Clawson, Ken 214
Clifford, Clark 164
Clinton, Bill 213, 226–227
Clinton, Hillary Rodham 121
Cohen, Mickey 98, 100
Cohn, Harry 96–98, 100
Cole, Nat King 127
The Colgate Comedy Hour (TV show) 72
Colson, Charles 159
Connally, John 178
Conniff, Ray 202
Cooper, Gary 90
Cosby, Bill 208
Coward, Neil 170
Cox, Archibald 206, 210
Cronin, John 51
Crouch, Hondo 178–179, 182–184
Crystal, Billy 221
Curb, Mike 172, 196
Curtis, Tony 81–82, 96, 170

Daley, Richard 120, 190
D'Amato, Paul "Skinny" 93, 217
Damone, Vic 206
Dancing Shoes (song) 71

243

Index

Davis, Altovise (Gore) 169–170, 173, 188, 191–192, 204, 218–219, 221–223
Davis, Elvira (Sanchez) 12–15, 29–30, 170
Davis, Miles 54
Davis, Ossie 208
Davis, Rosa 11, 14
Davis, Sam, Sr. 10–11, 14–15, 27–33, 35, 67–69, 78–80, 82–83, 91–92, 94–95, 98, 130, 170, 222
Davis, Sammy, Jr. 12, 14–15, 27–35, 67–72, 78–83, 90–103, 109–113, 126–133, 142–147, 166–173, 185–197, 202–208, 216–223, 226–227
Day, Roy 45, 47, 73, 75
Dean, John 200, 205, 210
De Gaulle, Charles 136
Denver, John 219
Dewey, Thomas 75–76
Dexter, Walter 24, 46
Diamond, Neil 219
The Dick Cavett Show (TV show) 174
Diem, Bui 156
Diem, Ngo Dinh 148–149
Dirksen, Everett 156
Dorsey, Tommy 32
Douglas, Helen Gahagan 73–74, 198
Drifting Way of Life (song) 62
Driftwood, Jimmy 117
Duke, James Buchanan 24
Duke University 24
Dulles, John Foster 49
Dylan, Bob 55–56, 114, 219

Eckstine, Billy 218
Edwards, Edwin 180
Ehrlichman, John 162, 186, 194, 206, 211
Einstein, Albert 154
Eisenhower, Dwight D. 44, 75–77, 81, 85, 87–89, 108, 120–122, 135, 150, 159, 178, 204, 209
Elkins, Hilly 142–145, 147
Ellington, Duke 13, 130, 132
Elliott, Ramblin' Jack 56–57, 62, 114
Ellsberg, Daniel 150, 164
Ervin, Sam 206

Faubus, Orval 88
Felt, Mark W. 198, 206, 214
Feraci, Carole 203
Fitzgerald, Ella 127
Ford, Gerald 211, 213
Ford, Thomas 73
Frost, David 157, 212

Garland, Judy 90, 102
Gaye, Marvin 171
Gerry, Elbridge T. 30
Gershwin, George 71, 101
Gershwin, Ira 71
Giancana, Sam 93, 98, 100, 112–113, 217
Glad to Be Home (song) 90

Golden Boy (Broadway play) 142–143, 145, 168, 170
Goldwater, Barry 20, 121, 139–140, 152
Goldwyn, Sam 92, 101–102
Gordy, Barry 171
Gore, Al 226
Graham, Billy 162
Graham, Katharine 213
Grant, Cary 129
Grateful Dead 151
Gray, Patrick L. 198
Gregory, Dick 144

Haig, Alexander 164
Haldeman, H.R. (Bob) 123, 152, 156–158, 160, 163, 205–206, 209, 211–212
Handy, W.C. 9
Hanks, Tom 179
Hanna, Jeff 118–119
Happy Days Are Here Again (song) 74
Harding, Warren 16
Harris, Emmylou 115
Harrison, Jim 174
Harvey, Paul 159
Hatcher, Andrew 130
Hayworth, Rita 96–98
Helms, Richard 200
Hemingway, Ernest 174
Hendrix, Jimi 151
Hey There (song) 79
Heyward, DuBose 101
Hiss, Alger 49–51, 125, 198
Holliday, Billie 70
Holly, Buddy 115
Holmes, Oliver Wendall 49
Hoover, J. Edgar 159, 198
Hope, Bob 192, 205–206, 218
House Un-American Activities Committee (HUAC) 49
Houston, Whitney 219
Hughes, Howard 123
Hughes, Langston 13, 130–131
Humphrey, Hubert 106, 152–153, 157, 187
Hunt, Howard 199–200

I Dream of Jennie (TV show) 173
Ibbotson, Jimmy 118–119
Imus, Don 20
I've Gotta Be Me (song) 169, 171, 204, 208

The Jack Paar Program (TV show) 135–137
Jackson, Jessie 207
Jackson, Mahalia 127, 130, 190
The Jackson 5 171
James, Daniel 193
Jaworski, Leon 210
Jefferson, Thomas 148
John Birch Society 121–123, 140, 152
Johnson, Lyndon 120, 138–139, 144, 149–150, 152, 154–157, 159, 161, 164, 175, 187, 206

Index

Jolson, Al 27, 30, 68, 167
Jones, Tom 169
Jorgensen, Frank 46–47, 73, 75, 106
Judgment at Nuremberg (film) 142

Kellogg, Lynn 191
Kennedy, Jackie 131, 138
Kennedy, John F. 74, 105–108, 112–113, 120, 124–127, 129–133, 138–139, 149, 158–159, 161, 164, 168, 206
Kennedy, Robert 108, 123, 127–128, 146, 152, 168
Kennedy, Ted 165
Khrushchev, Nikita 136, 140
King, B.B. 208
King, Coretta Scott 187
King, Larry L. 181
King, Marin Luther, Jr. 88–89, 107, 128–130, 132, 142, 144, 151, 166, 168, 188, 207
Kissinger, Henry 159, 164, 212
Kitt, Eartha 72, 83, 202, 207
Knowland, William 23

La Guardia, Fiorello 20
Laid, Melvin 159
Lancaster, Burt 142
Landsdale, Gen. Edward 149–150
Lawford, Peter 110–113, 127, 129
Lear, Norman 194, 196
Leary, Timothy 151
Leigh, Janet 83, 170
Lemay, Curtis 154
Lewis, Jerry 71, 90, 92
Liddy, G. Gordon 199
Lightfoot, Gordon 117
Lindbergh, Charles 36
Little Bird (song) 62
Lodge, Henry Cabot 108, 149
Lovett, Lyle 227
Lucas, Sam 8, 10, 216
Luckenbach, Texas 177–183
Luna, Barbra 109
Lunceford, Jimmie 14

Ma! He's Making Eyes at Me (song) 203
Maddox, Lester 186
Mailer, Norman 152
A Man Must Carry On (album) 182
Marcantonio, Vito 74
Martin, Dean 83, 90, 110–113, 129, 185, 204, 220, 222
Martin, Louis 130, 132
Marx, Groucho 68, 136
Mastin, Will 10–11, 14–15, 27–33, 35, 67–70, 78–80, 82–83, 90–92. 94–95, 100–101, 103, 128, 130, 145, 170, 185, 216, 220
McCain, John 205
McCarthy, Joseph 74, 84–86
McClaine, Shirly 110
McCord, James 199, 206

McEuen, John 118–119
McGovern, George 151, 199, 206
McGuane, Thomas 174
McKissick, Floyd 207
McNamara, Robert 164
Meet the Press 50
The Merv Griffith Show (TV show) 174
Minh, Ho Chi 148, 156, 158–159
Minnelli, Liza 222
minstrel shows 7–10
Mr. Bojangles (song) 5–6, 63–66, 114–119, 169, 175, 204, 219, 221, 225–228
Mr. Wonderful (Broadway show) 93–96, 128
Mitchell, John 152, 156, 200
Monroe, Marilyn 90, 112
Murphy, Michael Martin 62, 175
Murry, Bill 182
My Fair Lady (Broadway show) 94

Neil, Fred 118
Nelson, Willie 175, 180–182, 224
Newton, Huey 166
Nitty Gritty Dirt Band 116, 118–119, 219
Nixon, Don 123
Nixon, Frank 17–20, 46, 124
Nixon (Milhous), Hannah 17–20, 22, 46, 124, 151–152
Nixon, Pat 38–41, 44, 46–47, 74, 77, 81. 104, 108, 120–121, 157, 204, 211, 213
Nixon, Richard 16–21, 22–26, 36–51, 73–77, 81, 85–89, 104–108, 120–125, 135–141, 150–165, 185–190, 192–194, 196–207, 209–219
Novak, Kim 95–97, 100

O'Brian, Lawrence 200
Oceans 11 (film) 111, 145
O'Conner, Carroll 194
Odets, Clifford 142, 145–146
Oliver, Lawrence 146

Paar, Jack 137
Paige, Janis 70–71
Parks, Rosa 88
Pearson, Drew 84–85
Peele, Norman Vincent 162
Perry, Herman 45–46, 49, 73, 75
Poitier, Sidney 101, 127–128
Pope Paul VI 136
Porgy and Bess (film) 101–103
Presley, Elvis 171, 216

Queen (band) 219

Randolph, Phillip 132
Rather, Dan 227
Regan, Ronald 74, 101, 152, 213–214
Reynolds, Burt 220
Rice, Thomas 7
Richardson, Elliott 206
Rickles, Don 110

Index

Robin and the Seven Hoods (film) 133
Robinson, Bill "Bojangles" 31–32, 64
Robinson, Edward G. 34, 68, 71, 134, 221
Robinson, Jackie 89, 207
Robinson, Smokey 171
Rockefeller, David 213
Rockefeller, Nelson 105, 136, 152, 157
Rogers, Timmie 191
The Rolling Stones 179
Romney, George 121, 152
Rooney, Mickey 69
Roosevelt, Franklin 40, 44–45, 47, 49, 154, 159, 204
Roosevelt, Teddy 204
Ross, Diana 171
Rostow, Eugene 154
Rostow, Walt 154, 156
Ruckelshaus, William 210
Rumsfeld, Donald 187, 216
Rush, Barbra 134
Rustle of Spring (song) 210

Sachs, Alexander 154
Schlesinger, Arthur, Jr. 213
Seale, Bobby 166
Seasoned Greetings (film) 31
Sergeants 3 (film) 129
Shell, Joe 122–123
Shriver, Sargent 107
Simone, Nina 226
Sinatra, Frank 32, 34, 68, 70, 79, 81, 83, 90–92, 110–113, 126, 129, 133–134, 145, 170–172, 197, 204, 218, 220, 222
Sirica, Judge John 206
Six Bridges to Cross (movie) 81
Snider, Todd 227–228
Something for Everyone (album) 171
Stalin, Joseph 45
Starr, Ringo 221
Stennis, John 210
Stevenson, Adli 76, 88
Stewart, Jimmy 205
Stovall, Babe 57, 61, 63
Strouse, Charles 143
Struttin' Hannah from Savannah (vaudeville show) 27–28
Student Non-Violent Coordinating Committee (SNCC) 142, 167
Styne, Jule 93–95

Taft, Robert 75
Taft, William Howard 75

Taylor, James 115
Taylor, Laurette 12
The Ten Commandments (film) 99
Theater Owners Booking Association (TOBA) 11
Thieu, Nguyen Van 156
Thompson, Fred 209
Thompson, Hunter 174
Thurmond, Strom 113, 152, 185
Till, Emmett 88
Too Old to Change (album) 184
Tracy, Spencer 142
Truman, Harry 44, 74, 137–138, 148, 159, 164, 209

Vertigo (film) 97
Viva Terlingua (album) 179
Voorhis, Jerry 45–48

Walker, George 9, 11
Walker, Jerry Jeff 5–6, 52–59, 61–66, 114–119, 174–184
Walker, Susan (Streit) 179–184
Walker's Collectibles (album) 179
Wallace, DeWitt 202
Wallace, George 142, 144, 152–154, 157, 186
Wallace, Lila Acheson 202
Waller, Fats 13
Warren, Earl 75
Washington, Booker T. 204
Washington, Kenny 89
Waters, Ethel 31
Watson, Doc 56–57
Wayne, John 156, 205
Weiss, George 93
Welch, Raquel 195
Where the Boys Are (novel) 54
White, Loray 99
White, Theodore 121, 213
Williams, Burt 9–11, 216
Williams, Tennessee 174
Willie Wonka and the Chocolate Factory (film) 172
Wills, Frank 199
Wilson, Charlie 179
Winters, Shelley 144
Woodward, Bob 201, 206, 214

The Young Lions (film) 109

Zwicker, Ralph 86